AFRICA'S NEW PEACE
AND SECURITY ARCHITECTURE

Global Security in a Changing World

Series Editor: *Professor Nana K. Poku, John Ferguson Professor,*
Department of Peace Studies, University of Bradford, UK

Globalisation is changing the world dramatically, and a very public debate is taking place about the form, extent and significance of these changes. At the centre of this debate lie conflicting claims about the forces and processes shaping security. As a result, notions of inequality, poverty and the cultural realm of identity politics have all surfaced along side terrorism, environmental changes and bio-medical weapons as essential features of the contemporary global political landscape. In this sense, the debate on globalisation calls for a fundamental shift from a status quo political reality to one that dislodges states as the primary referent, and instead sees states as a means and not the end to various security issues, ranging from individual security to international terrorism. More importantly, centred at the cognitive stage of thought, it is also a move towards conceiving the concept of insecurity in terms of change.

The series attempts to address this imbalance by encouraging a robust and multi-disciplinary assessment of the asymmetrical nature of globalisation. Scholarship is sought from areas such as: global governance, poverty and insecurity, development, civil society, religion, terrorism and globalisation.

Other titles in this series:

Foreign Interventions in Ethnic Conflicts
Robert Nalbandov
ISBN 978-0-7546-7862-5

Cocaine Trafficking in Latin America
EU and US Policy Responses
Sayaka Fukumi
ISBN 978-0-7546-7043-8

A Decade of Human Security
Global Governance and New Multilateralisms
Edited by Sandra J. MacLean, David R. Black and Timothy M. Shaw
ISBN 978-0-7546-4773-7

Non-Traditional Security in Asia
Dilemmas in Securitization
Edited by Mely Caballero-Anthony, Ralf Emmers and Amitav Acharya
ISBN 978-0-7546-4701-0

Africa's New Peace and Security Architecture

Promoting Norms, Institutionalizing Solutions

Edited by

ULF ENGEL
University of Leipzig, Germany

JOÃO GOMES PORTO
University of Bradford, UK

ASHGATE

Published by
Ashgate Publishing Limited
Wey Court East
Union Road
Farnham
Surrey, GU9 7PT
England

Ashgate Publishing Company
Suite 420
101 Cherry Street
Burlington
VT 05401-4405
USA

www.ashgate.com

British Library Cataloguing in Publication Data
Africa's new peace and security architecture : promoting
   norms, institutionalizing solutions. -- (Global security in
   a changing world)
   1. African Union. 2. Peace-building--Africa. 3. National
   security--Africa. 4. Africa--Politics and government--
   1960-
   I. Series II. Engel, Ulf. III. Porto, João Gomes.
   341.2'49-dc22

Library of Congress Cataloging-in-Publication Data
Africa's new peace and security architecture : promoting norms, institutionalizing
   solutions / edited by Ulf Engel and J. Gomes Porto.
      p. cm. -- (Global security in a changing world)
   Includes bibliographical references and index.
   ISBN 978-0-7546-7605-8 (hardback) -- ISBN 978-0-7546-7606-5 (pbk) --
   ISBN 978-1-4094-0217-6 (ebook) 1. Conflict management--Africa.
   2. Peace-building--Africa. 3. National security--Africa. 4. Africa--Politics and
government--21st century. 5. Africa--Military policy. I. Engel, Ulf. II. Porto, João Gomes.

   JZ5584.A35A38 2010
   355'.03306--dc22

                                                                    2009040132

ISBN 9780754676058 (hbk)
ISBN 9780754676065 (pbk)
ISBN 9781409402176 (ebk)

Printed and bound in Great Britain by
TJ International Ltd, Padstow, Cornwall

Contents

This publication is supported by

gtz

List of Figures

List of Tables

Notes on Contributors

The Editors

Professor Dr Ulf Engel teaches "Politics in Africa" at the Institute of African Studies, University of Leipzig (Germany). He is the Director of Studies of the Masters in African Studies and the European Masters in Global Studies as well as spokesperson for a PhD research training program on Critical Junctures of Globalization, which looks at the implication of the so-called spatial turn in the humanities and social sciences. Dr Engel holds a PhD degree in Political Science; following a habilitation at the University of Hamburg his *venia legendi* is in Political Science. He has published widely on Africa's international relations.

Dr João Gomes Porto is a senior lecturer and director of undergraduate studies at the Department of Peace Studies, University of Bradford (United Kingdom). In his previous capacity as head of the African Security Analysis Program at the Institute for Security Studies (ISS), South Africa, he managed a multidisciplinary team of researchers dedicated to the analysis and provision of policy options on conflict situations in Africa. Dr Gomes Porto holds a PhD degree in International Conflict Analysis and Resolution from the University of Kent at Canterbury.

The Contributors

Fredrik Söderbaum is Associate Professor of Peace and Development Research at the School of Global Studies, University of Gothenburg (Sweden) and Senior Associate Research Fellow at the United Nations University-Comparative Regional Integration Studies (UNU-CRIS), Bruges (Belgium). Recent co-edited books include *EU and the Global South* (Lynne Rienner, forthcoming), *Afro-regions: The Dynamics of Cross-Border Regionalism in Africa* (Nordic Africa Institute, 2008), *The EU as a Global Player: The Politics of Interregionalism* (Routledge, 2006), *The Political Economy of Regionalism: The Case of Southern Africa* (Palgrave Macmillan, 2004), and *Theories of New Regionalism* (Palgrave Macmillan, 2003).

Dr Björn Hettne is Professor Emeritus in Peace and Development Research at the School of Global Studies, University of Gothenburg (Sweden). He has coordinated many international research programs and has a comprehensive record of publication, in fields such as South Asia, European studies, development theory, international political economy, and regionalism. His most recent publications are *Thinking About Development* (Zed Books, 2009) and *Sustainable Development in a Globalized World* and *Human Values and Global Governance* (both with Palgrave Macmillan, 2008).

Dr Klaas van Walraven is a researcher working on African politics and history at the African Studies Centre in Leiden (Netherlands). He holds a PhD degree from the University of Leiden, 1997. He has published on Africa's international relations (OAU, AU, ECOMOG), democratization and the politics of Niger. Currently, he is working on a history of the Sawaba rebellion in Niger in the period 1954–1975. He is also one of the co-editors of the *Africa Yearbook: Politics, Economy and Society South of the Sahara*, published by Brill Academic Publishers.

Dr Kathryn Sturman is acting Head of the Governance of Africa's Resources Program at the South African Institute of International Affairs (SAIIA, Cape Town office). She has worked previously as senior researcher for the Institute for Security Studies (Pretoria), and as speechwriter to the leader of the opposition in the Parliament of South Africa. Dr Sturman holds a PhD degree in International Relations from Macquarie University in Sydney (Australia).

Mrs Aïssatou Hayatou works as an expert in support of the Peace and Security Council Secretariat of the African Union. Mrs Hayatou holds a Masters Degree in International Relations from the Institute des Relations Internationales (Paris) as well as an MSc in Global Affairs from Rutgers State University of New Jersey. Mrs Hayatou is currently a PhD candidate at Rutgers.

Dr Tim Murithi is the Program Head of the PSC Report Program based at the ISS Addis Ababa Office in Ethiopia. From 2008 to April 2009 he was a Senior Research Fellow and Principal Coordinator of the post-graduate MA module in Applied Conflict Resolution Skills in the Department of Peace Studies at the University of Bradford (UK). He has held posts at the Centre for Conflict Resolution, University of Cape Town (South Africa); and the Program in Peacemaking and Preventive Diplomacy at the United Nations Institute for Training and Research (UNITAR), in Geneva (Switzerland). From 1995 to 1999 he taught at the University of Keele (UK), where he also obtained his PhD in International Relations. He has worked as a Consultant to the AU's African Citizens Directorate (CIDO). He is editor of *Towards a Union Government of Africa: Challenges and Opportunities* (Pretoria, 2007) and co-editor of *The African Union and its Institutions* (Johannesburg, 2008).

Mr Charles N. Mwaura is an Expert on the Continental Early Warning System and Preventive Diplomacy at the Peace and Security Department of the African Union. Mr Mwaura taught at the University of Nairobi's Department of Political Science and Public Administration (1995–2002) before joining the Intergovernmental

Authority on Development (IGAD) as the Coordinator for the Conflict Early Warning and Response Mechanism in the IGAD region. Charles Mwaura has, in the last several years, been working on the conceptualization, establishment and operationalization of conflict early warning systems both at regional and continental levels as well as implementation of the overall AU strategies for conflict prevention, management and resolution. Mr Mwaura graduated with a BA in Political Science from the University of Nairobi and holds a Masters degree (MSc Econ) in International Relations from the London School of Economics and Political Science.

Mr El-Ghassim Wane is the Acting Director of the African Union's Peace and Security Department and Head of the Conflict Management Division. Mr Wane has worked in various capacities in the AU/OAU for the last 14 years, and has been instrumental in the establishment, operationalization and functioning of the African Peace and Security Architecture (APSA) and the development as well as implementation of AU strategies for conflict prevention, management and resolution. Mr Wane graduated in International Law and International Relations at the University of Dakar, and International Relations and European Studies at the University Lille II, respectively.

Mrs Shewit Hailu works in the Conflict Management Division, Peace and Security Department of the African Union Commission. She is the Coordinator of the Situation Room, which is the observation and monitoring center of the Continental Early Warning System. Mrs Hailu holds a Masters Degree in Globalization and Development, from the University of London, Institute of Commonwealth Studies and a Bachelors Degree in Political Science and International Relations, from Addis Ababa University in Ethiopia.

Simone Kopfmüller is Coordinator for the German development cooperation with the African Union in the field of peace and security, which is implemented by GTZ – the German Agency for Technical Cooperation. Based in Addis Ababa, she is managing capacity development support for the Peace and Security Department of the African Union Commission. She has been working as an expert in the Horn of Africa, at GTZ headquarters in Frankfurt as well as at GTZ's liaison office in Berlin, Germany. Simone Kopfmüller has studied international politics and economics at the School of Oriental and African Studies in London and at the University of Augsburg, Germany.

Dr Doug Bond received a BS degree in Technical Communications from the University of Minnesota, an MA degree in International Communications and a PhD degree in Political Science at the University of Hawaii (USA). Upon completion of his PhD in 1985, he was a research fellow and held an assistant professorship at Kyungnam University in South Korea for three years. He moved to Harvard University's Center for International Affairs in 1988, where he has since led the development of the PANDA protocol used with news reports to identify, track and analyze the evolution of political conflict. Since 1994, Dr Bond has taught courses at the Harvard University Division of Continuing Education, where he has an appointment as Lecturer in Extension. He is employed by Virtual Research Associates, Boston MA, while maintaining his research staff and teaching appointments at Harvard.

Dr Jakkie Cilliers is the executive director of the Institute for Security Studies (South Africa), a pan-African applied policy research institute engaged on human security issues in Africa. He is an Extraordinary Professor in the Department of Political Sciences, Faculty of Humanities at the University of Pretoria, he serves on the International Advisory Board of the Geneva Centre for Security Policy (GCSP) and as independent non-executive director of the South African Banking Risk Information Centre (SABRIC). His current research interests are on African futures.

Captain (Navy) (rtd) Johan Pottgieter is a Senior Researcher with the Institute for Security Studies in Pretoria (South Africa). Towards the end of his long military career he served as Senior Military Liaison Officer, in Uganda, for the United Nations Missions in the DRC (MONUC). He has been deployed to Ethiopia as interim Military Attaché and was seconded, for a period of three years, to the African Union to assist in the establishment of the African Standby Force.

Acknowledgments

The inspiration for this volume originated in the editors' participation in several of the processes leading to the establishment of the African Union Peace and Security Architecture (APSA), with special reference to one of its pillars, the Continental Early Warning System (CEWS). Dr Engel and Dr Gomes Porto have been deeply engaged in the design and implementation of this important pillar of the APSA since 2005, when at the invitation of the African Union Commission they participated in the development of the first draft, *Roadmap for the Implementation of the CEWS*. Since then, their continued involvement has focused on the provision of policy advice, research support and training to the African Union Commission, more specifically its Conflict Management Division (CMD).

The editors' profound gratitude is expressed first and foremost to the management and staff of the African Union's Conflict Management Division. Our sincere thanks and appreciation go to El-Ghassim Wane, Charles Mwaura, Shewit Hailu, Kwaku Asante-Darko, Peter Okuhuangae, Ahmed Mokhtar, Aïssatou Hayatou, Faisal Alshaikh, Taye Abdulkadir, Merete Shawul, Orit Ibrahim and Alex Behabtu.

The editors would also like to express their gratitude to the AU Office of GTZ, and in particular Simone Kopfmüller (GTZ Support Project for the African Union's Peace and Security Architecture). GTZ's continued support and Simone's unwavering belief in the cause, coupled with her (and her family's!) welcoming hospitality in Addis Ababa have made the last four years a great pleasure.

Finally, the editors would like to express their gratitude to Kirstin Howgate at Ashgate who provided tireless support (and considerable patience!) during the writing of this volume.

List of Abbreviations

ACDS	African Chiefs of Defense and Security
AMIB	African Union Mission in Burundi
AMIS	African Union Mission in Sudan
AMISOM	AU Mission in Somalia
AMU	Arab Maghreb Union
APRM	African Peer Review Mechanism
APSA	African Peace and Security Architecture
ARS	Alliance for the Re-liberation of Somalia
ASC	African Standby Capability
ASEAN	Association of Southeast Asian Nations
ASF	African Standby Force
AU	African Union
C3IS	Command, Control, Communication and Information Systems
CAR	Central African Republic
CEN-SAD	Community of Sahel-Saharan States
CEWARN	(IGAD) Conflict Early Warning and Response Mechanism
CEWS	(African Union) Continental Early Warning System
CivPol	Civilian Police
CMD	(AU) Conflict Management Division
COA	Courses of Action
COMESA	Common Market for Eastern and Southern Africa
COPAX	Council for Peace and Security in Central Africa
CPMR	Conflict Prevention Management and Resolution
CSID	Cours Superieur Inter-Armees de Defense
CSO	Civil Society Organization
DFID	(British) Department for International Development
DSC	Defense and Security Commission
EAC	East African Community
EAPSM	Eastern Africa Peace and Security Mechanism
EAPSS	Eastern Africa Peace and Security Secretariat
EASBRIG	Eastern African Standby Brigade
EASBRICOM	EASBRIG Coordination Mechanism
ECCAS	Economic Community of Central African States
ECCASBRIG	Standby Brigade of the Economic Community of Central African States
ECOMOG	Economic Community of West African States Monitoring Group

ECOSOCC	Economic Social and Cultural Council
ECOWARN	ECOWAS Warning and Response Network
ECOWAS	Economic Community of West African States
EDF	Economic Development Fund
EEML	Ecole d'Etat-Major de Libreville
EFOFAA	Escola de Formação de Oficiais, Forças Armadas Angolanas/ Officer Training School, Angolan Armed Forces
ESF	ECOWAS Standby Force
EU	European Union
EWS	Early Warning System
FOMAC	Multinational Force of Central Africa
FNL	Forces nationales de libération (also known as PALIPEHUTU)
GTZ	Deutsche Gesellschaft für Technische Zusammenarbeit (German Development Agency)
HCNM	Office of the High Commissioner for National Minorities
ICC	International Criminal Court
IGAD	Intergovernmental Authority on Development
IGADD	Intergovernmental Authority on Drought and Development
IGOs	International Organizations
IncRep	Incident Report
MAES	African Union Electoral and Security Assistance Mission to the Comoros
MARACC	Early Warning Mechanism of Central Africa
MERCOSUR	Southern Common Market
MNC	Multi-National Company
MONUC	Mission de l'Organisation des Nations Unies en République Démocratique du Congo
MSC	Military Staff Committee
NAFTA	North American Free Trade Agreement
NARC	North Africa Regional Capability
NATO	North Atlantic Treaty Organization
NEPAD	New Partnership for Africa's Development
NGOs	Non-Governmental Organizations
OAU	Organization of African Unity
ONUB	United Nations Operation in Burundi
OSCE	Organisation for Security and Cooperation in Europe
PALIPEHUTU	Parti pour la libération du peuple hutu (also known as FNL)
PCIA	Peace and Conflict Impact Assessment
PLANELMS	Planning Elements
PRC	(AU) Permanent Representatives Committee
PSC	(AU) Peace and Security Council
PSOD	Peace Support Operations Division
PTA	Preferential Trade Area for Eastern and Southern Africa
RDC	The Rapid Deployment Capacity

RECs	Regional Economic Communities
RMs	Regional Mechanisms for Conflict Prevention, Management and Resolution
SADC	Southern Africa Development Community
SADCC	Southern African Development Coordinating Conference
SCA	Strategic Conflict Assessment
SHIRBRIG	UN Standby High Readiness Brigade
SitRep	Situation Report
SitRoom	(CMD) Situation Room
SOPs	Standard Operating Procedures
SRCC	Special Representative of the Chairperson of the Commission (AU)
UEMOA	West African Economic and Monetary Union
UMA	Maghreb Arab Union
UN	United Nations
UNAMID	United Nations/AU Mission in Darfur
UNDG ECHA	UN Development Group – Executive Committee of Humanitarian Affairs
UNDP	United Nations Development Program
UNDPKO	UN Department of Peacekeeping Operations
UNEP	United Nations Environmental Program
UNMIL	United Nations Mission in Liberia
UNMIS	UN Mission in Sudan
WANEP	West African Network for Peacebuilding
WB	World Bank

Chapter 1
Africa's New Peace and Security Architecture: An Introduction

Ulf Engel and João Gomes Porto

Africa is currently experiencing a potentially significant transformation with regard to the norms and institutions governing multilateral relations on the continent. This gradual shift has the potential to transform the way the continent addresses the mutually constituted challenges of peace, security and development and is likely to change the nature of bilateral relations within Africa as well as its interaction with the international system.

At the time it was founded in 1963, the Organization of African Unity (OAU) took it upon itself the duty of supporting collective struggles for national liberation from colonialism as well as the responsibility to act as the guardian of Africa's hard-won yet fragile independence from colonial rule. The principles of equality, respect for national sovereignty, non-interference as well as territorial integrity constituted cardinal principles that defined the modalities and parameters of multilateral cooperation within the OAU. Three decades later, the radically altered international environment that resulted from the collapse of the Berlin Wall in 1989 and the dissolution of the Soviet Union in 1991, the pressures of unrestrained globalization on an increasingly poor African continent in need of a new development paradigm, the unprecedented increase in the number and intensity of violent armed conflicts and the perception of the inability and gradual disengagement of the international community to respond to the worst forms of violence in the early part of the decade (Somalia and Rwanda come to mind) form part of the complex background within which the reinvention, repositioning and restructuring of the OAU took place. Furthermore, by the 1990s, the OAU had lost a great part of its credibility—often accused of indifference, of bureaucratic paralysis, of being an elite *club of dictators* far removed from the realities of daily life of the common African, too preoccupied with lofty political ideals and declarations, which bore little resemblance to the challenges posed by extreme poverty, conflict, governance or the respect of human rights in vast areas of Africa. A result of unwavering respect to the cardinal norm of non-interference in the internal affairs of member states, the OAU's lack of a more robust mandate on issues of peace and security had become unpalatable, difficult to justify and increasingly viewed as an obstacle to the repositioning of Africa in the new international post-Cold War environment. While the organization's traditional preference for softer options, such as consultation and mediation had had arguably some degree of success during the Cold War, these were seen as inadequate and insufficient to the problems of high intensity civil wars, genocide and gross violations of human rights perpetrated by regimes, many of whom were members of the OAU.

As a result, during the latter half of the 1990s, African states took a series of decisions to overhaul the continental organization, endorsing new norms and adopting new rules to govern their interaction on matters of peace, security and development and establish new institutions to enforce these norms. In legal and institutional terms, this transformation had taken a concrete turn when, on 9 September 1999 in Sirte, Libya, African Heads of State and Government declared their commitment to transform the OAU into a new organization, the African Union. On 11 July 2000, at the 36th Ordinary Summit of the OAU in Lomé, Togo, the legal-institutional framework for the new organization was adopted in the form of the *Constitutive Act of the African Union* (African Union 2000).[1] To be sure, while for most observers the institutional transformation was remarkably swift in politico-diplomatic terms, the final agreement by all 53 member states on the final shape of the *Constitutive Act* was not entirely devoid of patient negotiation and accommodation of different, often opposing interests and agendas as noted by Tieku (2004).

The adoption of the *Constitutive Act* was a decisive step, showing that African states were not only conveniently changing the name of their continental organization, but indeed giving it a radically new vision and mission, a set of clearly defined objectives and responsibilities, perhaps "more teeth" (see Cilliers 1999; Cilliers and Sturman 2004; Tieku 2004). This transformation has indeed expanded the sources of authority of the Organization: in addition to the Assembly of Heads of State and Government, a judicial pillar (the Court of Justice) and a democratic pillar (the Pan-African Parliament) have been created. In executive terms, the largely ad hoc (even if, over time, stronger) power of initiative of the OAU's Secretary-General and the Secretariat have been given a more precise substance by the creation of a fully fledged AU Commission with important responsibilities in moving the new organization forward, including a fully recognized political mandate. In addition, the Constitutive Act creates a civil society pillar, the Economic, Social and Cultural Council (ECOSOCC), whose objective is to forge strong partnerships between Governments and all segments of African civil society.

What then are the fundamental objectives of this new African Union? According to the *Constitutive Act*, the AU shall, among others, accelerate the integration of the continent, defend the sovereignty, territorial integrity and independence of its member States, promote peace, security and stability on the African continent, promote democratic principles and good governance, protect human rights and promote sustainable development (African Union 2000, §3 (c), (b), (f), (g), (j)). Politically, the African Union is guided by some of the principles which had

---

1   Note that the Constitutive Act supersedes and takes precedence of any other OAU treaty documents (Constitutive Act, Article 33 (2)).

characterized the OAU: peaceful settlement of disputes and conflicts; respect for the sovereignty equality of Member States; non-interference by any Member State in the internal affairs of another; sovereign equality and interdependence of the Member States; and respect of borders inherited on achievement of independence (African Union 2000, §4 (e), (g), (a) and (b)).[2]

Yet, a set of new principles is endorsed by Member States in Article 4, particularly the respect for democratic practices, good governance, the rule of law, protection of human rights and fundamental freedoms, and respect for the sanctity of human life (African Union 2000, §4 (m), (o)). Furthermore, while reiterating the principles of sovereignty, territorial integrity, independence and non-interference, the *Constitutive Act* gives the African Union a very important new right and as well as a new responsibility. Based on a decision by the AU Assembly of Heads of State and Government, the Union may intervene in Member States in respect of "grave circumstances, namely war crimes, genocide and crimes against humanity" (African Union 2000, §4 (h)). On 3 February 2003 this provision was amended also to include "serious threats to legitimate order."[3] In addition, the *Constitutive Act* gives member States the right to ask the Union to restore peace and security (African Union 2000, §4 (j)).

Core to the new organization's vision is therefore the active promotion of peace, security and stability on the continent as emphasized by Heads of State and Government in the preamble to the *Constitutive Act*. In their words: "conscious of the fact that the scourge of conflicts in Africa constitutes a major impediment to the socio-economic development of the continent", they recognize the "need to promote peace, security and stability as a prerequisite for the implementation of our development and integration agenda" (African Union 2000). In order to enable the organization to carry out its new peace and security mandate, and guided by the general principles detailed above and the need to establish "an operational structure for the effective implementation of the decisions taken in the areas of conflict prevention, peace-making, peace support operations and intervention, as well as peace-building and post-conflict reconstruction," the AU adopted *The Protocol Relating to the Establishment of the Peace and Security Council of the African Union* (hereafter referred to as the PSC Protocol) in Durban, South Africa on 9 July 2002. Less than two years later, member States would agree on a Common African Defense and Security Policy (CADSP) during the second extraordinary session of the Assembly of the Heads of State and Government, in Sirte, from 27 to 28 February 2004. These two important legal instruments are regarded by the Commission to form the legal underpinning of the continental peace and security architecture (African Union Commission 2004).[4]

---

2   Mirroring in this important regard Article III of the OAU Charter, which defined the organization's fundamental principles (OAU 1963, §3).

3   In this regard see Baimu and Sturman (2003, 39).

4   As noted in the Chairperson's report on the establishment of a continental peace and security architecture and the status of peace processes in Africa, "the CADSP, which is

In terms of source of finance for the new peace and security architecture, an unspecified amount of funds should be provided by member States and international donors to the Peace Fund (African Union 2002, §21).[5] However, at the time of writing, the peace and security architecture as well as ongoing AU peace support operations are being funded almost entirely via donor assistance, in particular the EU's *African Peace Facility* (APF) which was provided with €250 million by the EU for the period 2003–2007 (European Commission 2004). Four fifths of the APF are planned for spending in peace-supporting missions. In fact, the budget for the *African Mission in Sudan* (AMIS), which has meanwhile been transformed into the hybrid *United Nations – African Union Mission in Darfur* (UNAMID), to a large extent comes from the APF.[6] In June 2008, the EU decided to grant another €300 million from its 10th EDF for the period 2008–2010 (to illustrate the size: UNAMID's budget for the period 1 July 2008 to 30 June 2009 is $1.7 billion).

Also other key finance for the new peace and security architecture does originate from the regular African Union budget and Member State contributions, yet here too the contributions of the international donor community are critical. For instance the German *Gesellschaft für technische Zusammenarbeit* (GTZ) is going to provide the PSC and the *Peace and Security Department* with a new building in Addis Ababa;[7] while the People's Republic of China is building a new home for the rest of the African Union's institutions to the tune of some $150 million.

In the very year when the entire gamut of institutions and decision-making procedures of the African Union's Peace and Security Architecture (APSA) are set to be fully operational (i.e. 2010), this volume aims at providing the reader with an overview of this so-called architecture, the status of its implementation, as well as touching upon the some of the most pressing challenges of a political, financial and institutional nature. It is also our aim to reflect on a more conceptual basis on the principles underlying the architecture's design, and the conditions of its actualization through an emphasis on the gradual development of institutionalized behavior.

Africa's New Peace and Security Architecture: Promoting Norms, Institutionalizing Solutions is organized into eight chapters. Following this introduction, Chapter 1, written by Fredrik Söderbaum and Björn Hettne and titled *Regional Security in a Global Perspective*, introduces the reader to contemporary

---

largely premised on the concept of human security, identifies the common security threats to the continent; the principles and values underlining the CADSP; the objectives and goals of such a Policy; as well as the implementing organs and mechanisms, and the building blocks of the CADSP" (African Union 2004).

5   Under the former OAU Mechanism Member States had to contribute 5 per cent of their annual OAU membership fee to a *Peace Fund*.

6   After endorsement by the UN Security Council the AU mission (UN S/RES 1556, 30 July 2004) started in July 2004 with 80 military observers and 300 soldiers. In September 2004 it was enlarged to 3,320 troops and in April 2005 to 7,700 (AMIS II). UNAMID was given a mandate on 31 July 2007 (UN S/RES/1769).

7   See http://www.wb-ps-au.com/ (accessed 11 September 2008).

regionalisms that are seen as deeply linked to the changing nature of global politics and the intensification of globalization. With the aim of situating Africa's security regionalisms within this wider context and exploring their vertical linkages to global peace and security mechanisms, the chapter discusses the theory, practice, experience and rationale of security cooperation at a regional level in Africa, using several examples—including experiences at sub-regional level—to illustrate these points. The authors introduce a set of key conceptual tools necessary for a reflection on the relation between security and other forms of regionalism as well as a critical evaluation of the implementation of the African Union's ambitious and multifaceted agenda.

In order to understand the rationale, significance and potential of this peace and security architecture for the African continent and its peoples, a historical perspective is required. In Chapter 3, *Heritage and Transformation: From the Organization of African Unity to the African Union*, Klaas van Walraven provides such a critical retrospective by situating the current institutional transformation in context. Van Walraven's detailed discussion of the political record and legacy of the OAU in terms of conflict prevention, management and resolution, from its inception in 1963, provides a much needed contextualization to the rationale for the transformation of the OAU to the AU. Indeed, this reflection explores the extent to which the OAU's experiences in conflict management over the years affected the institutional and normative transformations that took place in the period 1990–1993—which van Walraven concludes affected the way that the AU was given form a decade later.

As far as the development and operationalization of the APSA is concerned, the ratification of the *PSC Protocol* by AU member states and its entry into force on 26 December 2003 stand as landmark achievements. It is in the *PSC Protocol* that we find the first specific articulation of the series of new institutions and decision making procedures (also known as *pillars*) that will form the new peace and security architecture: the Peace and Security Council (PSC); the Panel of the Wise; the Continental Early Warning System (CEWS); the African Standby Force (ASF) and the Peace Fund. It should be noted that this institutional design had been sketched in a decision taken by the OAU summit in Lusaka held between 9–11 July 2001 on the integration of the central components of the *OAU Mechanism for Conflict Prevention, Management and Resolution* (established in 1993) into the African Union.[8] It is, however, beyond the scope of this introduction, to provide a comprehensive discussion of the series of decisions and processes that eventually led to the adoption of the PSC Protocol, including the important contributions of Nigeria's President Obasanjo's Conference on Security, Stability, Development,

---

8   On the OAU Mechanism see Bakwesegha (1995), DeConing and Solomon (1994), Ibok and Nhara (1996), Kamto (1996), Muyangwa and Vogt (2003) as well as OAU (1994).

and Co-operation in Africa (CSSDCA), which was adopted at the Durban summit in July 2002.[9]

Furthermore, in what is the first indication of the true continental nature of this architecture as far as its components are concerned, Article 16 of the PSC Protocol states that "the Regional Mechanisms are part of the overall security architecture of the Union" – and it is here that, as will be discussed below, the harmonization and coordination roles of the Union, cushioned in an approach said to be that of "effective partnership," are first defined (African Union 2002, §16). Indeed, the Chairperson of the Commission is specifically tasked with involving the regional mechanisms in the establishment of two of the pillars of the architecture, the CEWS and the ASF.

The PSC has the far-reaching task to "promote peace, security and stability in Africa," to "anticipate and prevent conflicts," to "promote and implement peace-building and post-conflict reconstruction activities to consolidate peace and prevent the resurgence of violence," to "co-ordinate and harmonize continental efforts in the prevention and combating of international terrorism in all its aspects," to "develop a common defense policy for the African Union" as well as to "promote and encourage democratic practices, good governance and the rule of law, protect human rights and fundamental freedoms, respect for the sanctity of human life and international humanitarian law, as part of efforts for preventing conflicts" (African Union 2002, §3).

The PSC comprises ten representatives who are elected for a two-year period and five representatives who are elected for a three-year period (with an option for re-election) on the basis of regional representation.[10] Decisions shall by guided by the principle of consensus. And in cases where consensus cannot be reached, the PSC shall adopt its decisions on procedural matters by a simple majority, while decisions on all other matters shall be made by a two-thirds majority vote of its Members voting (African Union 2002, §8 (13)). But in contrast to the UN Security Council, no Member States has the right to veto Council decisions. While major decisions of the PSC—such as intervention—need to be authorized by the Assembly, in 18 clearly demarcated areas the PSC enjoys the right to initiate debate and action (African Union 2002, §7 (a-r)).[11] It also has a very important power: that of instituting sanctions in cases of unconstitutional changes of government.

---

9   See in this regard Kioko (2003); Tieku (2004) and Mwanasali (2004).

10   Currently Benin, Burkina Faso, Burundi, Chad, Mali, Rwanda, Swaziland, Tunisia, Uganda and Zambia have been elected for a two-year period while Algeria, Angola, Ethiopia, Gabon and Nigeria have been elected for a three-year period (the former were elected in January 2008 and the latter in January 2007).

11   In particular, authorizing the mounting and deployment of peace support missions; undertaking peace-making and peace-building activities; recommending intervention pursuant to article 4 (h) of the Constitutive Act as well as approving the modalities for intervention pursuant to a decision of the Assembly in light of article 4 (j) of the Constitutive Act.

Chapter 4 by Kathryn Sturman and Aïssatou Hayatou introduces this important structure, reflecting on its nature, objectives, composition, powers and functions. In addition, this chapter provides the first review of PSC operations since the first election of PSC members in March 2004, and its constitution on 25 May 2004, providing a detailed analysis of composition and membership dynamics within the PSC. While the PSC has met regularly since its inception (averaging three sessions per month), as poignantly noted by Sturman and Hayatou, this is an institution in the early stages of consolidation and its many challenges must be assessed against its achievements to date. Nevertheless, the PSC has, in a very short time, assumed an important profile as a focus of political discussions within the Union, naturally on situations of ongoing conflict but also importantly on other situations.

In terms of its focus and areas of operation, while routine decisions are usually taken at the level of a Permanent Representative to the African Union, in important crisis-related decisions, members of the PSC (at the level of Ministers of Foreign Affairs and, at times, Heads of State and Government) tend to prefer consensus- building, closely involving the Chairperson of the AU Commission, the Commissioner for Peace and Security as well as Special Representatives, who may be appointed by the Chairperson.[12] Administratively, the new peace and security architecture of the African Union rests on the *Peace and Security Department*, which oversees four divisions: the *Conflict Management Division* (CMD) (which evolved from a unit with the same name within the OAU Mechanism), two divisions for Peace Support Operations (*Peace Support Operations Division*, PSOD, and the *Defense and Security Division*), and the *PSC Secretariat*.[13]

It is important to highlight the importance that, on a principled and normative basis, conflict prevention—that is, the anticipation and early responses required to "contain crisis situations so as to prevent them from developing into full-blown conflicts"—assumes in the development of the architecture.

The Panel of the Wise is an institutional innovation as far as preventive diplomacy and conflict resolution are concerned. Its role is to advise the Chairperson of the AU Commission and the PSC, in particular on issues of conflict prevention (African Union 2002, §11). The members of this panel (which has often been misrepresented as a council of elders) shall be qualified by their "outstanding" past contributions to peace, security and development. Panel members are elected for a three year period by the AU Assembly, based on a proposal by the Chairperson of the AU Commission. At the request of the PSC or the Chairman of the AU Commission the Panel "shall take such action deemed appropriate to support the efforts of the [PSC] and those of the Chairperson of the Commission for the prevention of conflicts, and to pronounce itself on issues relating to the promotion and maintenance of peace, security and stability in Africa" (African Union 2002, §11 (4)).

---

12   In February 2008, the Foreign Minister of Gabon, Jean Ping, was elected as new Chairman of the AU Commission. The diplomat Ramtane Lamamra became *Commissioner for Peace and Security*. Like his predecessor, Said Djinnit, he is from Algeria.

13   The current commission plans to reorganize this set-up.

In Chapter 5, Tim Murithi and Charles Mwaura reflect on this pillar of the APSA, exploring its potential role in support of the AU's efforts in the area of preventive diplomacy, implementation of peace agreements and conflict resolution—including good offices and dialogue facilitation, mediation and support to the negotiations. As emphasized by the authors, the Panel's room to maneuver has only recently been demarcated.[14] According to the *modalities* document, the Panel of the Wise may play a variety of roles over and above advising the PSC and the Chairperson; in fact, the Panel may facilitate the establishment of channels of communication between the PSC/Chairperson and parties engaged in a dispute; carry out fact finding missions in areas where the Panel considers there is a danger of conflict breaking out or escalating; conduct shuttle diplomacy between parties in conflict; encourage parties to engage in political dialogue; adopt confidence building measures and carry out reconciliation processes; assist and advise mediation teams engaged in formal negotiations; and assist the parties and other agencies to resolve disputes that may arise during the implementation of peace agreements (African Union Peace and Security Department 2008). Nathan's reflections on the potential of this new institution are, in this regard, useful; in particular his emphasis on the importance of regarding mediation and related third-party activities as being highly specialized, requiring appropriate experience and technical expertise (Nathan 2004).

The appointment of members to the Panel of the Wise took some time. It was only in July 2007 that the first five members were named. They were inaugurated in December 2007. For the region of East Africa this was former OAU Secretary General Salim A. Salim (Tanzania, who also is the AU Special Representative for Darfur, Sudan); for North Africa, former president of Algeria, Ahmed Ben Bella; for West Africa, the president of Benin's Constitutional Court, Elisabeth K. Pognon; for Central Africa, the former president of São Tomé and Príncipe, Miguel Trovoada; and for Southern Africa, chairperson of the Independent Electoral Commission, Brigalia Bam. In Africa's more recent conflicts, the Panel of the Wise has attempted some level of involvement—particularly in Kenya and Zimbabwe—but also with very low-key visits to countries that will hold elections in 2009 (the case of South Africa, for example). However, as its modalities of action have only very recently been decided upon, one would expect to see the Panel have a more active stance on a much wider variety of situations. Nevertheless, this type of preventive diplomacy too requires precision—as the African Union favors a principle of regional subsidarity and expects the respective Regional Economic Communities (RECs) to be the first to get involved in conflict mediation—coordination at a sub-regional and international level is critical.[15]

---

14   On 12 November 2007 the PSC agreed on "Modalities of Functioning of the Panel of the Wise". See in this regard African Union Peace and Security Department (2008).

15   In the case of Kenya, former UN Secretary-General Kofi Annan became the chief mediator; in the case of Zimbabwe, the Southern African Development Community

As noted above, the PSC is first and foremost conceptualized as a "collective security and early warning arrangement" in its task as a standing decision-making organ for the prevention, management and resolution of conflicts. Perhaps not surprisingly, the *PSC Protocol* determines the establishment of a Continental Early Warning System (CEWS) meant to facilitate the anticipation and prevention of violent conflicts and tasked with gathering and analyzing information to enable the Chairperson of the AU Commission, the PSC and other actors of the new peace and security architecture to prevent violent conflict in a timely manner (African Union 2002, §12 (1)). Of importance as regards our discussion of Article 16 above, the PSC Protocol prescribes that the observation and monitoring units of the RECs are to form an integral part of the CEWS. Indeed, the Protocol states that the early warning system shall consist of the "observation and monitoring units of the Regional Mechanisms to be linked directly through appropriate means of communications to the Situation Room, and which shall collect and process data at their level and transmit the same to the Situation Room" (African Union 2002, § 12 (2) (b)).

This is a very important provision as regards our discussion in Chapter 8 of the conditions for the development of this architecture as a regime. In at least two cases, RECs have already established their own early warning systems (also referred to as *regional mechanisms* or *REMs*).[16] It should also be noted that the CEWS is also supposed to collaborate with the United Nations and its agencies as well as with—African and international—research institutions and representatives of what is labeled "civil society".

Chapter 6 is dedicated to the development and operationalization of the CEWS. Based on the direct experience of AU Conflict Management Division officials responsible for the operationalization of this key pillar of the APSA (El-Ghassim Wane, Charles Mwaura and Shewit Hailu) and the collaboration of Doug Bond, João Gomes Porto, Ulf Engel and Simone Kopfmüller, this chapter documents and reflects on the development of a conflict analysis and early warning methodology tailored to the specific needs of the AU. The establishment of CEWS started in 2003 with a series of workshops through which the CMD developed, with African and international consultants, a roadmap for its implementation. On 21 June 2006, the PSC, at its 57th meeting, reviewed the status of implementation of the continental peace and security architecture, urging the Commission to hasten the operationalization of the various pillars, including the CEWS. From 17 to 19 December 2006 in Kempton Park,

---

(SADC) mandated the then president of South Africa, Thabo Mbeki, to lead the regional mediation effort.

16   The Inter-Governmental Authority on Development (IGAD) at the Horn of Africa has established a *Conflict and Early Warning and Response Mechanism* (CEWARN; http://www.cewarn.org) which focuses on pastoral conflict. It is based in Addis Ababa, Ethiopia. The Economic Community of West African States (ECOWAS) is in the process of establishing the *ECOWAS Warning and Response Network* (ECOWARN; http://ecowarn. org) which is run by the ECOWAS Observation and Monitoring Centre in Abuja, Nigeria.

South Africa, the Commission convened a meeting of governmental experts on early warning to, amongst other things, review the Roadmap for the Operationalization of the CEWS. The results of the Kempton Park meeting were communicated to the Member States through a report of the Chairperson, and the AU Executive Council, at its 10th Ordinary Session held in Addis Ababa from 25 to 26 January 2007, finally endorsed the *Framework for the Operationalisation of the Continental Early Warning System* (for a more detailed explanation of these processes refer to African Union, Conflict Management Division 2008a).

As detailed by the authors, at the heart of CEWS lies a hybrid module that combines quantitative and qualitative methods of conflict analysis. It is based on general structural indicators (the so-called Indicators Module) and is fed by dynamic open source information, which is collected automatically through the internet. Analysis is based on standard Strategic Conflict Assessments techniques (African Union, Conflict Management Division 2008b). In the initial months of 2009, the CEWS had already implemented an important part of the data and information gathering infrastructure and had begun producing standardized early warning analysis and policy response options.

In terms of conflict management, and specifically for the deployment of peace support missions and intervention pursuant to Article 4 (h) and (j) of the Constitutive Act (African Union 2000), the African Union is setting up an African Standby Force (African Union 2002, §13). The African Standby Force (ASF) operates under the Chairperson of the Commission who will appoint a Special Representative and a Force Commander for every single operation. It comprises a military, a police and a civilian component. Member States are obliged to contribute troops to the ASF—a requirement which, as will be further discussed below, strengthens our emphasis on the need to think of the APSA as a regime. The African Standby Force shall perform tasks with regard to observation and monitoring missions; other types of peace support missions; intervention in Member States; preventive deployment; peace-building, including post-conflict disarmament and demobilization; and other functions as mandated by the PSC (African Union 2002, §13 (3)). In total, the ASF is planned to be composed of five regional standby brigades. A *Policy Framework for the Establishment of the African Standby Force and the Military Staff Committee* was approved by the African Chiefs of Defense Staff at their third meeting, on 14 May 2003 in Addis Ababa, Ethiopia, and revised at their fourth meeting, in January 2004, also in Addis Ababa. Depending on the deployment scenario, these brigades should be ready for deployment within 14 to 90 days—scenarios 1–4 in 30 days, scenario 5 full deployment in 90 days with a military component deployed in 30 days; and, finally, scenario 6 in 14 days.[17]

---

17   The six scenarios are: (1) AU/Regional Military advice to a Political mission; (2) AU/Regional observer mission co-deployed with UN mission; (3) standalone AU/Regional observer mission; (4) AU/Regional peacekeeping force (PKF) for Chapter VI and preventive deployment missions; (5) AU PKF for complex multidimensional PK mission-low level

Beginning with a detailed analysis of the ASF concept, Jakkie Cilliers and Johann Pottgieter critically review the development and implementation of the ASF in Chapter 7. The authors pay special attention to the issue of mandates of critical importance to understanding the relationship between the UN and the AU in this regard. In addition, Cilliers and Pottgieter provide a discussion on the Rapid Deployment Concept and conclude by reflecting on a set of critical challenges to the operationalization of the ASF. As noted in the chapter, the implementation status of the five brigades varies greatly (for an earlier overview cf. Kent and Malan 2003; for critical analysis of military and logistical capabilities cf. Kinzel 2007; Cilliers 2008). The most advanced region is East Africa with its EASBRIG.[18] In this case, only the civilian component and the standby roster have not been established. The other elements are in place: framework documents have been agreed upon, a memorandum of understanding has been signed, planning elements, a brigade headquarters and centers of excellence have been identified and units have been pledged by the Member States. The regional brigades for West Africa, ECOBRIG,[19] and Southern Africa, SADCBRIG,[20] are on the best way to reach a similar status. In contrast, ECCAS Brig in Central Africa[21] exits only in a rudimentary way and NASBRIG in North Africa[22] is embryonic at best. It is evident that in some of ASF regions complex violent conflicts are unfolding, making it difficult to imagine operations of the standby brigades in this particular region (for instance within the EASBRIG region with ongoing conflicts in Darfur/ Sudan, in Somalia or—at a lower level—between Eritrea and Ethiopia).

Finally, Chapter 8, entitled *The African Peace and Security Architecture: An Evolving Security Regime?*, provides a set of conclusions and directions for future research on the APSA. In this chapter, the editors suggest the need for thinking about the APSA as more than an architectural construct taking shape through the series of formal legal agreements, institutions and decision-making processes currently being implemented. Using regime theory, the authors reflect on the fundamental conditions determining the APSA's development as an effective, durable and resilient regime that binds all primary actors—as will be seen in the pages below, beyond the African Union itself, Regional Economic Communities (RECs) and of course member States—to the set of principles, norms, rules and

---

spoilers (a feature of many current conflicts); and, (6) AU intervention – e.g. genocide situations where international community does not act promptly.

18   Djibouti, Ethiopia, Eritrea, Kenya, Somalia, Sudan, Rwanda and Uganda.

19   Benin, Burkina Faso, Cape Verde, Côte d'Ivoire, Gambia, Ghana, Guinea-Bissau, Liberia, Mali, Niger, Nigeria, Senegal, Sierra Leone and Togo.

20   Angola (double membership, also in ECCAS!), Botswana, Lesotho, Madagascar, Malawi, Mauritius, Mozambique, Namibia, South Africa, Swaziland, Tanzania, Zambia and Zimbabwe.

21   Angola, Burundi, Cameroon, Central African Republic, Chad, Congo, Democratic Republic Congo, Equatorial-Guinea, Gabon and São Tomé and Príncipe.

22   Algeria, Egypt, Libya, Mauritania, Tunisia and West-Sahara.

decision-making processes that underpin the architecture itself. João Gomes Porto and Ulf Engel conclude by highlighting the usefulness of the concept of epistemic communities as central to the processes of internalization of those very principles and norms by actors involved in the APSA, in particular member States. In this, as the fundamental driver of this as-yet proto-regime, the AU Commission (in particular its Peace and Security Department), plays a central role in steering the political processes of cognition and learning through which collective behavior may, in time, be modified in line with the new norms—giving shape to a true, effective and durable peace and security regime in Africa.

Chapter 2
Regional Security in a Global Perspective

Fredrik Söderbaum and Björn Hettne

Introduction

Since the mid-1980s there has been an explosion of various forms of regionalist projects on a global scale. The widening and deepening of the European Union (EU) is the most pervasive example, but regionalism is also made visible through the revitalization or expansion of many other regional projects around the world, such as the African Union (AU), the Association of Southeast Asian Nations (ASEAN), the Economic Community of West African States (ECOWAS), the North American Free Trade Agreement (NAFTA), the Southern African Development Community (SADC), and the Southern Common Market (Mercosur).

Today's regionalism is closely linked with the shifting nature of global politics and the intensification of globalization. Regionalism is characterized by the involvement of almost all governments in the world, but the regional phenomenon also involves a rich variety of non-state actors, resulting in multiplicities of formal and informal regional governance and regional networks in most issue areas. This pluralism and the multidimensionality of contemporary regionalism give rise to a number of new puzzles and challenges for understanding security in today's world.

This chapter introduces the theory, practice, rationale and experience of security cooperation at a regional level. The aim of the chapter is to situate Africa's security regionalism within a wider context, explore its vertical linkages to global peace and security mechanisms and, through a reflection on the relation between security and other forms of regionalism (political, development, economic, etc.), provide the reader with the conceptual tools necessary to evaluate critically its development and implementation. The analysis is organized as follows. In the next section we discuss and conceptualize regionalism, development and security in a globalized world. The third section distinguishes between different dimensions of security regionalism. Thereafter, before rounding up the chapter, we analyze the management of African security regionalism, highlighting in particular the vertical linkages to global peace and security mechanisms.

Regionalism, Development and Security in a Globalized World

Regionalism is a key aspect in the post-Cold War period, and its relevance is not diminished by the current global crisis. It refers to a tendency and a political commitment to organize the world order in terms of regions; more narrowly, the concept refers to a specific regional project. In some definitions of regionalism the actors behind this political commitment are states (see for example Gamble and Payne 2003); in others non-state actors are given a crucial role (including Bøås et al. 2003). Regionalization refers to the more complex process of forming regions; whether these are consciously planned projects or caused by spontaneous processes is not agreed upon by all authors. As we noted elsewhere, "regionalization denotes the (empirical) process that leads to patterns of cooperation, integration, complementarity and convergence within a particular cross-national geographical space." Furthermore, we considered that a region can be more or less coherent, referring to this as the level of "regionness," or the "process whereby a geographical area is transformed from a passive object to an active subject capable of articulating the transnational interests of the emerging region" (Hettne and Söderbaum 2000, 461). A higher degree of regionness and regional identity therefore implies the capacity to act, or "actorness" (Hettne 2005). Lower regionness consequently implies greater impact on the region from the outside, which—as will be further discussed below—is the case with the African region. The level of actorness can best be assessed in the security field, where success or failure is more visible. A high level of actorness also means that security policy may reach outside the particular region and even influence or shape world order. This is so far the case only with the EU.

While the focus of first generation regional integration studies (1950s and 1960s) was ostensibly the economic sphere, it should be noted that peace and security were in fact a crucial underlying concern. Tending to see the nation-state as the problem rather than the solution, relevant theories for first generation regional integration approaches included federalism and functionalism/neofunctionalism and focused primarily on European integration (Rosamond 2000). More akin to a political program rather than a theory per se, federalism inspired the pioneers of European integration, underlying their skepticism of the nation-state—although, paradoxically, what was to be created was rather a new kind of state. There was no obvious theorist associated with federalism. In contrast, functionalism has been much identified with one particular name: David Mitrany. The question for functionalists was on which political level various human needs (often defined in a rather technical way) best could be met. While functionalism also proposed going beyond the nation-state, this did not necessarily imply going regional (Mitrany 1966). Thus, both federalism and functionalism wanted the nation-state to go, but through different routes and by different means. Neofunctionalism, on the other hand, more explicitly discussed integration as a region-building process— the positive implications in terms of security often taken for granted as part of processes of region-building, the assumption being of a spill-over effect from economic integration to political unity (Hettne 2003, 27). Ernst Haas' theory of European region-building remains key to an understanding of the neo-functionalist paradigm (Haas 1958). The security dimensions of regional integration would be further elaborated by Karl Deutsch, for whom, what was created in Europe was in fact a *regional security community* defined as "the attainment of institutions and practices strong enough and widespread enough to assure, for a long time, dependable expectations of peaceful change among its population" (Deutsch 1968, 194).

Today it has become commonplace to distinguish between an older wave or generation of regionalism ("regional integration") and a more recent, new "generation" of regionalism ("the new regionalism") starting in the latter half of the 1980s, and now being a prevalent phenomenon throughout the world. New regionalism studies have considered new aspects and dimensions of the phenomenon, particularly those focused on its relations to globalization. There are many ways in which globalization and regionalism interact and overlap, according to scholars of the new regionalism (Bøås et al. 1999; Cooper et al. 2008; Hettne et al. 1999; Söderbaum and Shaw 2003; Telò 2007). Yet, even if contemporary regionalism is intimately related to globalization it must be emphasized that regionalism needs to be understood both from an exogenous perspective (according to which regionalization and globalization are intertwined articulations of global transformation) and from an endogenous perspective (according to which regionalization is shaped from within the region by a large number of different actors) (Hettne 2002). As mentioned above, the exogenous perspective has primarily developed during recent new regionalism debates, whereas the endogenous perspective underlines, to an extent, some continuity with functionalist and neofunctionalist theorizing about the integration of Europe, the role of agency and the long-term transformation of territorial identities. In addition, and in contrast to the period in which Haas and the early regional integration scholars were writing, we find many different regionalisms today and thus a very different base for comparative studies. It is apparent that neither the object for study (ontology) nor the way of studying it (epistemology) has remained static.

One indication of the above is the emergence of a rich variety of theoretical frameworks for the study of regionalism and regional integration (Söderbaum and Shaw 2003). Indeed, current regionalism may be seen as a new political landscape in the making, characterized by an increasing set of actors (state and non-state) operating on the regional arena and across several interrelated dimensions (security, development, trade, environment, culture, and so on). Of particular importance is the way the dimensions of development and peace are related—as, over time, development has been increasingly linked to security, in an elusive development-security nexus. Often ignoring the empirical relations that always have existed between development and security, academia has produced two distinct discourses on the relationship between these factors. More recently, however, these two discourses have been converging through concepts such as human security and human development.

In the most general sense, development is a way to conceptualize those aspects of pervasive, continuous social change to which human actors attribute particular meaning and value, and which in some sense and to a varying extent are believed to be possible to influence. The conventional view of security emanates from the position of the individual nation-state in an anarchic international system; it basically concerns the survival of the state as such, that is to say, the preservation of its sovereignty. Security problems today, however, usually refer to much more than military threat. The UNDP's *Human Development Report* 1994 first took up the question of human security, defined as "safety from hunger, disease, and repression," thereby moving security towards the development corner. In later UNDP reports the concept was conceptually connected to 'human development', and ultimately to the whole complex of human rights. Other relevant links are "humanitarian emergency" and "humanitarian intervention." One can see this contemporary focus on "the human" as part of a paradigm shift that gives rise to a post-national logic. The frequent use of the concept "human" in different constellations points to an association with an assumption of transnational responsibility, as if one could no longer rely on states to fulfill their fundamental duties to their citizens.

In the 1990s, as a result of the spread of post-Cold War disorder, particularly in peripheral regions such as Africa, there emerged a qualitatively new discourse on intervention called "humanitarian intervention": a coercive involvement by external powers in a "domestic conflict" with the purpose of preventing anarchy, punishing human rights abuses, and promoting democracy and "good governance." Complex humanitarian emergencies thus refer to serious multidimensional crises in which the issue of coercive intervention from outside naturally arises.

Understanding the complex and intricate linkages between development and security is thus a demanding task. In this chapter we are mainly concerned with the relations between development regionalism and security regionalism. Development regionalism means concerted efforts from a group of countries within a geographical region to enhance the economic complementarity of constituent political units in order to strengthen the total capacity of the regional economy. Security regionalism, on the other hand, refers to attempts by states and other actors in a particular geographical area—a region in the making—to transform a security complex with conflict-generating interstate and intrastate relations towards a security community characterized by cooperative external (interregional) relations and internal (intraregional) peace.

In the more recent theoretical literature we find that security concerns still appear relevant but these are often seen as causal factors forcing countries to cooperate, due to the risk of regionalization of conflict. By this is meant both the outward spread or spill-over of a local conflict into neighboring countries, and the inward impact from the region, in the form of more or less diplomatic interference, military intervention and, preferably, conflict resolution, carried out by some kind of regional body. Security regionalism has now become a genre in itself, although there are different approaches as well as different dimensions, as will be discussed below.

Dimensions of Security Regionalism

Regionalism and security can be related in many different ways. One such way has to do with the choice of unit of investigation—e.g. a regional security complex—defined by Barry Buzan as "a group of states whose primary security concerns link together sufficiently closely that their national security cannot realistically be considered apart from one another" (Buzan 1991, 190). The concept has later been rethought in a multisectoral and social constructivist direction, making the actual delimitation of the unit more nuanced, but not easier since different security sectors (economic, environmental, societal) may define different regions (Buzan 2003). The idea of securitization further adds to this fluency of the concept (Buzan and Wæver 2003). In an alternative approach developed by Lake and Morgan regions are defined in terms of the mode of security management or "regional order" (Lake and Morgan 1997). Regional orders can shift from simple balance of power systems or concerts to more comprehensive communities or integrated polities. The authors also suggest an alternative definition of regional security complex: "the states affected by at least one transborder but local security externality" (Lake and Morgan 1997, 46). The region is nevertheless also primarily a level of analysis.

Another link between regionalism and security concerns the regional implications of a local conflict. These depend on the nature of the security complex and the way various security problems are vertically and horizontally linked in particular regions, which can and do vary highly. Some local conflicts may primarily affect relations with different forms of higher authority, while others may concern political rivalry among ethnic groups or cross-border competition for land and other natural resources. Yet another link between regionalism and security has to do with the conflict management role of the organized region, if there is one. This may include a role in internal regional security ("regional order"); a conflict management role in the immediate environment of the region (e.g. the neighborhood policy of the EU), as well as a role at the level of world order, to the extent that there may be 'actorness' enough to influence the shape of world order. Conflict management with regard to the immediate environment (outside the region) can refer to efforts at management of an acute conflict or aim at preventively transforming the situation, either by stabilization or by integration (enlargement of the regional organization).

The region can thus be the cause (the regional complex), the means (regional security management), and the solution (regional development). The level of regionness can be purposively changed in order to increase actorness and conflict management. For instance, security cooperation within a region would lead to improved stability, making the region more attractive for international investment and trade, and development regionalism would mean a more efficient use of available resources. There are, in terms of political stability and economic dynamics, of course different types of regions in the world where these approaches apply differently: core regions, intermediate regions and peripheral regions. Africa belongs to the third category (Hettne 2005).

The focus upon human security rather than state security is significant for understanding the change of the security and development discourse and the fundamental challenge to sovereignty during the 1990s. Implied in concepts such as "human security", "human development", "human emergency", and "humanitarian intervention" was the idea of a transnational responsibility for human welfare (the responsibility to protect, or R2P). While this discourse has, following the events of 9/11, been overshadowed by the discourse on global terrorism, R2P as a concept and norm still has wide support. In fact, this normative orientation has had a deep impact on regional organizations, not least in Africa where, as will be fully explored in the chapters to follow, the African Union's *Constitutive Act* concedes to it "the right to intervene" in another AU member state in respect of grave circumstances such as war crimes, genocide and crimes against humanity as well as against unconstitutional changes of government. In East and Southeast Asia on the other hand, there is an intense debate about "the Asian Way," in contrast to universal principles of human rights and liberal democracy (Acharya 2001). Is this evidence that the conventional hierarchical relationship between UN-based multilateralism and regionalism is being transformed even challenged?

Most observers claim that the UN constitutes the foundation of a rules-based world order. Go-it-alone strategies outside a UN framework—for instance, through NATO plurilateralism or US unilateralism—are controversial. Regionalism constitutes the main rules-based alternative to UN-based multilateralism, and its role has been intensively discussed at various junctures during the last century. In 1992, the UN Secretary-General's *Agenda for Peace* called for involvement of regional organizations in activities such as preventive diplomacy, peacekeeping, peacemaking, and post-conflict reconstruction (Boutros-Ghali 1992). Over the next 13 years, successive UN Secretary-Generals convened six high-level meetings with regional organizations from all the continents involved in security matters. In 2005, the Secretary-General's *In Larger Freedom* stated that "the United Nations and regional organizations should play complementary roles in facing the challenges to peace and security" (Annan 2005, 52). Likewise, the High Level Panel on Threats, Challenges and Change, set up by the Secretary-General to reflect on UN reform, acknowledged in its 2004 report that regional groupings have made "important contributions to the stability and prosperity of their members" (UN 2004, 85). The High Level Panel also urged the Security Council to make greater use of Chapter VIII provisions to use regional organizations to prevent and respond to threats. The critical requirements from a UN perspective are that: (a) regional action should be organized within the UN Charter and be consistent with its purposes and principles; and (b) the UN and regional organizations should collaborate more effectively and in a more integrated fashion than in the past (cf. Thakur 2005a).

Some proponents of this line have certainly developed greater recognition of the role of regional organizations. For example, Ramesh Thakur has acknowledged that there is an increasing gap between legality and legitimacy in multilateralism and that the UN cannot deliver a legitimate world order on its own. Regional arrangements closer to home can, in his view, counter perceptions of "external imposition" by a distant global UN. Yet, this approach stresses that to be legitimate such regionalism must be compatible with, and contribute to, UN-based multilateralism. For Thakur, regional organizations "may insert fresh blood into multilateralism" and fill some of its gaps, but they must do so within the UN framework (Thakur 2005b). In other words, it is a vertical order whereby multilateral sanction is necessary for regional interventions to be legal and fully legitimate.

With the rise of so-called "new regionalism" in recent decades, regional organizations have become actors in their own right. A number of them—including AU, ASEAN, ECOWAS, EU and SADC—have acquired some kind of institutionalized mechanism for conflict management. Regions, through their regional agencies, have transformed from objects into subjects, making their relationship to the UN much more complex than current policy and academic debates tend to recognize.

Regional Conflict Management in Africa

During the Cold War, most types of conflicts in Africa followed the systemic logic of that order. They formed part of the bipolar struggle or were "solved" by way of interventions from superpowers, former colonial powers or powerful neighbors. In the post-Cold War era a new pattern has emerged whereby conflicts are allowed to erupt and also continue, waiting for more appropriate solutions. Even though most contemporary conflicts in Africa are often defined as "domestic", they are deeply embedded in a regional and cross-border context. As illustrated by cases such as Liberia, Sierra Leone, the Democratic Republic of Congo (DRC) and more recently Sudan (Darfur)/Chad, most conflicts on the African continent spill over into neighboring countries or draw regional actors into what is often better understood as regional war-zones than simply "domestic conflicts." This pattern, leads in turn, to a much greater role for action, mediation and intervention at the regional level by affected neighboring countries and especially by regional organizations.

When African Heads of State and Government decided to reshape the Organization of African Unity (OAU) into the AU, one of the main impetuses behind the transformation was the declared will to "tackle African conflicts through African solutions." This vision has also been enthusiastically supported by the international community, in particular Western powers. Several of the other main regional organizations in Africa (ECOWAS, IGAD, SADC, etc.) have also developed distinct approaches to peace and security. There exist, however, fundamental differences of outlook and style among the regional organizations, reflecting different perceptions of threat, historical experience and cultural background, with correspondingly different strategies towards the maintenance of peace and security and the respective roles of the UN and regional and sub-regional organizations.

Based on actual cases of intervention, what follows is a discussion of some of the approaches to peace and security shown by African regional organizations, including the AU itself, but also ECOWAS, IGAD and SADC. These very different cases will allow us to conclude this chapter by reflecting on whether a region-centered approach can be more relevant than a UN-led approach in the emerging global security context; to what extent is a regional approach more efficient than multilateral mechanisms in terms of closeness and commitment; and, finally, are regional organizations better than multilateral efforts at addressing conflict prevention as well as post-conflict reconstruction? Ultimately, to be realized as a continent wide peace and security architecture where regional economic communities (RECs) are constituent, indeed critical components—an issue fully discussed in Gomes Porto and Engel's chapter on APSA as a security regime in the pages below—understanding the different trajectories, strategies and experiences of the AU and the RECs is key.

African Union

The AU was created in 2002 with the purpose of securing Africa's democracy, human rights, and sustainable development, in particular by bringing an end to intra-African conflict and creating the African Economic Community (AEC). As a successor to the OAU, the AU remains the primary forum for debating African unity and cooperation, with all African states having assumed membership (53 in total), except Morocco, which withdrew in the mid-1980s due the OAU's recognition of Western Sahara.

As noted by the editors in the introduction to this volume, the AU is guided by 14 objectives, designed to enhance political cooperation and economic integration, ranging from greater unity and solidarity between the countries and peoples of Africa, to promotion of democratic principles and good governance, to protection of human rights, to coordination and harmonization between the regional economic communities (RECs). The attainment of these objectives is to be achieved through the observance of a number of fundamental principles, in accordance with which the AU shall function. These principles include, among others, the participation of African people in Union activities, promotion of self-reliance within the Union's framework, promotion of gender equality and of social justice, respect for the sanctity of human life, prohibition on the threat of or use of force, the establishment of a common defense policy, and the condemnation and rejection of unconstitutional changes of government.

The AU remains consistent with the spirit of Pan-Africanism and many of the general principles and programs developed under the OAU. However, the AU's architects consider that the organization is not simply a continuation of the OAU under a new name. Three differences are worth highlighting: (1) the institutional structure; (2) the change in development thinking; (3) the new peace and security architecture. Although the AU has inherited many of the OAU's institutions, it has committed itself to a new and stronger institutional structure. In addition to the Assembly of Heads of State and the Council of Ministers, the AU also has the African Commission (headed by a Chairperson), and the Pan-African Parliament (launched in South Africa in 2004). It further plans a Court of Justice (to rule on human rights abuses) as well as various financial institutions (a central bank, a monetary fund, and an investment bank).

The actual impact and effectiveness of the new institutional structure is, at this point in time, rather uncertain. The OAU has long been criticized for having been solely an instrument for corrupt and authoritarian elites. Officially, the AU regards itself as different, with policies against unconstitutional changes of government and increased emphasis on good governance and democracy. Especially notable in this regard is the incorporation of the African Peer Review Mechanism (APRM) of the New Partnership for Africa's Development (NEPAD) as an instrument of the Union, with the potential of making African leaders accountable to one another and to the Union.

Regarding economic development and economic integration, the AU is based on two main mechanisms: (1) the Abuja Treaty (1991) which provides for a gradual establishment of the AEC with the RECs as building-blocks, and (2) NEPAD. As indicated above, there is a radically different "development thinking" and economic integration approach within the AU compared to the old OAU. From the 1960s until well into the 1990s, the dominant view within the OAU was that Africa was negatively affected by its dependence on the North and former colonial powers. De-linking and "collective self-reliance" were consequently advanced as ways to enhance Africa's economic, political and socio-cultural development. By contrast, the thinking dominating today's AU is that Africa's marginalization and underdevelopment should be overcome by closer integration into the world economy. Hence, there is a much stronger emphasis on outward-oriented regional economic integration through both the RECs and NEPAD, and a trading agenda that should be compatible with the World Trade Organization (WTO), although in practice trading arrangements with the US, China, and the EU tend to take priority.

The change in thinking is perhaps most dramatic in the case of NEPAD, which was launched through the then OAU in 2001 (NEPAD 2001; Taylor 2004). NEPAD is quite similar to many previous (yet failed) recovery plans in Africa in that it outlines a comprehensive list of development projects and programs. However, NEPAD is different in that it stresses a closer engagement (and "partnership") with the North, as well as good governance, democracy and an improvement in Africa's political-economic leadership. This reflects dominant understandings of capitalism and development, as espoused by the World Bank, the International Monetary Fund and the donor community. According to NEPAD's own logic, access to markets, aid, investment flows and debt relief are all deemed necessary for the continent's recovery (NEPAD 2001).

As discussed by Engel and Gomes Porto in the introduction to this volume, in sharp contrast to the OAU's rather poor record of mediating in disputes and conflicts on the African continent, the AU aims to develop a more relevant role for itself, having created, among others, a Peace and Security Council (PSC). While the old principle of non-interference in internal affairs of member states, which had paralyzed much of the OAU's work is still part of the AU's Constitutive Act, as already noted the AU has 'the right to intervene' in another AU member state in respect of grave circumstances such as war crimes, genocide and crimes against humanity (African Union 2000, §4 (h); African Union 2002, §4 (j)). The AU can monitor and intervene in conflicts, authorize troop deployments, and mandate peacekeeping operations. It plans to have a stand-by rapid-reaction force in place by 2010: the African Standby Force will be discussed at length by Cilliers and Pottgieter in Chapter Seven. These institutions are expected to make the AU much more relevant for dealing with so-called "new wars": that is, the civil wars and complex humanitarian emergencies that are developing in the context of globalization and after the end of the Cold War. However, two fundamental problems with these institutional developments point to a need for a deeper engagement beyond Africa itself. One is the lack of resources that African leaders are prepared to commit to joint security affairs. The other is a somewhat loosely defined relationship with the UN, which may challenge the effectiveness of collaboration between the two bodies—as evidenced by the levels of distrust and prevarication that marked the deployment of the hybrid mission to the Darfur crisis in Sudan.

While the AU has some experience in peacebuilding and peacemaking, the organization—often compelled by the international community—has tended to concentrate its response efforts on conflict management through peacekeeping and peace enforcement operations, as will be briefly discussed in the following pages. The AU has thus far deployed missions to Burundi, Sudan/Darfur, Somalia and Comoros. Military operations are, conventionally, deployed to supervise, observe, monitor, and verify the implementation of ceasefire agreements or to help broke cease-fires between government and rebel groups (Murithi 2005; Francis 2006).

The mandate of AMIB (African Union Mission in Burundi), which lasted from April 2003 to May 2004, was to supervise, observe, monitor and verify the implementation of the Ceasefire Agreement, signed in August 2000, in order to further consolidate the peace process in that country. In 2004, the UN took over the peacekeeping operations from AMIB with the creation of the United Nations Operation in Burundi (ONUB). Later, in January 2007, the AU Special Task Force in Burundi was deployed with the mandate to facilitate the implementation of the Dar es Salaam peace agreement of June 2006, between the government and the PALIPEHUTU-FNL (commonly known as "FNL")—the most extreme Hutu group, which had not taken part in the Arusha Agreement. Composed of the South African Battalion that served under the AMIB, the mission was re-hatted under an AU mandate when the UN mandate came to an end on 31 December 2006.

In Sudan/Darfur the AU helped broke a ceasefire between the government of Sudan and rebel groups. When launched in August 2004, the African Union Mission in Sudan (AMIS) initially had fewer than 100 observers in Darfur to monitor the agreement, but gradually increased its presence to include soldiers and police. By 2005, the AU had nearly 7000 troops in Darfur. A more sizable, better-equipped UN peacekeeping force was originally proposed for September 2006, but due to Sudanese government opposition, it was not implemented. AMIS's mandate was repeatedly extended throughout 2006 and 2007, while the situation in Darfur continued to escalate. On 1 January 2008, AMIS was finally replaced by a hybrid United Nations/AU Mission in Darfur (UNAMID).

The objective of the AU's mission in Somalia (AMISOM) since March 2007 is to carry out support for dialogue and reconciliation by assisting with the free movement, safe passage and protection of all those involved in a national reconciliation congress involving all stakeholders. It includes assistance with the implementation of the National Security and Stabilization Plan, and contribution to the creation of the necessary security conditions for the provision of humanitarian assistance. The mission has a UN Chapter VII mandate and is expected to comprise 8000 troops—yet, by March 2008, only 1500 AU peacekeepers from Uganda and around 400 from Burundi have been deployed.

The African Union Electoral and Security Assistance Mission to the Comoros (MAES) was deployed in May 2007 and is composed of approximately 300 soldiers and police. The fighting sparked when Mohamed Bacar, the leader of one of the islands (Anjouan) refused to stand down as the constitution demands if he wanted to run again for president. In October 2007, the AU decided to impose individual sanctions on 168 leaders of Anjouan by freezing their foreign accounts and restricting their ability to travel. And in March 2008, 1,500 AU troops (from Sudan, Tanzania and Senegal with logistical support from Libya) gave support to a military operation aimed at toppling Mohamed Bacar. The mission was successful, national rule of law was restored, and Mr Bacar sought political asylum in France. To date, the AU has deployed six missions with the objective of preventing electoral processes from mutating into political turmoil.

In addition to peacekeeping, the AU is engaged in the full spectrum of conflict management and conflict resolution, from conflict prevention to peacebuilding. It has sent election observers to approximately 20 countries and in 2002 adopted a *Declaration on the Principles Governing Democratic Elections in Africa*. The AU has served as a mediator or a third party on various instances. One example is in Rwanda-DRC (2004) (Murithi 2005, 108). Another is Sudan, where it helped negotiate an initial ceasefire and hosted peace talks from 2004 onwards between the Sudanese government and representatives of Darfur's rebel groups in Abuja, Nigeria. The talks, which proceeded with the support and close cooperation of international partners, including the United Nations, resulted in the signing of the Darfur Peace Agreement on 5 May 2006. In Togo, the AU reacted forcefully to the unlawful takeover of the Togolese presidency by Faure Gnassingbé following the death of his father, President Gnassingbé Eyadéma, in February 2005. More recently, in 2007, AU mediators visited Sudan, Chad and the Central African Republic (CAR) to try to ease tensions created by the Darfur crisis. In 2008, the AU attempted to mediate between government and opposition parties in Kenya.

Economic Community of West African States

Rooted in discussions dating back to the mid-1960s, the Economic Community of West African States (ECOWAS) was created in 1975 as the first West African organization that purported to bridge the Francophone-Anglophone gap. Nevertheless, many of the problems associated with the organization are related to the perception that it is a Nigerian-led instrument to enforce hegemony—a perception held especially by its Francophone members, who have continued to strengthen their ties with France, creating among themselves the West African Economic and Monetary Union (UEMOA).

ECOWAS has developed in a very volatile regional context. The diversity of West Africa is reflected in its history with a Francophone, Anglophone and Lusophone colonial divide, and socio-cultural, ethnic and linguistic differences. Moreover, West Africa "is the region *par excellence* of the military coup d'état" (Souaré 2006). West Africa can in fact be understood as a "regional conflict complex" because armed conflicts "are not just confined and localized within state borders, but the regional dimensions and dynamics often fuel and sustain these wars through the activities of the shadow economy and peace spoilers" (Francis 2006, 43). Although ECOWAS's original agenda was focused on economic integration and development, today it is probably best known for its security profile. In fact, ECOWAS is the African sub-regional organization with the largest operational experience in peace and security, encouraged by numerous UN Security Council Resolutions and Secretary General's reports.

The first ECOWAS mission was in Liberia between 1990 and 1997. Following the outbreak of civil war that pitted Charles Taylor (NPFL) against government forces (led by President Samuel Doe), ECOWAS deployed a mission with the mandate "to conduct military operations for the purpose of monitoring the ceasefire" and restore "law and order to create the necessary conditions for free and fair elections." The Economic Community of West African States Monitoring Group (ECOMOG), however, soon found its mandate complicated by the violent capacity of the warring factions. Not long after its deployment, ECOMOG shifted from being a peacekeeper to performing peace enforcement tasks. There was a second operation in Liberia in 2003. After President Taylor resigned office and departed into exile in Nigeria, conditions were created for the deployment by ECOWAS, in August 2003, of what became a 3,600-strong peacekeeping mission in Liberia (ECOMIL). The UN took over security in Liberia in October 2003, subsuming ECOMIL into the United Nations Mission in Liberia (UNMIL), a force that grew to its present size of nearly 15,000.

Other well-known ECOWAS operations included Sierra Leone during 1997–1999, Guinea Bissau (1998–1999) and Côte d'Ivoire (2003–2004). The mission in Sierra Leone was established after Nigerian leader, General Sani Abacha, diverted peacekeepers from the Liberia mission to Sierra Leone in an attempt to crush a military coup by the Sierra Leonean army in May 1997. Nigerian-led ECOWAS troops reversed the coup in February 1998 and restored President Ahmed Tejan Kabbah to power. The goal of the ECOWAS operation in Guinea Bissau (1998–1999) was to end civil conflict between President João Bernardino Vieira (backed by Senegalese and Guinean military forces), and his former army chief, Ansumane Mané. Given the continuous degradation of the conflict and its poor capacity to cope with it, ECOWAS withdrew its forces before the conflict was resolved. The ECOWAS mission in Côte d'Ivoire (2003–2004) was deployed in order to facilitate the implementation of the Linas-Marcoussis Agreement that put an end to the civil war that had broken out in September 2002. On 27 February 2004, the UN Security Council passed a Resolution authorizing a full peacekeeping operation for Côte d'Ivoire, and mandating nearly 7,000 UN troops to monitor and help implement the peace agreement. The ECOWAS forces have been, as a result, subsumed within the UN mandated operation.

ECOWAS military interventions have been marred by controversy. Critical analyses have demonstrated many operational weaknesses, including the lack of unified command and control, with troop-contributing countries keeping close national control of their forces. Other weaknesses have included the absence of community-wide logistical arrangements prior to the deployment of ECOMOG forces, which have led to "panicky responses to underestimated threats from rebel forces; and lop-sided national reinforcements that served to further complicate regional diplomacy" (Adibe 2002, 157–158). ECOMOG in all its operations relied on an inadequate and poor military capability, logistics and structure. The improvisatory nature of its deployments also catalyzed the lack of clarity of its mandate, especially relating to peacekeeping and peace enforcement (Ero 2000; Francis 2006, 177).

Intergovernmental Authority on Development

IGAD is the successor organization to the Intergovernmental Authority on Drought and Development (IGADD), created in 1986 by six drought-stricken East African countries—Djibouti, Ethiopia, Kenya, Somalia, Sudan, and Uganda; Eritrea joined in 1993—with a narrow mandate around the issues of drought and desertification. With the active encouragement of the United Nations Environment Program (UNEP), IGADD was created in order to improve the regional response to natural disasters (Berman and Sams 2000, 207). In the mid-1990s the founding members of IGADD decided to revitalize the organization into a fully-fledged regional political, economic, development, trade, and security entity similar to ECOWAS and SADC. One of the principal motivations for the revitalization of

IGADD was the existence of many organizational and structural problems that made the implementation of its goals and principles ineffective. In 1996, IGAD identified three priority areas of cooperation: (i) conflict prevention, management and resolution, and humanitarian affairs; (ii) infrastructure development (transport and communications); and (iii) food security and environmental protection.

The initial enthusiasm soon encountered various obstacles and the leaders quickly realized that the efficiency of IGAD was hampered by several factors, such as extreme poverty, natural calamities (floods, famine, water shortages, droughts), civil wars and political instability (not least a deadly conflict between Ethiopia and Eritrea). It has been contended that "IGAD's inability to foster peace and security cooperation among the countries in the Horn stems fundamentally from the persisting suspicions, geographical rivalries, and ideological differences among its members" (Lund and Betts 1999, 123).

IGAD has been involved in negotiating a peace settlement in Sudan since 1993. In 1999, a Secretariat was created in Nairobi to ensure continued engagement with the parties to the conflict. The process, however, has been stalled over the question of the separation of state and religion and the right to self-determination. In 2002, the Machakos Protocol agreed by the Government of Sudan and the Sudan People's Liberation Movement/Army (SPLM/A) under the auspices of IGAD opened the way for the signing of a peace agreement in 2005. The United Nations has closely followed and supported the regional peace initiative. The Secretary-General's Special Adviser, Mr Mohamed Sahnoun, and other senior officials represented the UN at IGAD summit meetings, and carried out consultations with regional governments and organizations in support of the peace process. They also took part in meetings of the IGAD-Partners Forum, composed of donor countries and organizations supporting the IGAD peace process and assisting the regional organization to enhance its capacity in several areas. The UN Advanced Mission in Sudan (UNAMIS) was set up in order to prepare for a fully fledged UN peace support mission to be deployed during the interim period following the signing of a Comprehensive Peace Agreement (CPA) between the Government of Sudan and the Sudan People's Liberation Movement/Army (SPLM/A) as the result of the IGAD-led negotiations. UNAMIS was transformed into the UN Mission in Sudan (UNMIS) in March 2005, after the UN Security Council adopted Resolution 1590, which tasked UNMIS with supporting the Government of Sudan and the SPLM/A in the implementation of the CPA.

Besides Sudan, IGAD is also involved in Somalia. In 1998, in cooperation with the IGAD Forum Partners Liaison Group, IGAD members created a Standing Committee on the Somali peace process, chaired by Ethiopia. This committee was mandated to organize a peace process in Somalia by providing a consultative forum for negotiations aimed at reconciliation and restoration of a government in Somalia. The current Transitional Federal Government is a result of Ethiopia's effort in finding a solution for Somalia, and it received the approval of IGAD. The UN offered its backing on the settlement of the Somalia situation. The Secretary-General's Special Adviser, Ambassador Mohamed Sahnoun, accompanied by his

Representative for Somalia, Winston Tubman, collaborated actively with IGAD leaders in efforts to re-energize the stalled reconciliation process during 2003–2004. In March 2005, IGAD proposed a Peace Support Mission to Somalia involving 10,000 troops, at a cost of $500 million for the first year (Tavares 2009). In order to allow the deployment of IGAD troops under Chapter VIII of the Charter, the UN Security Council approved a partial lifting of the arms embargo on Somalia. However this deployment never occurred and was replaced by a deployment of AU troops. IGAD's availability, unlike AU's, was not followed by international commitment to support the intervention. IGAD officials claim that the lack of international support was a result of the US's deliberate intention not to have any country or organization intervening in Somalia. However, when Islamists took power in Somalia in 2006, the US put the country on the map of the global war on terrorism, and withdrew its reservations over intervention (Tavares 2009).

Southern African Development Community

SADC was established in 1993, and replaced the Southern African Development Coordinating Conference (SADCC), which was established in April 1980. SADCC's goal was to foster regional economic cooperation, and diminish economic dependence on the outside world, especially apartheid South Africa. The new venture, SADC, has officially embraced more conventional regional economic integration together with sectoral cooperation. In the mid-1990s, SADC established the Organ for Politics, Defense and Security Cooperation. According to its mandate, the Organ operates in seven clusters: military issues; peacemaking, peacekeeping and peace enforcement; conflict prevention, management and resolution; crime prevention; intelligence; foreign policy; and human rights. Moreover, in 2003, SADC adopted a Mutual Defense Pact, whereby, "an armed attack against a State Party shall be considered a threat to regional peace and security and such an attack shall be met with immediate collective action" (§§ 6-1). By taking this step, the SADC became constitutionally equipped to operate not only as a Chapter VIII organization, but also as an alliance organization, with latitude of action under Art. 51 of the UN Charter.

Although the SADC has adopted a comprehensive and fairly agile organizational structure to handle issues of peace and security, it still has a limited record in the field with interventions in the area of peacekeeping and enforcement, having included Lesotho and the DRC. On 22 September 1998, South African troops entered Lesotho to prevent mutinous soldiers of the Royal Lesotho Defense Force (RLDF) from staging a military coup. The South African contingent was part of a SADC Combined Task Force. Their objectives were to prevent a military coup, to disarm the mutineers, and to create a safe and stable environment for the diplomatic initiative to find a peaceful solution to the political crisis in Lesotho. However, because of the way in which the intervention was authorized, structured and deployed, it has been marred by criticism on the basis that the intervention was in fact a South African intervention aimed at entrenching the rule of the governing Lesotho Congress for Democracy (LCD) party. It should be noted that the intervention in Lesotho did not have the approval of the UN Security Council.

The military intervention in the DRC by Angola, Namibia and Zimbabwe in 1998 has also been widely discussed, and views differ as to the appropriateness of the action. The participating countries argued that they were acting on the basis of collective self-defense. The fact that only some members of SADC participated has sparked controversy. There were claims of an intense internal rivalry in SADC. The intervention by only three member states was facilitated by the fact that until its 2002 restructuring, the Organ had a high degree of independence from the rest of SADC's institutions. The military intervention was only retroactively recognized by the SADC but it did not have the approval of the UN Security Council.

Apart from peacekeeping and peace enforcement, SADC has also been active in peacemaking. For instance, in October 1994, SADC members strongly pressured Mozambican RENAMO leader Afonso Dlakhama not to withdraw from the elections in Mozambique. Also in the late 1990s, the presidents of South Africa, Botswana, and Zimbabwe paid 'fatherly visits' to King Mswati III of Swaziland to advise him not to curb popular democratic demands. Finally, former South African President Thabo Mbeki was also engaged in mediation efforts in Zimbabwe on behalf of SADC.

Conclusion

This chapter has tried to situate security regionalism and conflict management in Africa in a global perspective. One of the initial assumptions was that purely state-centric approaches to understanding conflict and peace-building are problematic and at worst dangerous, at least for human security. The African experience shows that sometimes the state is not much more than a malfunctioning bureaucracy, and as an actor the state may also be fuelling conflict and threatening human security. At other times the state undoubtedly provides human security in a hostile environment. It is important to recognize that non-state actors are also part of the security logic, both in a positive and a negative sense. In this partly new situation it is relevant to unpack the state and investigate when and for whom the state is a threat or a shelter. Furthermore, even though most contemporary conflicts in Africa are defined as "domestic", they often quickly become regionalized, i.e. spill-over into neighboring countries or draw regional actors into the conflict. Such regionalization of conflict underlines the relevance of regional security cooperation.

There are undoubtedly some crucial problems and challenges with regional security mechanisms in Africa. First, the underlying reasons (as opposed to the official declarations) for military interventions are often closely associated with myopic regime interests. Indeed, several regional peacekeeping missions have more or less been 'manipulated' by governments seeking to camouflage and legitimize their individual regime interests, jeopardizing, in this way, the regional agenda. This is closely related with the fact that regional institutions can show a lack of neutrality and there has even been abuse of regional security mechanisms, as most evidently seen in the case of SADC and ECOWAS. According to Diehl, such problems weigh more heavily on regional as compared with multilateral peace-keeping (Diehl 1994, 131).

Second, the operational and bureaucratic ineffectiveness and resource constraints of African security mechanisms present another set of challenges. All regional security mechanisms in Africa are spectacularly under-resourced. For an organization that is mandated to prevent, resolve, and reconstruct countries in the aftermath of conflicts, the AU possesses neither enough physical nor qualified human resources to meet the challenges. Third, and intimately related to the previous point, the African Union's operational capacity in peace and security is almost fully dependent on external development assistance: infrastructure, salaries, and professional training are covered by contributions from the EU (African Peace Facility), Germany, Denmark, the US, China, the United Nations Development Program (UNDP), and Canada.

This chapter shows that security regionalism in Africa has to be understood in relation to the fundamental question of what is the optimal relationship between global bodies and regional agencies in global security. This question has been intensively discussed at various junctures during the last century, including at the establishment of the United Nations (UN) in the 1940s. The long-standing prevailing view of the global-regional relationship in security matters has posited that a dominant UN would delegate tasks to subordinate regional institutions, especially under Chapter VIII of the Charter. In this conception the region is simply an intermediate actor that undertakes tasks determined at the multilateral level. Today, the debate between the UN and regional organizations has resurfaced— among policymakers as well as the research community—as one of the most important issues in the global security architecture, not only regarding the reform of the UN Security Council but also with regard to the emerging regional security architectures in Europe, Africa, Asia and to some extent also in the Americas.

In spite of the problems associated with security regionalism mentioned above, there are at the same time many reasons why a region-centered approach can be more relevant than an UN-led approach in the emerging global security context. For instance, the regional spill-overs and regionalization of many so-called "domestic" conflicts require regional solutions, which is particularly evident in most cases in Africa. The regional approach is also more efficient than multilateral mechanisms in terms of closeness and commitment. In many cases, regions can be more suited to deal with their own conflicts compared with a distant and sometimes paralyzed UN. Moreover, regional organizations are often better than multilateral efforts at addressing conflict prevention as well as post-conflict reconstruction. The region has to live with the consequences of unresolved conflicts, and cannot simply withdraw from such a conflict. One must also concede that multilateral peacekeeping is not always forthcoming, and even when it does arrive, it usually comes late and not infrequently for the wrong reasons. Hence, regional security operations are often faster and more relevant.

Clearly global and regional approaches can potentially be competing authority structures; hence, the challenge is to construct arrangements in which the two logics complement one another. Insistence on the vertical UN-led approach, which seeks to subordinate regions, will only reinforce competition between the two logics. Likewise, an ideological regionalism that ignores wider multilateralism cannot address the links between conflicts within the region and wider global politics. Instead, complementarity can be encouraged through interregional arrangements that support the values and principles associated with the idea of multilateralism. The UN would still be needed but it would be a rather different organization compared with the present one.

Thus, some kind of horizontal and more balanced combination of regional and multilateral agencies, each having its own basis of authority, should provide the predominant form of future global security governance. Both the UN and regional bodies need each other and must assume shared responsibility for resolving security problems. For its part, the UN has suffered a decline in power and authority and therefore needs support from regional bodies. Meanwhile many regional formations (particularly in Africa) are still embryonic and need support from global arrangements. A combined multilateral-regional strategy provides the most feasible solution for the future.

Chapter 3

Heritage and Transformation: From the Organization of African Unity to the African Union

Klaas van Walraven

Introduction

It is now almost ten years since the *Constitutive Act* of the African Union came into force (African Union 2000). The transformation of the Organization of African Unity (OAU) into the African Union (AU) and the significance for Africa's politics of this new institution has attracted a flurry of scholarly interest. Many publications have pointed to the potential of the Union in contributing to a more stable political order in Africa. Others emphasize the limitations the African Union has with regard to conflict management and internal functioning (see Francis 2006; Makinda and Okumu 2008). In many cases these assessments are made against the backdrop of the problems experienced by the OAU in its 40 year history, but usually not more than by passing reference. Such mention is often affected by the negative image that the organization developed in the first 30 years of its existence.

While much of this stereotype is deserved, it does not do complete justice to the complexities of the practices established by the organization. This chapter analyses the essential elements of OAU functioning during its first 30 years (1963–1993), concentrating on its role in conflict management. It discusses how this function evolved and how the accumulated experiences affected the institutional and normative transformations that took place in the period 1990–1993. It contends that the essence of these experiences, as laid down in the reforms of the early 1990s, affected the way that the AU was given form a decade later, in particular in the areas of conflict management and budgeting. In fact, it concludes that many of the problems that beset the OAU still haunt the African Union and that the latter's functioning cannot be properly gauged without understanding the fundamentals of OAU history.

The first section of this chapter outlines the historical causes underlying the formation of the OAU, reflecting on the rationale for the organization's creation stemming from the views of those that controlled it at the time. This precedes a discussion of the OAU's internal functioning, focusing on key institutions and how they interacted, as well as the nature of OAU budgeting. The final section of the chapter is devoted to the normative and institutional dimensions of the organization's approach to, and record in, conflict management. The restructuring that took place in the early 1990s is discussed, showing how this culminated in and affected, to some extent, the formation and institutional character of the AU.

The Birth of the OAU: Formation and Rationale (1958–1963)

It was the politics of decolonization that lay at the basis of cooperation between African states. Nationalist struggles did not simply follow territorial frontiers. Colonial territories were composed of different communities and cultural complexes, which often cut across state boundaries, with people moving to link up with others in neighboring colonies, and with many of whom they shared a common language and culture. Introduced by Europe's colonial powers just 80 years previously, the colonial territories had, by the 1950s, barely "hardened", let alone formed state boundaries. Indeed, one salient feature of the nationalist struggles of the epoch was how rapidly political agitation spread across the continent, carried by strong social impulses that required little organization and were difficult to curb (Low 1982, 26–9).[1]

If particularist loyalties weakened the appeal of territorial nationalism in colonies such as Uganda, Nigeria or French Equatorial Africa, nationalist agitation was further complicated from an opposite angle, i.e. by the partly federal, rather than territorial, nature of anti-colonial politics in French Africa as well as the lure of Pan-Africanism. France had organized most territories into federations whose governing structures and resources provided a focus for political mobilization, especially in the poorer territories. Pan-Africanist discourse, an amalgam of aspirations to dignity, freedom and unity originating in the Diaspora, had struck a note among (proto) nationalists even before the Second World War. After 1945, it gained in popularity among students, unionists and activists, principal among who was Kwame Nkrumah of the Gold Coast. The colonial powers, however, as well as leaders of richer territories such as Nigeria and Côte d'Ivoire, saw little use for larger territorial structures. Colonial authorities were lukewarm to allowing the break-up or merger of territories—or changes in state boundaries—which were constructed in the preceding decades and more easily allowed the authorities to retain influence upon independence (Davidson 1992, 6). In 1956, the French proceeded to weaken federal structures, shifting the focus to the territorial level where political elites mobilized followings that guaranteed the capture of state power that they, with few exceptions, were unwilling to forego in favor of shared influence in region-wide federations. The fruits of enduring cooperation with the metropole reinforced this (Mortimer 1969, 303–25; cf. Ansprenger 1961; Dugué 1960; de Benoist 1982; Schachter-Morgenthau 1964).

---

1   Modern territorial nationalism itself was 'Pan-Africanist' in the sense that its goal of resistance to colonial rule brought together different groups living in the same territory, which until then had often had little in common in terms of shared political organization.

Against this, some leaders articulated international ambitions. Kwame Nkrumah was a convinced Pan-Africanist. He believed that supranational cooperation involving unification of individual territories would enhance several key common interests and, of course, further his own prestige. As with every self-styled messianic leader, he imagined himself to be at the helm of such a grand project. This personal ambition, in turn, made the realization of such an undertaking even more difficult—as it resulted in competition with rival political tycoons such as Félix Houphouët-Boigny of Côte d'Ivoire, Egypt's Gamal Nasser, or the leaders of Nigeria. Nevertheless, with Nkrumah having managed to wrest independence from the British relatively early, the focus of international cooperation centered on Ghana at first. Nationalist movements gathered in Accra in December 1958, unleashing a wave of anti-colonial rhetoric, adopting resolutions full of nationalist fervor and hazy appeals for Pan-African unification and the abolition of "artificial" borders (Munger 1961, 81–3). In fact, the previous April, leaders of African states that were already independent had convened separately in Accra for their own meeting, marking off non-governmental groups from state elites in a way that was to bedevil African politics for the coming decades. This state conference listened to Nkrumah's visions but did not commit itself beyond general pronouncements on assistance to colonial peoples and the importance of non-alignment. Reference was made to an African common market, but no obligations entered into, and a Ghanaian proposal to establish a secretariat to institutionalize cooperation was rejected in favor of a decision to organize African ambassadors at the UN into an informal pressure group. This was not yet the time for strategies to manage Africa's own conflicts—their very existence was ideological anathema against the background of anti-colonial euphoria (Conference of Independent States n.d.).

Francophone leaders meanwhile tried to salvage something of their inter-territorial federations. Politicians such as Barthélémy Boganda (Central African Republic) and Djibo Bakary (Niger) were impassioned federalists, but the former died in an air crash and the latter was deposed by the French for preferring immediate independence to continued autonomy in a greater Franco-African framework (Kalk 1971; Van Walraven 2009). Even the Mali federation, a supranational undertaking between Soudan (Mali) and Senegal, was stymied by French-Ivorian pressure, disintegrating under the weight of internal rivalries (Foltz 1965). However, the "Entente" framework that Côte d'Ivoire initiated with Dahomey, Niger and Upper Volta—a loose structure without central institutions based on a customs union, French backing and Ivorian largesse—proved more enduring. It contrasted sharply with the grandeur with which Nkrumah and his charismatic colleagues of Mali and Guinea, Modibo Keita and Sékou Touré, proclaimed a "Union of African States" (UAS). Presented as the nucleus of supranational unification, the UAS broke through colonial language barriers but, dependent on headstrong personalities, did not form common institutions beyond the heads of state assembled in conference. As Touré and Keita consolidated themselves in the face of French hostility, the UAS disintegrated (Welch 1966).

The UAS and the Entente showed that cooperation was quickly becoming a feature of Africa's emerging international relations, even if carried by the somewhat inarticulate notions of common interest declared (and shared) by the new state elites (Van Walraven 1999, 99–100). However, if both organizations varied little structurally, they represented different forms of cooperation, not just in style and rhetoric but also in their underlying conception. These became apparent during the crisis in the former Belgian Congo (1960–1962), whose ill-conceived independence led to civil war between factions distinguishing themselves by left-leaning currents of nationalism and pro-Western postures supported by white settlers—in the process inviting elements of Cold War rivalry that crystallized a simmering continent-wide split between what were now seen as "radical" (left, Eastern Bloc-leaning) states and conservative-moderate (pro-Western) powers. In December 1960, 12 Francophone countries came together in Brazzaville to hammer out a pro-Western stand on both the Congo as well as Algeria's war of independence, in addition to emphasizing respect for existing borders and non-interference in internal affairs and deciding on close political and technical cooperation built on continuing ties with the metropole.

More militant states, some of which had troops in the Congo as part of a UN enforcement mission, responded with a conference in Casablanca the following month, where they adopted resolutions on Algeria and Congo and agreed a charter calling for a "Joint African High Command"—Nkrumah's idea for a common defense policy—and an "African Consultative Assembly" bringing together African parliamentarians. These decisions provided the Casablanca group with a supranational image, even though the institutional framework was purely inter-governmental and, apart from Nkrumah, the other states did not wish to accept unnecessary limits on state sovereignty.

As the Brazzaville group structured its institutions in similar ways, this raises the question where these alliances—including the Monrovia group made up of the Brazzaville 12 and moderate English-speaking powers—diverged. For the Casablanca countries, inter-state cooperation was directed primarily against the continued influence of non-African powers in continental affairs, something that found expression in resolutions on "neo-colonialism", the liquidation of colonial and settler regimes, on Israel, on French nuclear tests in the Sahara and non-alignment in world affairs among others. Brazzaville, on the other hand, stood for an inward-looking form of cooperation among former French colonies, largely favoring the continental status quo, staying close to France and accommodating existing patterns of foreign influence. Understating decolonization and disarmament, they stressed economic and technical cooperation all the more. The Monrovia group, originally intended as a rapprochement between the "militant" and "conservative" states, had a more forceful posture on decolonization and disarmament but stressed especially a common African strategy in the UN and peaceful settlement of disputes.

Monrovia, however, helped to harden the continental divide. In the emotionally charged atmosphere marking the immediate post-independence era, it was impossible to heal the rift before the situation in Congo had ameliorated (with UN troops ending the settler-inspired secession of the Katanga region at the end of 1962) and Algeria's nationalists achieved independence in July of that year. From early 1962, moves were initiated to reconcile the opposing alliances, facilitated by disagreements inside these blocs themselves[2] and reflections shared by governments in both groups that divisions weakened Africa's voice in the global arena and endangered everyone's security since all regimes were vulnerable to the possibility of foreign powers supporting their domestic opposition. These elite security considerations and reflections on Africa's external influence drove governments from both groups[3] to prepare the ground for a conference where all countries would participate to found a continental structure.

The outcome of this conference—held in Addis Ababa, Ethiopia, in May 1963 and embodied by the Charter establishing the OAU—represented a brilliant ideological compromise but one inclining towards the position of the Monrovia-Brazzaville powers. The Charter bore a striking resemblance to the treaty establishing the Monrovia institutions,[4] catering for strictly inter-governmental cooperation and emphasizing sovereign equality of member states, non-interference in each other's internal affairs, respect for member states' territorial integrity, peaceful settlement of disputes and condemnation of subversion. The last point alluded to the recent assassination of the president of Togo, involving one of the first coups d'état of the post-independence era. As Ghana was suspected of meddling in Togo's—and other conservative states'—affairs, it symbolized Nkrumah's isolation in the OAU's formation, even if its name represented an ideological concession to his Pan-Africanist scheme.[5] Non-alignment, an issue dear to the more radical states was emphasized, as was decolonization—with a decision establishing a committee to assist liberation movements.

The OAU Charter essentially institutionalized a form of 'state nationalism' and not Pan-Africanism, i.e. post-independence nationalism as embodied by state elites emphasizing the status quo through concepts such as sovereignty, equality of member states (or, rather, their elites), territorial integrity and non-interference. Nevertheless, the Pan-Africanist doctrine of unity did provide the OAU with a dualist rationale: to improve reciprocal security (against, especially, domestic opposition groups) as well as increase the global influence of Africa and its states

---

2   These included rivalry between Nkrumah and Nasser, Ghanaian support for Mauritania (angering Morocco, which claimed Mauritania as part of its territory), Mali's need for better economic ties with Côte d'Ivoire, cooling relations between Côte d'Ivoire and Senegal, and resistance of the Monrovia powers to French nuclear tests and Africa's association with the European Community (Van Walraven 1999, 120–1).

3   Led by Guinea, Ethiopia, Côte d'Ivoire and Nigeria.

4   Called the Inter-African and Malagasy Organisation (IAMO), established December 1962.

5   The name was suggested by the Dahomeans, who may have acted on a suggestion of Nkrumah, and the Liberians. In addition, the first paragraph of the Charter preamble came from a resolution drafted by Nkrumah at the Fifth Pan-African Congress held in Manchester in 1945.

and claim equality of status with non-African elites. It should also be noted that the OAU's birth left non-governmental groups in independent states, which had relied predominantly on the support of the Casablanca powers, in the cold.

The OAU's Structure and Internal Functioning

While the Casablanca alliance had disintegrated (Gallagher 1963), the OAU did not do away with the broad ideological distinction between radical and moderate-conservative states, merely papering over differences in foreign policy orientations. At a deeper level, this reflected a structural feature of Africa's international relations, i.e. the absence of undisputed leadership in the relations between African states themselves. Especially at independence, disparities in power were far from obvious, as some states—even when small like Ghana— carried by the energies of a charismatic leadership, developed forceful postures in foreign affairs, while other countries—even when bigger, richer—exercised limited influence as a result of domestic instability. It took some time before the differentiation in power (through development or build-up of a country's armed forces, for example) became apparent.

Thus, in the course of the first three decades of independence, Nigeria, Algeria, Zaire[6] and, from the mid-1990s, South Africa,[7] established themselves as the primary actors of the African state system—a result of large populations, mineral wealth, industrial base or armed forces. On the basis of similar or other indicators, Ethiopia, Morocco, Egypt, Côte d'Ivoire, Libya, Kenya, Senegal, Gabon, Angola, Zambia and Zimbabwe, among others, developed into second-tier powers. This influence could make itself felt more easily in regional arenas, where leading states were confronted with fewer actors and rival powers and the effect of their preponderance was greater—even if limited intra-African trade and intrusive action from extra-African powers at the behest of neighboring countries mitigated against such influence. At the continental level, the larger number of actors—further increased following Southern African countries' independence from colonial or settler rule—reduced the relative weight of the more important states, forcing them to negotiate to arrive at Pan-African decisions rather than simply impose them.[8]

In the background, this effect—readily explained in game theory (Oye 1986, 18–20)—influenced the OAU's evolution and functioning in several ways:

---

6   Although this country suffered high levels of instability, making it often an object rather than an autonomous agent in international politics.

7   Apartheid South Africa, while a matter of fact, was deliberately isolated diplomatically and, until 1994, could therefore not participate in any normal sense in continental procedures of cooperation.

8   See for an analysis of such internal decision-making, involving the dispatch of Nigerian troops to Tanzania to maintain security after an army mutiny in 1964, Van Walraven (1999, 200–3).

affecting its ability to create strong institutions autonomous from member states, build a solid financial basis and develop forceful policies. The organization always lacked the clout provided by one overwhelmingly powerful ("hegemonic") state—or group of states—necessary to impose discipline with respect to regulations or decisions to be taken (see Van Walraven 2005, 81). Thus, looking at the OAU's structure, the centrality of the Assembly of Heads of State and Government is clearly evident. As the "supreme organ of the Organization" it could rescind the decisions of all other institutions including the General Secretariat and its head, as well as the Council of Ministers,[9] the next policy organ in line. Plenary in composition, Assembly members were sovereign equals, in theory and in a diplomatic practice marked by circumspect handling of fellow heads of state—all towering *patres familias* at home—an inclination to keep quarrels *in camera* to avoid public criticism, and caution in treating controversies or violation of rules. Decision-making was cumbersome, as consensus rather than stipulated (two-thirds) majorities was the practice. In addition, presidential non-attendance slowed down action as lower-ranked representatives lacked adequate mandates. Reflecting domestic hierarchies, even foreign ministers, officially assembled in Council to prepare Assembly conferences (OAU 1963, §13(1)), were regularly confronted with the monopolistic penchant of the presidential organ, forcing referral of even the simplest of details to the overburdened agenda of the heads of state. Indecision and deferment were thus part of Assembly functioning.

Against this, the Council of Ministers—also plenary in composition—provided some resolve, benefiting from two, as opposed to one, statutory annual meetings, sessions longer than those of the Assembly, and, preparatory duties which allowed for policy development and troubleshooting. This role, however, was not codified—as a consequence, because the position of the Council, which also decided the OAU budget, was never formally upgraded, its autonomy remained liable to presidential repudiation. Nevertheless, the Council did provide limited continuity as it was easier to convene in extraordinary session and at short notice. This, to some extent, balanced the cumbersome nature of the Assembly, which needed two-thirds of Africa's heads of state to convene outside its normal schedule (Van Walraven 1999, 190).

The Assembly Bureau, made up of an annually rotating chairman elected from the heads of state and seconded by eight (similarly presidential) vice-chairmen representing the five continental regions, initially did not provide the necessary follow-up as its role was limited to managing the annual summit, being dissolved upon its conclusion. Theoretically, it was possible to reconvene during the following year to handle a particular crisis but, until the 1990s, this remained unusual. The Chairman himself, however, while having modest powers on paper, developed into a major spokesman between sessions, especially from the early 1980s onwards, when serious conflicts deepened the rift between moderate-conservative and radical states and ineffectual operating of the Secretary-General over the Western

---

9   OAU (1963, Article 8) and AHG/Dec. 21 (V).

Sahara crisis led to efforts to reinforce Assembly control—with the Assembly Chairman ("OAU president") overshadowing the head of the Secretariat.

Consequently, marked by the predominance of plenary organs[10] the OAU developed few institutions limited in member state composition or staffed by autonomous officials representing the Organization as a whole. The "General Secretariat", based in Addis Ababa, built up a modest personnel base, growing to around 600 people by the 1980s, including regional offices and staying at a comparable level until the OAU's transformation into the AU.[11] Until 1979, the head of the Secretariat was officially known as the "Administrative Secretary-General" (ASG). This title was no coincidence as member states did not wish for a strong political position, having the controversial role of the UN Secretary-General in the Congo crisis still in mind when they drafted the Charter.[12] Saddled with administrative and financial duties, the ASG, appointed by the Assembly,[13] had no formal right to take part in Council or Assembly meetings (although in practice he always attended these), nor did he have the power to convene these organs on his own initiative. He lacked the equivalent of the explicit right to develop peace and security initiatives as enjoyed by his UN colleague.[14]

However, ASG reporting duties made it possible to develop a political role to some extent, depending on the circumstances, the attitude of the policy organs and the character of the Secretariat's chief. Thus, the first ASG, the Guinean Diallo Telli, proved a dynamic personality who used his reports to the Council for political *tours d'horizon*, attended mediation missions, held press conferences and inserted items on the Council agenda he deemed important. After two consecutive terms, however, this militancy proved his undoing.[15] The next most political ASG was the Togolese Edem Kodjo. Yet, Kodjo would only serve one term following his admission of Western Sahara as a formal member in 1982, as desired by radical member states but opposed by conservative ones—a decision that plunged the organization into one

---

10   The plenary 'Specialized Commissions', tasked with among others socio-economic and technical cooperation, knew a checkered existence as member states logically preferred to pursue many of these objectives in regional international organizations such as SADC and ECOWAS.

11   For these 'organigrams' see Van Walraven (1999, 164, 166).

12   At the OAU's founding conference even Nkrumah, who had sent troops to Congo and disagreed with UN policy, resisted political prerogatives, proposing to call the Secretary-General 'Administrative Secretary' and leave out the word 'General'. He added scathingly: 'We don't want a super-something. Executive Secretary, simple. He would think he is Hammarskjold' (Van Walraven 1999, 146).

13   Which theoretically could also fire him.

14   'The Secretary-General may bring to the attention of the Security Council any matter which in his opinion may threaten the maintenance of international peace and security.' UN Charter, Article 99.

15   His stature was considered a threat by Sékou Touré, accounting partly for his arrest and tragic demise in 1977, starved to death after a political purge the previous year. See Lewin (1990, chapters 6–7).

of its most serious crises and led to Morocco's withdrawal, unique in OAU history. Before and after Kodjo, ASG's were mostly bureaucratic personalities bowing to the policy organs and the political role of the Assembly chairman, until the ascent of Tanzania's Salim Ahmed Salim in 1989 (see below). Even so, in 1977, the Assembly granted the ASG the provisional prerogative to investigate conflicts that, in his opinion, could endanger peace and security, and to submit a report to the Assembly chair for further action. Two years later, the epithet "Administrative" was dropped from the title, though without expansion of powers, and in 1982 the Charter Review Committee proposed an explicit right to develop peace and security initiatives along the lines of Article 99 of the UN Charter. However, it took until the early 1990s before this suggestion was acted upon.

Naturally, many of these institutional features cannot be explained entirely by the absence of continental leadership. They were, in the final analysis, also tied to the nature of Africa's domestic polities, marked as these were during most of the OAU era by presidential supremacies if not personal despotism, escalating cultures of corruption, absence of the rule of law shielded by impunity, and concomitant political lethargy. An expression of state elite interests, free-rider behavior became a structural characteristic of the OAU, shown nowhere more clearly than in its budgeting. Finances grew slowly in the course of the decades, climbing from around $2–4 million during the 1960s to around $25 million by the mid-1980s—a level at which it stagnated for much of the rest of the Organization's life span. In itself this was not unreasonable[16] considering that many of its objectives found expression in the organization of conferences, although it proved grossly insufficient for the development of forceful postures in conflict management, among others.

Without hegemonic discipline, moreover, arrears in contributions—which were compulsory—became a structural feature of OAU budgeting. Even if member states paid their dues, consistent delays in actual transfers complicated functioning. While members owed around $4 million in 1971, debts had grown to 16 million a decade later and, by 1986, never dropped below the $35 million mark, i.e. well over an entire annual budget. For the period 1965–80 only half the membership could retrospectively boast a payment record not marred by arrears (although this excluded past arrears or delay in payment). Some countries managed to develop arrears over every annual budget (Van Walraven 1999, 185). If some of these countries battled against extreme poverty or turmoil, others used non-payment to express dissatisfaction with OAU policies.[17] While some countries, by contrast, were committed to respect financial obligations more generally, arrears— besides indicating limited priority attributed to the OAU as compared with other spending—were the result of a free-rider context where countries could misbehave

---

16   However, in view of inflation and the depreciation of the dollar, the budget level decreased.

17   Libya, for example, during the 1980s developed arrears after member states torpedoed the Tripoli summit and Libya's presidency of the Assembly in 1982 (Van Walraven 1999, 187).

at will. In fact, while the Charter did not provide for enforcement measures, in 1979 the Financial Rules and Regulations introduced the possibility to bar defaulters from voting. Yet, the Assembly could still allow them to participate if it concluded that arrears were due to circumstances beyond their control. In fact, throughout the 1980s, the sanction was never implemented.[18] Instead, the Secretariat and other member states resorted to political pressure, notably ahead of annual summits, which would generally lead to back-payments that could run into considerable sums of money. While the Organization was marred by weak financial norms, these back payments often gave it a source of additional income that enabled it to make do.[19] These arrears nevertheless show that the fact that a small number of more important countries[20] were always responsible for half of the budget or more, did not add up to a hegemonic bloc able to enforce continental discipline.

The Management of Inter-state Conflicts

As Africa's continental organization, the OAU had a broad palette of objectives: coordinating Pan-African standpoints in the UN and other world forums, assisting the struggles against colonial and settler regimes in Southern Africa—a goal that, generally, had a unifying effect on the collectivity of member states—and encouraging cooperation on economic issues (OAU 1963, § 2). Both these latter two objectives were given more tangible form in smaller contexts such as the alliance of Southern African Frontline states and regional organizations such as the Southern African Development Coordination Conference (SADCC later SADC) and the Economic Community of West African States (ECOWAS). In the economic field, the OAU limited itself to adopting resolutions on a vast variety of subjects, many of which were highly unrealistic or impossible to achieve in a continental framework, imparting a surreal image that, more often than not, served to soothe simmering elites' anxieties about their vulnerability and lowly status in the global order of things.[21]

While originally anathema to the OAU's ideological underpinnings, the mediation of intra-African discord forced itself onto the agenda of the organization with an immediacy that reduced the importance of other objectives. Here, too, elite self-esteem was at stake, as the *Times of Zambia* graphically expressed when the ineffective response of the 1977 Libreville summit to the crises in Shaba (Zaire)

---

18   A proposal of the Charter Review Committee in 1982 to bar any member defaulting longer than two years, from participating in meetings as such, was not accepted either (Walraven 1999, 188).

19   'Operating on arrears', as the Assistant Secretary-General for Administration and Finance called this. Interview with Brownson N. Dede, Addis Ababa, 22 September 1989.

20   Nigeria, Egypt, Libya, Algeria and, for some time, Morocco.

21   The OAU's role in the political psychology of Africa's state elites is extensively treated in Van Walraven (1999).

and the Horn caused it to lament that Africa's conflicts made the continent "look like the village idiot of the world."[22] The remark reflected concern not just about violent conflicts and their repercussions, jeopardizing inter-state relations and detracting from Africa's collective influence, but also about the consequences they had on a mental plane, calling into question a much desired equality of status with non-African elites. At worst, this informed a minimalist strategy towards conflicts, stimulating Assembly and Council not to try to resolve crisis situations as such but prevent them from causing the state elites' global embarrassment by reducing their extent or intensity or, if need be, by keeping discussion *in camera* (i.e. protecting the village idiot from the glare of outsiders), or plain denial as to the conflicts' existence. The reverse side of this was, in the words of Botswanan President Khama, the right of Africa's peoples (he must have meant the state elites) to "be left alone to manage *or mismanage* their own affairs."[23] The rationale of OAU conflict management until the early 1990s thus evolved from its general ideology and was aimed at keeping conflicts within bounds—and, as much as possible, discouraging extra-African interference (for details, Van Walraven 1999, 267–9 and 383–4).

In itself this was a rational approach since the lack of continental leadership militated against the design of forceful strategies aimed at wholesale resolution of conflicts. Institutional practice with regard to conflict mediation or "management"— a term implying not resolution but a conflict's transformation in less violent or non-violent forms—was based on the procedures allowed for by the OAU Charter. Yet, the Commission of Mediation, Conciliation and Arbitration, one of the Organization's four "principal organs"—made up of 21 legal experts (OAU 1963, §7 (4))—was never seized with any dispute. It was considered too unwieldy, with an image of independence that repelled belligerent states from taking recourse to it. While, legally, member states were obliged to settle conflicts peacefully (OAU 1963, §3 (4)), the Charter did not require them to do so through the Commission of Mediation. Other organs took its place. The officials of the General Secretariat, for example, had the duty to draft reports on political developments for the attention of the Secretary-General and therefore monitored, although not on a permanent basis, conflicts. However, in view of the politically marginal role of the Secretary-General, this was not the most important institutional arrangement, at any rate until the 1990s. Thus, it was sessions of the Council of Ministers and especially the Assembly that served as important instruments in the mediation of conflicts. They allowed belligerents to restore communication, as well as diplomatic activity behind the scenes, such as the seeking or offering, on an *ad hoc* basis, good offices or mediation by third parties, preferably by another head of state or a group of them.

---

22   *Times of Zambia*, 6 July 1977.

23   Text speech in *Botswana Daily News*, 26 July 1978 (emphasis added), in response to discussions at the Khartoum summit of Western proposals for a Pan-African peacekeeping force in the wake of the Shaba crisis, where Zaire's national government was saved by Western-backed intervention.

The institutional contribution of the OAU was often no more than to ratify the role that a head of state took upon himself at his own initiative or on the request of the belligerent(s), or to request a particular head of state to mediate. Operating on the basis of the principle of flexibility so important for all international organizations (Bennett 1991, 102), member states considered it more important that a conflict was managed *within* the OAU's institutional framework than *by* it. That it was especially heads of state who got involved in *ad hoc* mediation, rather than professional diplomats, reflected the concentration of power at the domestic level of African states and the enormous prestige presidents carried. A special role in this respect was played by the head of state who occupied the Assembly chair and therefore enjoyed added prestige. Alternatively, it was particular heads of state who had made their mark on continental politics—such as Ethiopia's Haile Selassie—who were sought out to try to mediate a conflict. In other cases, it was done by a group of heads of state, their composition usually reflecting a careful political balance in order to maximize their influence vis-à-vis both belligerents.

The absence of hegemonic leadership made reliance on the power of persuasion (Princen 1992) particularly relevant and presidential mediation simply had a better chance that a settlement would stick. In addition to this pragmatic arrangement, the Organization sanctified certain fundamental norms for Africa's continental order that member states had to respect. Although these were generally cast in the form of—legally non-binding—Assembly resolutions or declarations, they could carry considerable political import. Usually, they were introduced in the course of a particular conflict between member states.

Thus, with the establishment of the OAU in 1963, member states implicitly confirmed their aspiration to settle conflicts in an African framework first, something that was a logical corollary of the OAU's conflict rationale to discourage extra-African intrusion, and the universal basis for which lay in Article 52 of the UN Charter. This, what could be coined a 'competence of initial concern' was explicitly confirmed by the Council of Ministers in the course of the Algero-Moroccan border war of 1963, when it called to attention the "imperative need of settling all differences between African States [...] within a strictly African framework."[24] The wording showed that it was not necessarily through the OAU that states had to resolve their problems but that, in any case, they should not take recourse to the United Nations—or request the one-sided help of an extra-African power in their struggle against another member state—and that the OAU's competence of initial concern revolved around inter-state conflicts or the inter-state dimensions of domestic crises.

While the UN Security Council backed this arrangement and the OAU and OAU-coordinated group of African ambassadors in New York were by and large successful in discouraging members from taking inter-state disputes to the United Nations, from the mid-1970s serious intra-state conflicts triggered massive interference from extra-African countries, notably the superpowers. These

---

24   ECM/Res.1 (I).

intrusions were usually the result of a combination of factors, i.e. superpowers meddling on their own initiative but also of OAU members themselves seeking extra-African support in order to get the upper hand in conflicts with other states or domestic opposition groups. These developments, consequently, went directly to the heart of the Organization's conflict settlement rationale, demonstrating the declining effectiveness of the continental regime.

Another important norm, set in the legal framework of the Charter (and thus legally binding) and later solemnly confirmed in resolutions, concerned the prohibition on subversive support to each other's (violent) opposition. In view of part of the dualist rationale underlying the OAU's formation—enhancing inter-state cooperation so as to improve reciprocal (state elite) security—this, too, touched on the core of the OAU's continental regime. The anti-subversion norm, however, never enjoyed any effectiveness. While for most governments embroiled in inter-state conflicts conventional warfare was no viable option, the cultural, social and regional heterogeneities of African states made recourse to supporting foreign nationals in conflict with their own government cheap, easy and harder to prove. As noted above, the OAU's founding conference was already bedeviled by the fall-out of the assassination of Togo's President Olympio, widely—although probably falsely—attributed to Nkrumah's government,[25] and the OAU Charter therefore explicitly confirmed, as one of its solemn principles, the 'unreserved condemnation, in all its forms, of political assassination as well as of subversive activities on the part of neighboring States or any other State' (OAU 1963, §3 (5)).

Resolutions of Council and Assembly two years later demonstrated what was considered as subversion in the continental order, and that this went far beyond armed support of, or political and material assistance to, armed opposition groups. These resolutions were adopted in the wake of failed guerrilla operations in Niger by the Sawaba movement of Djibo Bakary—who had been toppled by the French in 1958—which culminated in an all-out invasion of Niger's borders and an attempt on its president's life during the autumn of 1964 and spring of 1965.[26] The Ghanaian government was deeply implicated in these operations and conservative Francophone countries and Nigeria used the events to try to cut Nkrumah down to size. The adopted resolutions condemned the presence on the territory of African states of foreign exiles hostile to their own government, although adding that "refugees" should return home voluntarily and that political refugees of dependent territories (colonial or settler-dominated countries in Southern Africa) should have their safety guaranteed.

---

25 While certainly trying at the time to overthrow Olympio, the Ghanaians were probably overtaken by internal Togolese developments. See for a discussion Thompson (1969, 308-12).

26 The infiltrations spanned the period 1960–66 and are the subject of my monograph entitled 'The Yearning for Relief: A History of the Sawaba Rebellion in Niger 1954–1974' (manuscript in progress).

The OAU's plenary organs further called for the prohibition of the formation of foreign political groups on a country's territory, whose aim was to oppose fellow OAU members. Member states were asked not to create dissension within or among other member states by fomenting racial, religious, ethnic, linguistic or other differences, with the Assembly adding that media campaigns to this effect should be eschewed.[27] "Subversion" was thus broadly defined, and at best had an uncomfortable relation with the humanitarian handling of refugee problems (i.e. "non-refoulement"), and reflected the vulnerable character of Africa's "national" polities. The OAU's norm on this displayed a focus on state elite interests, but without strong continental leadership it was to remain an empty promise.

This was not the case with that other, infamous, OAU norm—the sanctity of colonial borders—but this was more a function of the interest that state elites had in not calling these into question and the relatively low incidence of pure frontier disputes in the total of inter-state conflicts during the OAU's life span.[28] The OAU norm, known in international law as *uti possidetis (iuris)*, could be said to be ingrained in the principle of respect for the territorial integrity of member states (OAU 1963, §3 (3)) and as such was legally binding. It was given more explicit formulation, however, in the course of Somalia's conflicts with Ethiopia and Kenya in 1964, fuelled by Somali irredentist claims on part of their territories. In an attempt to nip potential conflicts in the bud the Assembly declared that "all Member States pledge[d] themselves to respect the borders existing on their achievement of national independence."[29] While Somalia and Morocco, spurred on by irredentist aspirations, had no respect for this principle and member states embroiled in conflicts could occasionally resurrect border or demarcation problems, or simmering territorial claims, simply to get even, there is no question that the OAU norm helped to contribute to the stability of Africa's international relations—even if *uti possidetis* or, rather, strict border regimes, were a reflection of the interests of state elites as opposed to those of the population at large.

Thus, set against a background of absent continental leadership and the specificities of Africa's domestic orders, OAU mediation in inter-state conflicts followed a minimalist strategy that concentrated on persuading, not bullying, belligerents, delaying their actions and containing (potential) hostilities. Employed on a decentralized *ad hoc* basis, this approach was averagely successful—contrasting with popular perceptions in this respect. A quantitative assessment

---

27   See ECM/Res.9 (V); AHG/Res.27 (II). Also CM/Res.253 (XVII) in which these guidelines were used to settle a conflict between Guinea and Senegal during the early 1970s.

28   While indeed cutting across ethnic communities and wider cultural complexes, something that may cause problems for the communities concerned, the factual permeability of inter-state boundaries balances this. Elite African criticism of colonial frontiers as the cause of Africa's political miseries is possibly more related to their symbolic significance as markers of Africa's past encounter with European imperialism (Van Walraven 1999, 283).

29   AHG/Res.16 (I).

of mediation efforts in inter-state conflicts in the period 1963 to 1993 (Van Walraven 1999, 295) shows that, during the first two decades, 18 out of 28 inter-state conflicts or (non-violent) disputes were settled—i.e. abated or, occasionally, resolved—by or in the institutional-normative framework of the OAU. If one were to include the category of intra-state conflicts during this period up to 1983, the figure would drop to some 20 percent, thus fairly representative of the track record of multilateral institutions during this era.[30] By the early 1980s, however, a decline in effectiveness set in because of the general intensification of (intra- and inter-state) conflicts as a result of superpower meddling and growth in armaments. In the period 1976 to 1981 alone, the success rate dropped to 10 percent, while during the next decade mediation led to some sort of settlement in only four out of 13 cases. This figure, however, included the—rising—number of intra-state crises.

The OAU's Approach to Intra-state Conflicts and Internal Crises

It has been widely argued that the OAU was never allowed to concern itself with conflicts within member states. Indeed, in contrast to UN practice, the concept of "non-interference in internal affairs" (OAU 1963, §3 (2)) was given an extensive interpretation, disallowing not just tangible action towards or within a member state (such as sending in troops against the wishes of the government concerned), but even the very *discussion* of intra-state developments or the passing of resolutions on such events by the OAU's organs against the will of the member state government (Kunig 1981).

Nevertheless, and in contrast to popular perception, the Organization *did* at times concern itself with domestic conflicts, even before the 1990s. The historical record shows that conflicts that were marked by involvement of extra-African actors or carried that risk, or otherwise generated major consequences for Africa's international relations, could trigger some sort of reaction on the part of the OAU. Conversely, intra-state conflicts that largely lacked these features failed to elicit any response. Thus, during the mid-1960s another crisis broke out in the former Belgian Congo, this time marked by massive aid from the United States and Belgium, in addition to action by white mercenaries from Southern Africa, to quell a revolt against the "national" government in the capital, led at the time by Moise Tshombe, *bête noire* of Africa's radical nationalists. These developments tore open the simmering rift between moderate-conservative and militant member states, papered over at the OAU's establishment, and led to debates in the Council of Ministers that condemned foreign intervention and mercenary action at the behest of Tshombe and appointed a ten member state *ad hoc* committee, led by Kenya's Jomo Kenyatta, to mediate between Tshombe and his domestic enemies—a decision strongly resented by Tshombe's government. The committee even invited Congolese rebels fighting

---

30   The Council of Europe scored 18 percent, the Arab League 15 percent, the OAS 34 percent and the United Nations 23 percent (Haas 1983, 198).

Tshombe to one of its sessions (something that clearly violated the OAU's own non-intervention norm) and sent a delegation to Washington to try and stop arms deliveries to Tshombe. The latter then broke off cooperation and the conflict was in the end settled, provisionally at least, on the battlefield, with the help of Western troops (Van Walraven 1999, 304–6 and 324–6).

The point is not that the OAU's actions were counterproductive—reflecting the fact that the absence of hegemonic leadership meant that the Organization lacked sufficient clout to impose its will on a member state. The relevant argument here is that the OAU's plenary organs *did* decide to talk and concern themselves, in some ways, with an intra-state conflict, albeit one with major extra-African implications. Those dimensions were less pronounced in the context of Nigeria's civil war (1967–70), where, as a consequence, the Organization proceeded far more cautiously, possibly also because it had learned from its mistakes in the Congo. Although both the federal government and the Biafra rebels received aid from outside, including in the latter case from South Africa and the Portuguese, and the humanitarian plight of the civilian population in Nigeria's south-east generated worldwide concern, most member states were firmly against condoning any act of secession. As an institution expressive of state elite interests the OAU could hardly pose differently and thus had little leverage or persuasive power vis-à-vis the belligerents.

Still, at several instances the OAU did concern itself with the civil war. A six nation "consultative" mission was formed to offer its services to the federal government, something that could hardly be seen as an attempt at impartial mediation but provided the Organization with a potential say in any future settlement. Later, Haile Selassie managed to organize talks between the belligerent forces in Niger's capital, Niamey, focusing on the humanitarian dimensions of the conflict. Four countries, Côte d'Ivoire, Gabon, Zambia and Tanzania, even granted recognition to Biafra, something that actually violated the OAU's standpoint, implicit in its principle of respect for the territorial integrity of member states, rejecting attempts at secession. The 1968 Assembly summit was marked by drawn-out discussions between the four states, which recognized Biafra and the OAU majority supporting Nigeria's federal government. While the Assembly called on the Biafrans to end their secession and restore Nigeria's territorial unity, it also called for a cessation of hostilities, recommending an amnesty for all concerned and cooperation with the OAU to ensure the safety of all Nigerians.[31] Thus, the fact that this conflict was, in the end, "resolved" through the barrel of a gun does not gainsay the fact that the organization concerned itself in some ways with intra-state developments, even by mere discussion.

Similarly, by the early 1980s the OAU again focused on a domestic conflict, this time in Chad, and here it even sent in peacekeepers—the first in the Organization's history. While its maneuvers were successful in the sense that they led to a withdrawal of Libyan forces present on Chadian soil, the nature of

---

31   See Van Walraven (1999, 306–10) and AHG/Res.54 (V)2.

the conflict and ensuing hostilities made it not amenable to mediation by third parties. Hostilities escalated to a high level of intensity and Egyptian and Sudanese support for one rebel faction neutralized the clout that leading troop contributor Nigeria could have mustered as a potential regional hegemon. Space does not allow for an extended discussion but here, too, the failure of the OAU's efforts point more to the importance of the structural features of Africa's international relations—the lack of hegemonic leadership—than of the (alleged) lack of interest of the Organization in intra-state conflicts.

Nevertheless, during much of the OAU's life span, large segments of Africa's population remained on the receiving end of collective state elite neglect. The Southern Sudanese, for example, but also other communities such as the Eritreans, suffered for three decades of purposive disregard of their plight, aspirations and humanitarian state. This triggered widespread condemnation by non-governmental groups, which as Africa's conflict potential steadily worsened, expressed ever more biting critiques of the continent's Pan-African institution. The metaphor of the OAU as a trade union of tyrants is certainly the most famous critique, coined originally by the Sawaba movement of Niger in the run-up to the Organization's establishment.[32] The allegory was taken up by other groups later[33] and by the early 1990s had established itself as one of the sharpest non-governmental views of any international organization. In one way this was related to the OAU as the institutional embodiment of the continent itself. Because of this, people would, rightly or wrongly, attribute objectives to the Organization, some of which it could never hope to achieve and which made it into an easy target of popular denunciation.

On the other hand, until the 1990s, the OAU catered predominantly to the narrow interests of Africa's state elites, something that even found expression in instruments purportedly to help refugees or protect human rights. The *OAU Convention Governing the Specific Aspects of Refugee Problems in Africa* (1969), while stipulating the international legal norm of "non-refoulement" laid strong emphasis on keeping refugees away from state borders and discouraging subversive activity on their part. Humanitarian concern was, until the late 1980s, a side issue left in the lap of the United Nations High Commissioner for Refugees (UNHCR). By then, however, the continent counted up to five million refugees and the issue became increasingly difficult to ignore. Similarly, human rights violations in member states, sometimes on a massive scale, for long met

---

32   Its leader Djibo Bakary in February 1963 warned that African unity should not result in a kind of trade union of men in power seeking to support each other against popular currents. *Révolution Africaine*, February 1963. The fact that Bakary and fellow Sawabists had had a solid footing in the union world was surely relevant in the metaphor's birth.

33   The metaphor was reiterated in one way or another at several stages during the OAU's first three decades and in the 1990s contrasted with ideas about a Pan-African institution open to non-governmental voices. See below and for an overview of the union metaphor, Van Walraven (1999, 313–14).

with deafening silence. The murder of up to 100,000 Hutus in Burundi in 1972 was dismissed by the then Secretary-General as an internal affair and President Bokassa's personal participation in the murder of prisoners in the CAR that same year did not elicit any response, just as the death in one of Guinea's dungeons of former OAU Secretary-General Diallo Telli and the Red Terror campaign in Addis Ababa (both in 1977)—on the very doorstep of the OAU Secretariat—also did not warrant a reaction by the Organization.

However, the spectacular excesses in the Central African Republic (CAR) at that time, the horrors in Equatorial Guinea and Idi Amin's regime in Uganda made for increasingly bad publicity and finally forced the Organization to come up with at least a response in the form of the *African Charter on Human and Peoples' Rights* (1981, in force since 1986). Yet, this too was largely tokenistic in light of the numerous flaws contained in the Charter—the most remarkable of which was that the Human Rights Commission lacked judicial powers and could only recommend action by the Assembly of Heads of State and Government, which, once again, retained the final word. The instrument thus primarily addressed the "syndrome of the village idiot", rather than human rights protection *per se*, and did not immediately herald a rupture with the way in which the Organization had approached intra-state conflicts. The above suggests that this was essentially due to two fundamental features, i.e. the repressive character of domestic ruling elites and the absence of hegemonic leadership, militating against a forceful OAU posture on these issues.

Reform and Transformation (1977–2007)

It took until the early 1990s—with the subsidence of the Cold War, restive populations in Eastern Europe and continuous resistance of Africa's peoples to their own state elites, which culminated in the toppling of one single-party regime after another—before the time arrived for more far-ranging reform. These reforms, while couched in the parlance of "conflict prevention" and "early warning" then popular in international diplomacy, were to a considerable extent grafted on the specificities of the OAU's own experiences. Already in 1977 some soul-searching had taken place that resulted in the acceptance of a Nigerian proposal to establish a more or less permanent "*Ad Hoc* Committee" for the settlement of inter-state disputes and conflicts. As the Organization was threatening to become overwhelmed by the eruption of several serious conflicts—including the Somali invasion of Ethiopia's Ogaden region—member states felt the need for a standing committee that could meet at short notice. Faced with protracted conflicts, some of them raging at a high level of intensity, the Committee had to ensure greater coordination and continuity of mediation efforts. A novel aspect of the Committee was that it had a restricted membership of nine states,[34] something that went against

---

34   Nigeria, Zaire, Zambia, Tunisia, Togo, Gambia, Madagascar, Gabon and, ironically, CAR (Van Walraven 1999, 296).

a long-standing preference for sovereign equality of member states and plenary composition of the OAU's organs. This *Ad Hoc* Committee could nevertheless be expanded with three other members by the Assembly chair.

The Committee, however, was regarded as a stop-gap measure and the idea was followed quickly by a new proposal, supported by Sierra Leone, Liberia and Sudan as well as the Secretary-General, for a "Political and Security Council" (1978– 1980). Just as the *Ad Hoc* Committee, it would be limited in composition: a Sierra Leonean proposal suggested 15 members—like the UN Security Council—from the five African regions, who would have an "appropriate mandate" to identify "trouble spots" and "effect a rapid response" to situations that might threaten peace and security. While it is doubtful whether this included intra-state conflicts, the notion of speeding up OAU responses was to prove important for the future. The plan, however, was rejected at the time, principally for its restricted membership that originally was supposed to be permanent and would probably have gone to the more important states. Even a Secretariat proposal to let membership rotate annually on the basis of election could not mollify the majority of members, whose comportment in this so clearly alluded to the non-existence of continental leadership (Van Walraven 1999, 297–8).

The fundamental changes, however, that heralded the beginning of the following decade strongly affected overall attitudes of state elites—many of which were new on the political scene or had changed in composition. In 1990, the Assembly adopted a *Declaration on the Political and Socio-Economic Situation in Africa and the Fundamental Changes Taking Place in the World*. In it, the OAU announced that it committed itself to the settlement of "all the conflicts on the continent", thus formally arrogating intra-state conflicts to its mandate.[35] With the principle of non-interference in internal affairs still part of its legal basis, however, it meant that it would be interpreted more restrictively. Exactly in what way was not made clear but the ensuing context clarified that it involved an interpretation comparable to the way mainstream international law had approached these matters since 1945: something only represents "interference" in internal affairs, without a state's consent, if it involves an activity amounting to a denial of that state's independence, i.e. some sort of *tangible action*—not mere debate or the adoption of resolutions (Brownlie 1979, 291–5).

Hence, the "village idiot" was out and the embarrassment he caused no longer relevant: from now on, everything could be discussed head-on and even lead to denunciation of member state behavior, whether or not domestic developments were marked by extra-African factors or generated significant repercussions for Africa's international relations.[36] The easiest part of the new dispensation was the reform and upgrading of the General Secretariat and its head. In 1992, the Secretariat opened a new Conflict Management Division in order to conduct

---

35 AHG/Decl.1 (XXVI), paragraph 11.

36 With the end of the Cold War and Africa's strategic marginalization such factors carried less weight.

monitoring of (simmering) conflicts on a more permanent basis as well as to improve fact-finding (Van Walraven 1999, 168). While this could be seen as a response to the Secretariat's past institutional underdevelopment, in terms of finance and staffing (cf. Van Walraven 2005, 83), the changes were also part of a bigger plan, as inspired and launched in 1992 by the ambitious new Secretary-General Salim.[37] This aimed at the establishment of a comprehensive system of peacekeeping and peacemaking and would involve a whole process of prevention, management and resolution of conflicts, including their political, judicial and military dimensions.

This comprehensiveness in approach nevertheless led to resistance on the part of several member states, many of which opposed a blanket right of intervention in member states' internal affairs. The result was that for the external effects of tangible action—sending civilian/military observer missions or fact-finders to the territory of a member state, executing a mediated settlement—the OAU still required the consent of the belligerent parties.[38] In his 1992 proposals, Salim had argued for a right to intervene in situations marked by a total breakdown of order, attendant humanitarian suffering and regional spreading. In addition, however, he had claimed the right of pre-emptive action in situations where this stage had not yet been reached. While he was supported in this by Senegal, other countries such as Sudan and Rwanda were opposed and in the end it was decided that the OAU would not get a general right of intervention and that, moreover, it would be the Assembly Bureau that would decide on tangible intervention in practice. Still, the 1993 summit did agree that contexts marked by severe human suffering as well as the collapse of the state gave the Organization a right to intervene. What this entailed was not clarified, but presumably alluded to the simple fact that in situations where the state, to all intents and purposes, ceased to exist, the issue of member state consent in multilateral intrusion lost much of its salience (Van Walraven 1999, 299–300, 320).

Judicial elements of conflict management were nevertheless dropped,[39] and the military dimensions of OAU involvement circumscribed to the consensual dispatch of observer missions of restricted scope and duration. This was justified by the preventive focus of the new conflict management strategy the Organization was said to be developing and an explicit referral of crisis management to the UN in case situations deteriorated. However, this was a far cry from Salim's 1992 proposals, which catered for a role by the OAU Defense Commission to standardize training and harmonization of member state contingents of a prospective inter-African peace-keeping force. These ideas elaborated on long-

---

37   CM/1710 (LVI) Rev.1: Report of the Secretary-General on Conflicts in Africa: Prospects for an OAU Mechanism for Conflict Prevention and Resolution in Africa (June 1992).

38   AHG/Decl.3 (XXIX)/Rev.1, para. 14.

39   Involving a Border Commission, the Court of Justice of the newly-launched African Economic Community (AEC) and an Interim Arbitral Tribunal.

standing plans for a collective defense arrangement, debates on which had been raging ever since Kwame Nkrumah came up with an African High Command structure during the first session of the OAU Defense Commission (October 1963). Ideas for such an arrangement, which focused on inter-state conflicts, extra-African "aggression" and the dangers posed by colonial and settler regimes, continued to be aired fruitlessly as many states feared the potential abuse of a collective defense structure and they did nothing to tackle intra-state conflicts or the murky waters of inter-state subversion—the principal threats to peace and security on the continent. Proposals in 1965 by the Defense Commission, which usually assembled interested countries but could only recommend to the plenary Council, thus came to naught, as they did later in the 1970s, resurrected in the wake of incidents with colonial regimes or major extra-African intervention, such as in Zaire. The ideas concerned were dismissed by the more conservative member states as 'grandiloquent notions' and, though they received more serious treatment in a draft convention for an "African Defense Force" in August 1981, they got buried in the sands of the Chadian quagmire, only to be resurrected by the mid- and late-1980s in a draft protocol intended as an annex to the OAU Charter. This protocol, while still focusing on inter-state conflicts and extra-African aggression, catered for a panoply of institutions including an African Defense Force, Defense Council, Committee of Chiefs of Staff and Force Commander. It was, in its turn, overtaken by the strategic transformations of the early 1990s and the new round of reforms of 1992–93.[40]

The essence of what was approved by the 1993 Cairo summit as the Mechanism for Conflict Prevention, Management and Resolution revolved around intensified cooperation between the Secretary-General and the Bureau of the Assembly. In line with the original 1982 proposal of the Charter Review Committee, the Secretary-General received a broad right of diplomatic initiative to identify (impending) conflicts, whether intra-state or inter-state ones, and launch mediatory initiatives. This side of the arrangement was meant to speed up the OAU's responses, which had always suffered from the cumbersome functioning of the Assembly—an issue which, as noted above, had already informed the ideas for a Peace and Security Council launched in 1978–80. The Assembly Bureau (the so-called 'central organ') was meant to provide the mediation initiatives of the Secretary-General with political clout, while it should also handle the more far-reaching aspects of decisions (such as deployment of military observers), bear political responsibility and exercise overall supervision.

Part of the success of these reforms, which were swiftly put into practice, was that they worked on the basis of existing institutions (the Bureau) as well as past ideas—speeding up response time and restricting member state membership in relevant organs. Thus, the Bureau, which had a semi-permanent existence in the past and was very occasionally activated between Assembly sessions to tackle

---

40   For an historical overview of the Pan-African security debate between 1963 and 1989 see Van Walraven (1999, 329–37).

crises (Angola 1976, for example), had its membership expanded from nine to eleven (including the outgoing and future chairmen[41]) to represent the five African regions—membership rotating annually by way of elections, just as in the earlier plans for a Peace and Security Council. The Bureau was put on a more permanent footing and would now meet once a month at the level of ambassadors, twice a year at ministerial level and once at the level of heads of state. More importantly, it could be convened at short notice by the Assembly chairman, the Secretary-General or any OAU member state (Van Walraven 1999, 299–301).

In fact, the Bureau did begin to meet far more often than before and, more generally, OAU institutions including the Secretary-General managed to increase their activities in conflict management, including by dispatching military (observer) missions to Burundi, Rwanda and Liberia.[42] Reactive capacities thus increased, yet, on closer inspection, it becomes clear that the old minimalist strategy of reducing and containing rather than resolving and settling conflicts continued to obtain. This remained grossly deficient with regard to high intensity (often intra-state) conflicts, for which recourse to the UN, with its larger resources, was still necessary. At a deeper level, this had much to do with a lack of hegemonic leadership, something that was ingrained in the structures of continental relations and could not simply be "reformed away." Budgetary and staffing problems thus persisted, despite the introduction of a new biennial budget regime in 1994 and sanctions on defaulters, which actually began to be applied, excluding member states from certain rights.[43]

These problems became potentially more acute as the new conflict mechanism was said to be oriented towards prevention, thus requiring a substantial increase in monitoring capacity, and as the OAU's agenda expanded under the influence of the Secretariat's ambitions and the shifts in Africa's new political culture of democracy and multipartyism. That certain shifts in the political culture underlying inter-state cooperation were taking place can be seen from the acceptance of restricted member state representation in organs with increased powers, the tightening of budget rules, and, more generally, the new interest of the OAU in developments inside member countries. The Organization began to dispatch election monitors; some of its meetings invited representatives of non-governmental groups to give their views on OAU business, make suggestions or air criticism; and perverse events like the 1993 coup attempt in Burundi met with swift condemnation of the Bureau, demanding a return to democratic government and the rule of law.

All these dimensions—truly novel against the backdrop of OAU history— became part of new soul-searching in response to persistent economic miseries,

---

41   Reminiscent of the 'troika' idea in the European Union.

42   The last one would involve Ugandan and Tanzanian troops (*Africa Confidential*, 4 November 1994).

43   At the end of 1995 ten countries were barred from certain rights, such as participating in or taking the floor at meetings, putting up candidates for posts, or voting (Van Walraven, 1999, 189–9).

the strategic marginalization of the post-Cold War order and continued deficiencies in meeting large-scale crisis situations such as the genocide in Rwanda, the trench slaughter between Ethiopia and Eritrea, and the collapse of Mobutu's Zaire, soon culminating in a complex maze of intra-state and region-wide conflicts ("Africa's First World War"). Amidst the rivalry and jockeying for position among the more influential states typical of maneuvers towards new continental set-ups, OAU members began to move towards an entirely new international institution—the African Union.

If history repeats itself, the first time as a tragedy, the second time as a farce (see Marx 1852, ch. 1), the way that Libya's Colonel Gaddafi sprang his treaty for an "African Union" on unsuspecting delegates at an extraordinary Assembly summit in the Libyan town of Sirte (September 1999), bore at least some resemblance to the bravado of Kwame Nkrumah in the run-up to the OAU.[44] Other countries, including Egypt, Mali, South Africa and Nigeria were actively engaged to affect the outcome of Libya's surprise tactics. Moreover, some were entertaining their own ideas on a more effective continental order. Nigeria was at the forefront of the semi-permanent Conference on Security, Stability, Development and Cooperation in Africa (CSSDCA, born from the so-called Kampala forum in 1991). South Africa, as well as Senegal, was developing ideas for Africa's economic regeneration, which the South Africans propagated through the concept of an "African Renaissance" and these ideas were soon to become institutionalized in the New Partnership for Africa's Development (NEPAD) program. This is not the place to discuss all these visions, but the point is that the more cautious member states managed to neutralize the Libyan proposal through the *Sirte Declaration*, which referred the OAU's transformation to the agenda of the Council of Ministers. Duly taking into account the OAU and AEC Charters (see Van Walraven 2004), the Council of Ministers produced a draft *Constitutive Act*, finally adopted by the Assembly in Lomé in July 2000. It made not a single provision for a supra-national structure— in much the same way as Nkrumah united Africa *against* his grand vision by way of the OAU.[45]

While the overall structure of the OAU was retained, the names of some of its organs were altered—betraying the inspiration of European integration—in addition to providing for new organs (although some of these had already been planned earlier), such as the Court of Justice, Pan-African Parliament, the Permanent Representatives Committee and the Economic, Social and Cultural Council (ECOSOCC). The Parliament and ECOSOCC, launched in 2004 and 2005, demonstrated the growing importance of non-governmental voices in the new continental set-up. The Secretary-General, now called "Chairman" of the

---

44   A fortnight before the OAU's founding conference Nkrumah published his *Africa Must Unite* (1984 [1963]).

45   See on the African Union's establishment Mathews (2001, 2003), Cowling (2002), Cilliers (2003), Schoeman (2003), Van Walraven (2004), Francis (2006), Makinda and Okumu (2008).

"Commission" (formerly the General Secretariat) retained much the same powers of political and diplomatic initiative as bestowed in the 1992–93 reforms, while in 2003 a "Peace and Security Council" (PSC) was introduced under a protocol replacing the 1993 Cairo declaration that introduced the Mechanism for Conflict Prevention, Management and Resolution. Thus, since the reform proposals of 1978–80, when the notion of such a Council was discussed for the first time, the wheel had turned full circle: looking much like the semi-permanent Assembly Bureau (it was made up of state delegates represented at the AU Headquarters in Addis Ababa), the PSC is composed of 15 countries—as in the original Sierra Leonean proposal: ten members selected for a term of two years and five for a period of three. Together with rotating membership this should ensure continuity while realizing equitable regional representation.

In line with the changing times, however, members were explicitly expected to show commitment in the field of conflict management and respect for constitutional governance at the domestic level. Meeting twice a month in Addis Ababa at the level of permanent representatives and yearly at the level of ministers and the heads of state, the Peace and Security Council obtained a broad mandate—defined in minute detail—including, among others, peace-making and peace-building functions and the authority to deploy "peace support" missions. With a strong focus on prevention, the Council (as noted by Engel and Gomes Porto in the introduction to this volume) was intended as a "collective security and early-warning arrangement to facilitate timely and efficient response to conflict and crisis situations in Africa", while also charged with implementing a common defense policy, as referred to in the Union's *Constitutive Act* (see African Union 2000). The PSC was ostensibly given the discretion to determine its own "entry point" to intervene in countries but since "non-interference by any Member State in the internal affairs of another" was part of the principles guiding the Council's work, the presumption is that any tangible action inside or towards a member state would require the latter's consent (African Union 2002, §4 (f) and (9)).

However, an exception was made for "the right of the Union to intervene in a Member State pursuant to a decision of the Assembly in respect of grave circumstances, namely war crimes, genocide and crimes against humanity in accordance with Article 4(h) of the Constitutive Act." This was in line with some of the novel principles guiding the Union, which, for example, rejects "unconstitutional changes of governments" and provides for sanctions against member states not just when violating financial obligations but also in case "any Member State [...] fails to comply with the decisions and policies of the Union"—alluding more broadly to political principles. Sanctions can go beyond the institutional framework of the Union and, for example, involve the rupture of communication links and punitive measures of an economic nature (African Union 2000, §4 (p), §23 (1) and §23 (2)).

In its work, the Council is to be supported by the Commission and its Chairman, and a Continental Early Warning System, African Standby Force and Special Fund are to be established later, in addition to a Panel of the Wise, an organ launched in

2007 and composed of five "highly respected African personalities from various segments of society" mandated to advise Council and Commission (African Union 2002, §11).

Some Concluding Reflections

Clearly, Africa's principal continental institution has undergone a long-term process of change, in which factors of heritage and transformation have produced a complex interplay of forces leading to the reproduction of the essential structures of the OAU while at the same time providing for genuinely novel organs and principles. Whether, however, this transformation has—so far—led to a completely new, more effective approach towards the handling of conflicts is open to question, especially with regard to the intra-state level. This is not the place for a full analysis of the African Union's performance in this field, yet an initial glance shows that the old problems have not immediately withered away. To be sure, the Union took a tough stand on the problems on the Comoros, extending sanctions against the rebel leader of Anjouan (2007) and together with government forces taking the island by force the following year. A coup d'état in Mauritania (2005) led to the suspension of that country's membership. Yet, comparable developments in Togo, while leading to public denunciations, did nothing to prevent the consolidation of the old ruling clan and led to a public falling out between Nigeria's President Olusegun Obasanjo, then chairman of the AU Assembly, and the Commission's chairman, the outspoken Malian Alpha Oumar Konaré. Against this background the degeneration of the situation in Zimbabwe, shielded by ineffective mediation of the South Africans, was even more difficult to handle, as were the scandalous presidential elections in principal AU funder Nigeria (2007), left to the accommodating observers of ECOWAS.[46] Thus, Konaré, deeply disappointed about the AU's practical functioning and the thwarting of his ambitions for the Commission's role, did not seek re-election at the end of his term.

It would be unfair, however, to judge the Union's performance on the basis of intractable conflicts such as Darfur or Somalia, as it is doubtful whether these crises were, at this stage, amenable to effective third party intervention. The African Union certainly put up a brave stand with its AMIS mission in Sudan but the "rehatting" of its peacekeepers to a hybrid AU/UN force in 2007–2008 (UNAMID)[47] showed that its presence, so far, was incapable of making a change, principally because of the behavior of the Sudanese government and the splintering of the rebel factions, but also because of the Union's chronic financial and logistical underdevelopment

---

46   These reported that the presidential elections, seriously marred by violence and fraud, passed off in a 'relatively more secure environment' than the preceding state and gubernatorial polls.

47   AMIS: AU Mission in Sudan; UNAMID: United Nations and African Union Mission in Darfur.

and Western powers failing to live up to past pledges in this area. Yet, it cannot be denied that the African Union has designed a very ambitious program for handling the continent's conflicts—an area in which it continues to feed expectations. It will, therefore, be judged by many precisely on the basis of developments in this field.

Continuous soul-searching in the purely institutional realm, such as in 2007 when the Assembly summit hotly debated the question of Pan-African government, risks diverting attention from underlying fundamentals, such as political commitment to the Union as such and the need for effective leadership in Africa's inter-state relations.[48] Free-rider behavior has not vanished, complicating the life of new organs such as the Pan-African Parliament and risking stymieing institutional evolution. The entry of post-apartheid South Africa onto the Pan-African scene did, in this respect, not do much to ameliorate the situation. Whereas five major African powers (South Africa, Nigeria, Libya, Algeria and Egypt) agreed in 2005 to shoulder 75 percent of the regular budget with a 15 percent share each, their leadership did not produce more discipline on the part of other member states, who in 2007 were indebted to the Union to a staggering amount of $100 million.[49]

---

48   The Addis Ababa summit in February 2009 agreed to transform the Commission once again, this time into an 'Authority', ostensibly with a broader mandate.

49   Twenty-one of the 53 member states faced arrears of at least one year.

Chapter 4

The Peace and Security Council of the African Union: From Design to Reality

Kathryn Sturman and Aïssatou Hayatou

Introduction

In its fifth year, the Peace and Security Council (PSC) has become a focus of collective security decisions by Africans for Africans. It has been at the centre of reforms of the Organization of African Unity (OAU) into the African Union (AU), changing both the procedures and norms of the continental organization. Procedurally, the 15-member council has been able to act more decisively than the larger Assembly of 53 member states in response to urgent political crises and conflicts. At the level of norms and principles, the PSC has shifted the AU from a tradition of strict non-interference in the affairs of member states to a new *modus operandi* of peace operations, sanctions and more assertive regional diplomacy.

This chapter reviews the development of the PSC since its launch on 24 May 2004. It traces the history of an idea, through to its grand design in the *Protocol Relating to the Establishment of the Peace and Security Council* (hereafter called the PSC Protocol) adopted by AU member states in Durban, South Africa on 9 July 2002 and entering into force on 26 December 2003. The chapter then outlines the more modest reality of an institution in the early stages of consolidation, with many challenges to be weighed against its achievements to date. The future of the PSC depends on maintaining the political will and practical commitment of member states, increasing staff and resources to support its work, and streamlining its working methods.

Historical Context

In current debates on Africa's new peace and security architecture, it is often forgotten that the Pan-Africanism that inspired the formation of the OAU in 1963 advocated a common approach to addressing conflicts in Africa. Indeed, long before the notion and practice of regional security (including but not limited to peacekeeping) gained currency in global affairs, Kwame Nkrumah noted that African leaders together could have prevented the interference of Cold War powers and foreign business interests in the independence of (former Belgian) Congo: "If at that time, July 1960, the independent states of Africa had been united, or had at least a joint military high command and a common foreign policy, an African solution might have been found for the Congo; and the Congo might have been able to work out its own destiny, unhindered by any non-African interference" (Nkrumah 1963, 138).

At the first meeting of the OAU Defense Commission in 1963, Nkrumah's representative proposed a "Supreme Military Command Headquarters" which would oversee four regional headquarters, and a "Union Defense Council" to issue the political directives for collective defense (Van Walraven 1999, 330). In fact, as will be discussed below, this structure is much like that of the Peace and Security Council and the African Standby Force arrangements adopted by the African Union in 2003. As noted by Klaas Van Walraven in the previous chapter, these proposals were rejected in 1963 mainly as a result of "different patterns of external dependence" among the recently independent states, as well as a "lack of hegemonic leadership", whereby a dominant member state could have pushed the group to accept such an arrangement (see also Van Walraven 1999, 332).

In the context of decolonization and the Cold War, the 30 new states that formed the OAU sought to consolidate their national sovereignty, independence and territorial integrity. They were threatened with interference from several sources: (1) the "neo-colonialism" of former ruling powers from Europe; (2) Western and Soviet rivalries played out through strategic support for or sabotage of African governments and political movements; and (3) their own African member states supporting rival groups and mercenaries in neighboring countries. Nkrumah himself was accused of the latter form of interference. Thus, proposals for supranational structures, including the Union Defense Council, were blocked by the adoption of the OAU's most enduring principles of non-interference and respect for state sovereignty and territorial integrity.

These were enshrined in the OAU Charter of 1963, which begins with an assertion of "the inalienable right of all people to control their own destiny [...]", and in Article 3: i.e. (1) sovereign equality of member states; (2) non-interference in the internal affairs of member states; (3) respect for sovereignty; (4) peaceful settlement of disputes; (5) condemnation of subversive activities by neighbors or other states; (6) total emancipation from colonialism; and (7) non-alignment. As it turned out, adherence to the principle of non-interference would lead to a softer approach to dealing with conflicts than the proposal for a Union Defense Council. The result was that a Commission on Mediation, Conciliation and Arbitration was established. According to Omar Touray, "[this] quasi-legal body was stillborn. Its mandate was limited to inter-state conflicts, and few such conflicts were referred to it" (Touray 2005, 638). The Defense Commission conceded the need for a common defense policy at the 1963 meeting, and two years later recommended the creation of an "African Defense Organization." But these and subsequent proposals put forward in the 1970s were resisted by the majority of member states and did not go beyond the level of the Council of Ministers (Van Walraven 1999, 332–3).

Civil wars and intra-state conflict tested the OAU's conflict resolution ability to the limit, challenging the very principle of non-interference as well as the efficacy of the then preferred method, that of ad-hoc dispute settlement committees. The problem of how to deal with a coup d'état, for example, vexed the Organization early in its history and often thereafter. Togo's President Sylvanus Olympio was ousted on the eve of the OAU's launch. The portrait of the "Founding Fathers of the OAU", which hangs in the Africa Hall in Addis Ababa, has a blank frame painted in between the other leaders as testimony to Togo's absence. Yet sudden and often violent leadership changes passed without comment in the official texts of OAU summits for decades.

This changed in 1997, when leaders meeting in Harare finally took a stand against unconstitutional changes of government. In 2000, the Lomé Declaration on Unconstitutional Changes of Government defined the modalities for the OAU's response in cases of unconstitutional changes of government, going beyond situations where power is taken by force (military coups d'état; intervention by mercenaries to replace a democratically elected Government or replacement of democratically elected Governments by armed dissident groups and rebel movements) to include situations where there is a "refusal by an incumbent government to relinquish power to the winning party or candidate after free, fair elections" [AHG/Decl.5 (XXXVI)].

When in 1979, Tanzanian troops intervened in Uganda, a heated debate between Member States at the OAU Assembly in Monrovia resulted in the first two significant challenges to the norm of non-interference. As noted by Thomas (1985, 112) these were: (1) "the idea of establishing an African peacekeeping force gained credibility" and (2) "a declaration of human rights was drafted". When, shortly thereafter, the OAU mounted a peacekeeping mission in Chad, the idea of a peacekeeping role for the organization had finally become a reality—the lack of success of the intervention notwithstanding (see Mays 2002).

The end of the Cold War provided new space and need for African-led peace initiatives. The withdrawal of Western and Soviet strategic support for many African regimes led to state collapse and an increase in the number and intensity of civil wars on the Continent. Conflict erupted in Liberia in 1989, in Somalia and Sierra Leone in 1991, in Algeria in 1992 and Burundi in 1993. Nine out of ten of the worst conflicts in the world in the 1990s took place on African soil (Hawkins 2003). An initial increase in United Nations (UN) peacekeeping operations in Africa in the early 1990s dwindled after the embarrassing failures of Somalia in 1993 and Rwanda in 1994. Thereafter, the OAU was encouraged to take regional responsibility for peacekeeping.

A new team of OAU officials initiated a *Report of the Secretary-General on the Fundamental Changes taking place in the World and their Implications for Africa: Proposals for an African Response*, which resulted in a declaration of the same name by the Assembly in 1990. The declaration committed the member states to "further democratization" and to "the consolidation of democratic institutions" in their countries, to human rights and conflict resolution [AHG/Decl. 1 (XXVI)].

It also spoke of "reviving the ideals of Pan-Africanism", associating the older rhetorical constructs of unity and solidarity with the regional enforcement of human rights and conflict mediation.

A meeting of around 500 government and civil society delegates took place in Kampala in 1991, thereafter called the Conference on Stability, Security, Development and Cooperation in Africa (CSSDCA). The CSSDCA policy document made a range of commitments, including to constitutional governance, the rule of law, democracy and human rights as prerequisites for human security. The security proposals included the development of "continental peace-keeping machinery" and an "Africa Peace Council" made up of eminent persons.

Institutional reform of the OAU was undertaken in the form of a treaty to create an African Economic Community (AEC) in 1991. Article 5(3) of the treaty enabled sanctions by the Assembly against member states that failed to "honour its general undertakings under the Treaty." Although it was never used in practice during the 1990s, this clause set the precedent for the sanctions mechanism in Article 23(2) of the AU *Constitutive Act*.

In Chapter Three, Van Walraven discussed in detail the developments that would lead to the proposals for the creation of a Bureau of the Summit as well as a Conflict Management Division within the OAU. It suffices to say that this division was indeed set up in 1992 within the Political Affairs Department, with the aim of providing institutional support for the Bureau, a smaller decision-making structure. In his proposal, Salim had argued that the OAU, "should be enabled to intervene swiftly in situations where tensions evolve to such a pitch that it becomes apparent that a conflict is in the making" [CM/Res. 1710 (L.VI)]. The need for such an instrument became increasingly apparent in the 1990s as the litany of atrocities grew from Somalia, Rwanda, Sierra Leone, Liberia, the DRC and elsewhere.

The proposal was adopted in modified form by the Assembly at the Cairo Summit of 1993, where member states agreed to establish a Mechanism for Conflict Prevention, Management and Resolution (AHG/Decl. 3). The difference between the Mechanism and the Secretary General's proposal was that the Bureau was meant to have decision-making powers above those of the Assembly, while the Mechanism was a subordinate commission (Clapham 1996, 117). The mechanism was to have a 'Central Organ' to decide on matters of continental security. The institution gained standing within the OAU from the mid- to late-1990s, as the mechanism facilitated the Arusha Peace Agreements for Rwanda, engaged in peace processes and deployed military observers to Burundi and the Comoros. Following the adoption of the Constitutive Act of the African Union in 2000, the Assembly decided to elevate the status of the Central Organ of the Mechanism for Conflict Prevention, Management and Resolution, making it into an organ of the African Union (Lusaka Summit July 2001, Assembly decision AHG/Dec.160 XXXVII). The Assembly requested a review of the Central Organ, which set in motion the process of designing the more aptly named Peace and Security Council.

To conclude this section, the long-standing idea of *Pax Africana* within the OAU explains to some extent why—with the adoption of the PSC Protocol in 2002—

the AU was able to make such a seemingly radical switch from non-interference to "non-indifference" principles. The Pan-Africanist vision held prototypes for an "African Army" and human rights regime, which gathered momentum from democratization across Africa in the 1990s and found institutional form in the new millennium. However, national interests of member states have remained a countervailing force within the Organization. As will be discussed below, the balancing act required between state sovereignty and regional governance remains a significant challenge for the PSC.

Design: The Peace and Security Council Protocol

The *PSC Protocol* emerged from the review of the Central Organ, during the pivotal year of transition from the OAU to the AU in 2002. At a "brainstorming retreat" held in South Africa in March 2002, the ambassadors of the Central Organ, the New Partnership for Africa's Development (NEPAD) Implementation Committee and the interim AU Commission worked out the details of the new institution. Their deliberations ranged from choosing the new name, to setting out the terms and criteria for membership and considering its relations with other institutions, including the UN Security Council, the Regional Economic Communities (RECs) and other organs of the AU.

The Protocol was adopted by the AU Assembly in Maputo in July 2003 and entered into force on 26 December 2003—the PSC having been launched in May 2004. The Protocol defined the Peace and Security Council as a "standing decision-making organ for the prevention, management and resolution of conflicts" and "a collective security and early-warning arrangement to facilitate timely and efficient response to conflict and crisis situations in Africa" (African Union 2002, §2 (1)). Its objectives were to anticipate conflicts and to resolve them. Conflict prevention was defined broadly to include the promotion of democracy, good governance and the rule of law, and the protection of human rights. The principles of the PSC reflect those of the AU's *Constitutive Act*, including the groundbreaking Article 4(h) right of the Union to intervene—pursuant to a decision of the Assembly—in a member state in "grave circumstances" of genocide, war crimes and crimes against humanity.

It is a function of the PSC to authorize the mounting and the deployment of peace support missions as well as recommend to the Assembly a military intervention by the Union pursuant to Article 4(h) of the *Constitutive Act*, or Article 4(j), in which a member state may request an intervention by the AU. This means that the PSC may recommend an intervention with or *without* the consent of the member state in which a conflict takes place and approve the modalities of such intervention. Yet, more crucially, this reflects the fact that the decision-making powers of the PSC are limited in that it may only recommend an Article 4(h) intervention to the Assembly, the highest decision-making body of the AU (African Union 2002, §6 (e)). Moreover, according to the rules of procedure of the Assembly, a two-thirds majority of the Assembly of 53 heads of state must authorize an Article 4(h) intervention.

Nevertheless, while the powers of the PSC are limited as regards military intervention, the PSC has a second tool of enforcement, in that it may recommend sanctions against unconstitutional changes of government (African Union 2002, §7 (g)). In terms of the Assembly's *Rules of Procedure*, whenever an unconstitutional change of government takes place, the Chairperson of the Assembly and the Chairperson of the Commission are to take a range of actions, including requesting the PSC to convene to discuss the issue (African Union 2002, Rule 37, §4 (d)). The Member State in question is to be immediately suspended from the African Union. The Assembly is required to "immediately apply sanctions against the regime that refuses to restore constitutional order", on the recommendations of the PSC (African Union 2002, Rule 37, §5).

It should also be noted that the composition of the PSC reflects a limitation placed on the ambitions of the big states during the drafting of the *PSC Protocol*. There was an intense debate over this in the preparatory meetings of ambassadors and at the Durban summit in 2002 (Mwanasali 2004, 14). The draft supported by the "big five" (South Africa, Nigeria, Algeria, Libya and Egypt) was to have five permanent members of the PSC (modeled on the UN Security Council), which they argued would encourage those member states with the greatest military and economic capacity to play a leading role in the AU peace and security structures. This was rejected by the others, who appealed to the AU Act's principle of equality between member states (Mwanasali 2004, 14).

A 15-member council with equal voting rights was the result of this compromise. The *PSC Protocol* allows for five members with a three-year term, and ten members with a two-year term, all of which are renewable. Members are elected by the Executive Council pursuant to a permanent delegation of power by the Assembly on the basis of regional representation. Each of the five regions of the AU, North, East, West, Southern and Central Africa, present candidates for election; however, because of the different sizes of these regions, East, Southern and Central Africa may elect three PSC members each, while North Africa elects two members and West Africa elects four. The Protocol sets out detailed criteria for election to the PSC, including a member state's capacity and commitment (including financial and troop commitments) to the functions of the PSC. Significantly, respect for constitutional governance, human rights and the rule of law are required as criteria for membership (African Union 2002, §5 (2) (g)).

Procedures are set out in the *PSC Protocol* and elaborated in the *Rules of Procedure* adopted in March 2004. The PSC normally meets in Addis Ababa, Ethiopia, at the headquarters of the AU Commission. It may hold a meeting outside the AU headquarters. Such meetings have taken place in Libreville, Gabon in January 2005, in Abuja, Nigeria, 2007, in New York, USA in 2007 and 2008 and in Sharm El Sheikh, Egypt in 2008. The PSC meets at three levels without prejudice to the strength of its decisions: (1) Heads of State; and (2) Ministers at least annually; and (3) Permanent Representatives at least twice a month. It should be noted however, that the PSC is in permanent session as the Permanent Representatives (ambassadors stationed in Addis Ababa) are able to meet at any time to receive up-to-date briefings and reports by the Commission on conflict situations in the field, including in the event of a crisis such as a coup d'état or armed violence.

The PSC is chaired by each member on a rotating basis, for one month each. The chairperson of the PSC, in consultation with the Chairperson of the Commission, sets the agenda for meetings held during that month. It generally meets in closed session, although there is provision for open meetings to be held. The Council may invite parties to a conflict to present their case, or experts from other organizations such as the UN, RECs or NGOs to attend meetings. An important provision of the Protocol is that any member that is party to a conflict under deliberation must recuse him- or herself from the discussion, and may not take part in any decision relating to such conflict (African Union 2002, §8 (9)). Voting may take place if there is no consensus on a decision, by simple majority for procedural issues and by two thirds majority for substantive matters.

The AU Commission plays a critical role in the operations of the PSC. It gives support to the PSC to enable it make the most informed decisions. In particular, the Commission supports the PSC's decision-making process by providing expertise in various domains of peace and security including analysis, reports and briefings on conflicts situations. The AU Commission also makes recommendations to the PSC on the way forward and follows up on the implementation of PSC decisions. For this reason, a Peace and Security Council Secretariat was established within the AU Commission to support the work of both the AU Chairperson and the PSC (African Union 2002, §10 (4)). The PSC is also supported by a Panel of the Wise, a Continental Early Warning System and an African Standby Force, each of which is covered in subsequent chapters of this volume.

Article 17 of the Protocol acknowledges that the UN Security Council is the ultimate authority on matters of peace and security, and that the AU PSC "shall maintain close and continued interaction" with the UNSC. Moreover, it is in recognition of the critical role played by Regional Economic Communities (RECs) in the prevention and management of conflict in their respective regions that the Protocol provides for close working relations between the PSC and these sub-regional organizations—including the Southern African Development Community (SADC), the Economic Community of West African States (ECOWAS), the Intergovernmental Authority on Development (IGAD), the Economic Community of Central African States (ECCAS), the East African Community (EAC), the Common Market for Eastern and Southern Africa (COMESA), CEN-SAD and the Maghreb Union.

The PSC is required to liaise closely with other organs of the AU, including the Pan-African Parliament (PAP) and the African Commission on Human and Peoples' Rights (ACHPR). Civil society engagement is provided for in Article 20 of the *PSC Protocol*, with specific reference to the role of women in promoting peace and conflict resolution. A Peace Fund is established to finance the activities of the PSC, made up of appropriations from the AU budget, additional voluntary contributions from member states and external sources (such as international donors' contributions).

Having sketched the design of the PSC, we now consider how the institution has worked in practice. The areas of the *PSC Protocol* featured above serve as a framework for analysis of the development of the PSC in its first five years. Three aspects are to be considered: (1) the composition of the PSC and membership dynamics; (2) working methods and procedures of the institution, including questions of capacity and funding; and (3) a review of the activities of the PSC, focusing primarily on the deliberations of over a 150 meetings held since 2004.

Institutionalization of the PSC: Composition and Membership Dynamics

The first Council elected by the AU Assembly in March 2004 (Table 4.1) consisted of Algeria, Nigeria, Ethiopia, Gabon and South Africa (as three-year members) and Libya, Togo, Senegal, Ghana, Sudan, Kenya, Cameroon, Republic of Congo (Brazzaville), Lesotho and Mozambique (as two-year members). This line-up included the major troop-contributing countries to peacekeeping operations in Africa, such as in Liberia, Sierra Leone, Burundi and the DRC as well as four of the big five financial contributors to the AU budget (with the exception of Egypt, which became a member following the second two-year term election).

Apart from the long-running civil war in Sudan, there were no major wars taking place in any of these member states. Thus, while some of the criteria for membership set out in the PSC Protocol were adhered to in each of the five regions' choices, it was immediately apparent, however, that respect for constitutional governance, human rights and the rule of law, was less of a rule than a guideline for electing members. Sudan was among several choices considered controversial in light of this requirement. Indeed, this country was among those replaced in 2006, when the second rounds of two-year members were elected.

Table 4.1   The first Peace and Security Council, 2004–2006 (top row elected 2004–2007)

Algeria	Nigeria	Ethiopia	Gabon	South Africa
Libya	Senegal	Sudan	Cameroon	Lesotho
Togo	Ghana	Kenya	Congo	Mozambique

The principle of rotation of members within each of the five RECs has been adhered to in the election of two-year memberships. However, only SADC has applied this rule to the three-year membership of South Africa, replaced by Angola in January 2007. The difference between Southern Africa and the other four regions is quite marked in this respect. West and North African member states, such as Nigeria and

Mali, Libya and Egypt, have competed openly for seats on the PSC, while SADC has taken a more cooperative approach. Foreseeably, Southern Africa's approach could undermine the AU's good governance criteria for membership, should Zimbabwe's current regime gain a seat by a process of automatic rotation, rather than principled selection. South Africa's overwhelming economic and military power in the region lends a different dynamic to SADC, as the regional hegemon exerts considerable influence on the PSC from behind the scenes through SADC members represented in the PSC.[1]

This is not to say that might is always right on the PSC. Some of the smallest member states have been among the best performers on the Council, with Botswana, Senegal and Ghana making important contributions. The quality of debate within the PSC has much to do with the experience, capacity and preparedness of the member states' delegations. Small countries such as Botswana can sometimes be less reckless, more independent and more effective than the representatives of the bigger powers. The knowledge and experience of delegates to the PSC meetings is an important factor. This diplomatic influence is linked to the level of human and financial resources at a government's disposal.

Table 4.2   The second Peace and Security Council, 2006–2008 (top row 2004–2007, South Africa replaced by Angola, 2007–2010)

Algeria	Nigeria	Ethiopia	Gabon	South Africa/ Angola
Egypt	Senegal	Rwanda	Cameroon	Botswana
Burkina Faso	Ghana	Uganda	Congo	Malawi

The declining overall strength and capacity of the PSC from the first to the second and third configuration of members is a concern for the AU (Tables 4.2 and 4.3). Only a third of the current PSC members have troops committed on the ground to African peace missions. Chad and Burundi are embroiled in serious conflicts and find it difficult to contribute effectively to the PSC meetings. Angola has yet to contribute its sizeable army to an AU mission, and remains disengaged from regional conflict prevention efforts (the exception being its, at least declared, pledge to ECCASBRIG – the Standby Brigade of the Economic Community of Central African States – with two battalions). Perhaps more crucially, while Presidents Thabo Mbeki and Olusegun Obasanjo were leading figures in the development of the AU since 1999, leadership changes in both South Africa and Nigeria have seen these countries stepping back from their commitments to the AU.

In practice, the deliberations and decision-making of the PSC have not followed the PSC Protocol to the letter. Despite the provision for voting on both procedural and substantive issues, consensus has remained the norm by which all decisions

---

1   Interview conducted by the authors with South African diplomat, September 2008.

Table 4.3   The third Peace and Security Council, 2008–2010 (top row 2007–2010)

Algeria	Nigeria	Ethiopia	Gabon	Angola
Tunisia	Benin	Rwanda	Chad	Swaziland
Burkina Faso	Mali	Uganda	Burundi	Zambia

have been reached. However, face-saving language is often used to create the impression of consensus, so that observers need to read between the lines of press statements and communiqués. Although debate within the Council meetings is often heated, the communiqués issued afterwards are carefully worded to reflect consensus. The wording of these public documents is usually scrutinized intensely and subject to drafting and redrafting until all members are satisfied.

This mode of decision-making is not only time-consuming but it allows member states with a strategic interest in a particular conflict or political crisis to block a particular action or intervention by the PSC. The stalemates reached by the UN Security Council could be replicated by the PSC, even without veto powers afforded to any member states. The countervailing norm that mitigates this outcome is the rule that any member that is party to a matter under consideration by the Council may not participate in the discussion or decision-making process, as noted above. Members of the PSC have upheld this rule in most cases, although it has proved controversial in several instances. For example, the Government of Sudan objected to the rule when the conflict in Darfur was first raised on the PSC agenda. On the insistence of other member states, the Sudanese delegation did eventually recuse themselves from these discussions. The Ethiopian government did not, however, when the PSC met to debate their incursion into Somalia in January 2007. Several PSC members were astonished when the Ethiopian Ambassador insisted on chairing the PSC meeting held to discuss the situation in Somalia, on the grounds that Ethiopia was not a party to the conflict, rather it was invited by the Government of Somalia.

Several PSC members voiced their disapproval at this meeting and afterwards, which suggests that this particular norm has gained acceptance within the PSC. As international relations theorist Nicholas Wheeler argues, the violation of a norm by one party does not invalidate the norm itself. Rather, the reaction of others to the rule-breaking behavior demonstrates the extent to which they collectively subscribe to the norm (Wheeler 2000, 5). A question arising from this is whether adherence to this particular rule of the PSC waxes or wanes according to: (1) the membership composition of the Council, and (2) the status within the PSC of the implicated member state in a matter raised for deliberation by the Council. The fact that Ethiopia is the host nation of the AU and PSC meetings may have dampened the objections of the Council members in the discussions of intervention in Somalia.

The compromise reached between big and small AU member states when designing the PSC was to avoid an overly hierarchical structure with no permanent members and no veto rights. In practice, this has allowed delegations from less powerful countries to use their wits and sound preparation to contribute effectively to PSC decision-making. However, the continued reliance on the consensus principle rather than voting provisions means that all 15 members may exercise a kind of veto. With the exception of Southern Africa, a pattern has also emerged in which regions re-elect their three-year members (Nigeria, Algeria, Ethiopia and Gabon). This suggests that the political heavyweights in each of these sub-regions play a leading role on the Council and that a two-tiered hierarchy exists to some degree.

Operationalization: Institutional Strengths and Weaknesses

This section reflects on the institutional challenges of capacity and resources needed to implement the mandate of the PSC. The workload of the PSC has increased rapidly since its establishment in 2004. In accordance with Article 10(4) of the *PSC Protocol*, a Secretariat to the PSC was set up in 2006. The original plan to have ten full-time staff supporting the PSC within the Peace and Security Department of the AU Commission has not yet been realized. Recruitment began in 2005/06, followed by the appointment of the Secretary to the PSC, three policy experts and two administrative support staff. Meanwhile, a fourth researcher has been appointed, but hiring of additional experts has been delayed.

The small team of the PSC Secretariat quickly became overburdened, as the number of meetings held from 2005–2006 doubled in the period 2006–2007. To put their workload into perspective, there are 64 well-paid bureaucrats supporting the UN Security Council compared with the PSC's four. These four staff members have to follow several different conflict situations at once, and do not have the luxury of specializing in particular countries or regions. They are also required to assist the Conflict Management Division of the Peace and Security Commission in drafting reports for a range of purposes beyond the meetings of the PSC. This small team is therefore able to perform only very limited secretarial duties for the Council. For example, they cannot produce verbatim or even summary records of PSC meetings in all cases and in all the working languages of the AU. Despite being overworked, these experts are well placed to influence the decisions of the PSC, simply because many of the government delegations have even less expertise available to them. In this way, the PSC Secretariat is ironically in a better position to shape policy for the PSC than their more numerous counterparts at the UN Security Council, despite the fact that most UNSC members have the capacity to prepare thoroughly for their meetings.

A review of the working methods of the PSC was conducted during 2007 and a number of recommendations were made aimed at strengthening and consolidating the institution (see in this regard "Background Paper on the Review of the Working Methods of the Peace and Security Council of the African Union", African Union

Peace and Security Council 2007). It was suggested that recruitment of more staff for the PSC Secretariat be made a priority, to achieve a more appropriately-sized and skilled team of five political officers (each one dedicated to one of the five regions of the AU); professional editors of documents into (at least) French, Arabic and Portuguese; one bilingual political expert; four interpreters/translators dedicated to the PSC meetings only, a technician, an administrative assistant and a messenger. Sufficient operational equipment was requested, including computers, laptops for reporting on PSC meetings, projectors, photocopiers and fax machines. In addition, the review emphasized the need for PSC member states to contribute more to the functioning of the Council. First, it was recommended that the chairperson of the PSC should take greater responsibility, during their one month incumbency, to set the program of work and oversee its implementation in consultation with the other members and the AU Commission. To date, the chairperson's role has been primarily to chair the PSC meetings. This position could be made a more active one, in which the chairperson drafts and circulates the agenda and presides over a monthly program of activities for the PSC.

Recently, the member state in the position of chairperson has briefed the media after a PSC meeting. This promotes transparency on the part of the PSC itself and takes some of the political responsibility off the bureaucrats. A further recommendation of the Review of Working Methods was that the PSC chairperson should reside in Addis Ababa during their month of duty. Their close proximity to the AU Headquarters would enable the member state to contribute more to the everyday functioning of the PSC and to field missions taking place. Second, it was suggested that a number of subcommittees of member states should be set up to support the work of the PSC. Six were recommended, including: (1) a drafting committee to word the decisions and communiqués of the Council; (2) a "follow-up committee" to oversee the implementation of decisions; (3) a "resource mobilization committee" to raise funds and build capacity for PSC activities; (4) a standing committee on procedure and working methods of the PSC; (5) a committee on procedures and mechanisms for peace support operations; and (6) a sanctions committee. Each of the five regions would be represented on these committees.

The formalization of a sanctions committee could be the most significant innovation for the PSC, since it would operationalize one of the two enforcement mechanisms at the Council's disposal. An ad hoc committee to apply sanctions in the Comoros proved effective, as discussed further below. Such a committee would also have a strong historical precedent in the OAU Sanctions Committee, which coordinated African sanctions against the Apartheid regime in South Africa and Ian Smith's Southern Rhodesia.

The format of PSC meetings has been loosely structured, with a mix of consultations, informal discussions, procedural debates and decision-making. The result has been extremely long sessions that lack direction or clarity on occasion. The Review of Working Methods therefore suggested a structure for meetings similar to that used by the UN Security Council. Four types of session would be held, namely: public meetings (at which the media may be present); private or closed meetings with other AU member states or AU organs; consultations—at which the Council receives briefings from the AU Commission and drafts decisions; and 'Aria type meetings', to which civil society actors, think tanks and academics are invited.

There is a need for greater civil society engagement by the PSC, as well as closer coordination with other AU organs, such as the African Commission on Human and Peoples' Rights, the Pan-African Parliament and the Economic, Social and Cultural Council (ECOSOCC). This is also mentioned in the Review of Working Methods document. In implementation of Article 17 of the *PSC Protocol*, the PSC holds annual joint meetings with the UNSC. Two such meetings, in Addis Ababa in June 2007 and in New York in April 2008, gave the two bodies the opportunity to exchange views on conflict situations they are both involved with, as well as to strengthen their cooperation in terms of conflict prevention and management. With regard to relations with RECs in the five regions of Africa, in addition to inviting the concerned RECs to contribute to its meetings on specific conflicts, the PSC may lead decisions on the basis of recommendations made by RECs, in particular by ECOWAS on Côte d'Ivoire and by IGAD on Somalia.

From Design to Reality: The PSC in Action

Since 2004, the PSC has met over 130 times to deliberate on more than 12 conflict situations. The focus has, of necessity, been on conflict management and resolution, rather than conflict prevention, due to the capacity constraints of the PSC and the intensity of conflict in numerous African countries, but also to a lack of political will. Director of the PSC Secretariat, Dr Admore Kambudzi describes this as an approach of "putting out fires, where we have to check the colour of the coals to see where it is hottest."[2]

A simple way of determining where these conflict 'hotspots' are considered to be, is to compare the number of times they have met to discuss the various conflicts and political crises in Africa since 2004. This offers a rough indication of where the PSC's priorities lie. It should be noted, however, that the PSC meets more often to discuss situations in which the AU has taken the lead, which may not be a reflection of the seriousness of one crisis over others. For example, the UN has been responsible for the MONUC (Mission de l'Organisation des Nations Unies en République Démocratique du Congo) peacekeeping operation in the DRC, which has allowed the AU to concentrate its limited military capacities elsewhere. The conflict in the DRC has received more attention from the Council after the Nairobi and Goma ceasefire agreements were broken in the North Kivu province on 28 August 2008. Of the conflict situations deliberated upon by the PSC, Sudan, Somalia and the Great Lakes region (DRC and Burundi) have

---

2   Interview by the authors, 12 January 2007.

received the most attention, followed by West African conflicts in Liberia and Côte d'Ivoire. Ongoing conflict mediation in the Comoros and renewed tensions between Eritrea and Ethiopia appeared on the agenda, as did concerns regarding Chad and Guinea-Bissau.

As discussed at length in the following chapters, the AU's mission to Burundi (AMIB) was the first AU deployment, authorized by the Central Organ before the PSC came into being. The peacekeeping force was made up of contingents from South Africa, Ethiopia and Mozambique, with South Africa as the lead nation, providing the Force Commander, Major General Sipho Binda. AMIB had a one-year mandate, which was extended twice before the UN took over from the AU in July 2004. In practice, this meant the South African and other troops were 'blue helmeted' and given reinforcements and, critically, financial support from the UN Department of Peacekeeping Operations (DPKO). Unlike a UN mission, in which troop contributing countries may be keen to participate for the compensation received (in terms of training, equipment as well as financial contributions), the cost of AU military interventions has to be carried by the contributing member states and by donor assistance.

The second major troop deployment by the AU was to Darfur, Sudan in July 2004. The PSC approved the modalities for the African Mission in Sudan (AMIS), following a decision of the Assembly, as a 'fully fledged peacekeeping mission', with a mandate that included the protection of civilians (PSC/PR/2(XLII). The difference between the conflict in Darfur and that in Burundi was that the Government of Sudan was implicated in the situation in their country, while AU troops in Burundi were protecting a fragile new government against rebel attacks. The situation in Darfur, and its spillover effects into Chad, occupied the agenda of the PSC more than any other matter, including the ongoing crises in Somalia and the DRC. AMIS focused most of the attention and resources of the PSC over three years, from 2004–2007.

Thus, AMIS has been a test case for the AU's foray into peace operations—even though it was never regarded as a substitute for a larger, stronger UN intervention. However, the UN failed to achieve even a semblance of consent to a UN peacekeeping deployment to Darfur. Eventually, the unprecedented step was taken to create a "hybrid" mission under the joint command of the UN and the AU in 2007. Although the PSC must have been greatly relieved to hand over some of the financial and logistical burden of this mission to the UN, the African member states expect to retain a degree of political leadership over the current operation.

In January 2007, the PSC met to discuss a military intervention by Ethiopian troops into Somalia. They agreed to follow this up with an African Mission in Somalia (AMISOM), although this decision proved controversial and difficult to follow through. The first consideration was that African troops would be entering a terrain of ungovernability since 1991, from which the US army and the UN had been forced to withdraw. The chances of achieving sustainable peace and order in Somalia were slim, despite the Ethiopian government's rout of the Union of Islamic Courts (UIC) from Mogadishu. Secondly, the mission was premised on a request for assistance from the Transitional Federal Government (TFG) of Somalia, even though the legitimacy and viability of this entity had not been established on Somalian soil. Finally, the danger of AMISOM being seen as a proxy for US strategic interests in the "War on Terrorism" made most PSC members reluctant to contribute troops.

So far, none of the interventions undertaken by the PSC have invoked the controversial article 4(h) of the *Constitutive Act*. That is to say, none of the conflict situations have been defined as "grave circumstance, such as war crimes, genocide or crimes against humanity", nor has the PSC intervened without the consent of the government concerned. In each case, and even in Sudan and Somalia, the PSC has been careful to argue that their action has been at the request of the government of the territory in which the conflict is taking place. This suggests that the norm of "humanitarian intervention" has not yet been institutionalized by the PSC (Williams 2007). While, as discussed in the pages above, this norm has been agreed to in principle by AU member states, in practice it has not yet been applied. The tension between this principle and the more entrenched norm of non-interference has resulted in a diplomatic egg-dance around questions of sovereignty and consent each time the PSC has built consensus for troop deployments to conflict situations.

There has been more significant progress in the institutionalization of a norm of non-military intervention, namely the application of sanctions by the PSC, specifically in cases of unconstitutional changes of government (Williams 2007). The mechanism of condemning and suspending any member state from the AU has been applied to a number of coups d'état, for example, in Togo, Mauritania and Guinea. Applying sanctions in response to unconstitutional changes of government has proven complicated in practice, however. Francis Ikome makes a convincing argument that there are "good coups" and "bad coups." He points out that there are two reasons why coups take place: (1) the ambitions and opportunism of the coup plotters, and (2) bad governance, which has shut down peaceful, democratic methods of changing a government (Ikome 2007, 23). This has quickly become apparent to the PSC, when it has had to apply the new rules in a number of cases, as discussed below.

In Togo, the AU followed the lead of ECOWAS, in responding to a coup d'état in February 2005. The death of Africa's longest running military dictator, Gnassingbe Eyedema, prompted his son, Faure Gnassingbe to assume the presidency unconstitutionally. This time, instead of looking the other way, the AU suspended the "de facto authorities of Togo [...] in the activities of all the AU policy organs until the restoration of constitutional legality in that country." The PSC "endorsed the sanctions adopted by ECOWAS [... and] requested all Member States to scrupulously implement the sanctions" (PSC/PR/Comm.(XXV).

As it turned out, the AU did not have to implement these sanctions, as Faure Gnassingbe resigned from the presidency on the same day and agreed to hold elections. ECOWAS immediately lifted sanctions, and Gnassingbe was allowed to run and win the presidency in an imperfect election marred by violence and allegations of rigging. The result was upheld by Togo's Constitutional Court and the AU subsequently dispatched an observer mission to monitor the ongoing humanitarian situation.[3]

This outcome went against the recommendations of the Chairperson of the Commission to the AU in 2003, when he argued for the need to strengthen the Lomé Declaration: "[…] including the rejection of the participation, especially as candidate, of the authors of unconstitutional change, in elections aimed at restoring constitutional order."[4] The Member States did not adopt this recommendation, showing the limits of their new norm of rejecting unconstitutional changes of government.

In response to coups in the Central African Republic (CAR) in March 2003 (prior to the PSC launch), and Mauritania in August 2005, the AU took a relatively muted stance in line with popular sentiment in these two countries (Ikome 2007, 38–41). The Central Organ discussed the coup in CAR, condemned it as an unconstitutional change of government and recommended that it be suspended from AU activities. This suspension was lifted by the PSC on 24 June 2005, after elections were held. Mauritania was suspended from the AU until after presidential elections held in March 2007. On 6 August 2008, however, newly elected President Sidi Abdallahi was overthrown by another coup. This time, the AU did not hesitate to condemn this coup in no uncertain terms. Meeting in New York on 22 September, the PSC demanded the "return to constitutional order" in Mauritania and issued a warning to "the authors of the coup d'état and their civilian supporters against the risk of sanctions if they do not respond positively to this demand."[5] The case of Mauritania thus illustrates the problem with a one-size-fits-all rule against any and all unconstitutional changes of government.

A way out of this dilemma would be to point out that the AU's definition of an unconstitutional change of government applies to coups d'état against *democratically elected* governments only. This could be used to understand the rationale for a lesser response to "good coups" than to "bad coups", provided there was some attempt at consistency and objective criteria in making these decisions on a case by case basis. There is no getting around the required suspension of membership, however, as the Constitutive Act explicitly prohibits "governments which shall come to power by unconstitutional means … [to] participate in the activities of the Union" (African Union 2000, §30), whether they seize power from a democratic or an authoritarian incumbent. The AU would have to maintain this blanket rule against all coups, in order to push those who take power unconstitutionally towards the ballot box.

---

3   See Report of the Chairperson of the Commission on the Developments in Togo, 27 May 2005, PSC/PR/2(XXX).

4   See Communiqué of the 93rd Ordinary Session of the Central Organ on Conflict Prevention, Mediation and Resolution, 24 July 2003.

5   See Communiqué of the 151st Meeting of the Peace and Security Council, 22 September 2008, PSC/MIN/Comm.2.

Unsurprisingly, the most comprehensive sanctions passed by the AU to date have been against a secessionist group rather than a government. The secession of the islands of Anjouan and Mohedi from the Comoros in August 1997 was condemned as "totally unacceptable" by the OAU (Naldi 1999, 45). The Organization mediated the conflict and, in 2001, brokercd an agreement to share power with a rotating presidency between Grande Comore and the "autonomous islands." Legislative elections were held in 2004 and a National Union Government formed in July 2005.[6]

Anjouan continued to defy the new dispensation, howevcr, and held its own presidential election in June 2007, against a presidential decree from the National Union Government. The AU then applied sanctions against "the illegal authorities of Anjouan and all other persons that impede the reconciliation process and constitute a threat to peace and security in the Comoros."[7] Sanctions included a travel ban implemented by all member states of the AU and the freezing of financial assets "owned or controlled by the illegal Anjouanese authorities."[8] The PSC agreed to draw up a list of the individuals concerned, to be circulated to all member states, and to monitor all air and sea transport to and from Anjouan. Concern that sanctions should not cause undue harm was expressed in the communiqué, "bearing in mind the need to limit, as much as possible, the impact of these measures on the civilian population."[9]

These sanctions were extended by a month on 21 January 2008, and again on 18 February for a further two months. However, the next report of the Chairperson of the AU Commission noted that the Comorian president lost patience with the process, and "announced his government's determination to use all available means, including force, given the failure of all attempts to resolve the Anjouan crisis peacefully."[10] The AU then agreed to plans for a military intervention, although this support was not unanimous among AU member states. In late March 2008, armed forces of the federated islands of the Comoros routed the "illegal" leadership of Anjouan with the backing of troops and logistical support from Tanzania, Libya, Sudan and Senegal. Colonel Mohamed Bacar fled the island on a boat for Mayotte. The Comoros situation raises questions at the heart of the AU agenda, about secession and Africa's famously fixed boundaries, and about the use of sanctions versus military intervention.

Apart from military intervention and sanctions, the PSC has sent diplomatic and observer missions to mediate, observe or investigate a range of conflicts and

---

6　See Report of the Chairperson of the AU Commission to the PSC on the situation in the Comoros, 21 March 2006.

7　See Communiqué of the 95th Ordinary Session of the PSC, 10 October 2007.

8　Ibid.

9　Ibid.

10　Report of the Chairperson of the Commission on the Situation in the Comoros since the 10th Ordinary Session of the Assembly of the AU held in Addis Ababa from 31 January–2 February 2008, PSC/PR/2(CXXIV).

political situations throughout Africa. PSC meetings have been used to pronounce an African position on certain cases, for example electoral problems in Kenya in 2007, Zimbabwe in 2008, and the indictment of Sudanese President, Omar al-Bashir by the International Criminal Court in 2008. In cases of Kenya and Zimbabwe, however, the PSC merely received briefings on the evolution of the situations without making any significant decision. The PSC did not even identify, let alone condemn, the parties involved in perpetrating violence. The mediation processes led by a joint AU-UN team in Kenya and by South Africa in Zimbabwe were decided respectively by the Chairperson of the AU and the Secretary General of the UN and by the Assembly of States of the AU.

Conclusion

This chapter has reviewed the development of the PSC since its launch in May 2004. It traced the establishment of the PSC and its operationalization, through an analysis of its activities and the challenges it faces, including the implications of the nature of its membership for the effective execution of its mandate. It appeared that, during its first four years of operation, the PSC gained clout and authority not only on the continent, but also in the global arena. Its decisions have been respected by the international community in a number of cases, for example, with respect to the conflict in Côte d'Ivoire, and implemented by all concerned, including the private sector. The implementation by private companies of sanctions imposed on the Comoros Island in Anjouan is also good case in point.

Notwithstanding the progress made in respect of the prevention and management of conflicts in different parts of the continent, the PSC, particularly during its fifth year of activity, fell short of its primary role in the resolution of a number situations, such as the post-electoral violence that erupted in Kenya in 2007 and in Zimbabwe in 2008. The resurgence of violence in the DRC in the last quarter of 2008, raised the expectation that the PSC, having once considered authorizing a peace enforcement mission in Eastern DRC, would react forcefully to protect civilians. The low profile adopted by the Council since the resurgence of fighting in that area, compared with the more prominent role played by other institutions, in particular the UN and the Process of the International Conference on the Great Lakes Region, does not preclude a decisive role for the PSC in the region in the near future. The presence of Rwanda in the Council and the Chairmanship of Uganda in November 2008, two countries directly concerned with the situation, may explain the silence of the PSC despite the humanitarian disaster that is unfolding in the region.

The marginal role played in many cases discussed above, and its lack of decisive initiative, undermines the PSC's image as the premier institution for the prevention and management of conflicts on the continent. And yet the PSC cannot be regarded as a standalone institution. Rather, it should be seen in the context of the AU conflict prevention and management regime, where the Assembly, the Chairperson of the Commission and the Chairperson of the AU also play critical roles. Where the PSC fails to act, these other institutions, and the Assembly in particular, take up the task. This was the case regarding the situations in Zimbabwe, Kenya, and the tensions between Ethiopia and Eritrea. Thus, while the PSC is certainly important, it is still only one element of a larger architecture, with the ultimate goal of bringing about peace, security and stability on the continent.

Chapter 5

The Panel of the Wise

Tim Murithi and Charles Mwaura

Introduction

The African Union Peace and Security Architecture is designed to promote conflict prevention, peacemaking, peacekeeping and post-conflict peacebuilding. The Panel of the Wise has been established as part of the peacemaking component. Specifically, the Panel is an integral aspect of the African Union's (AU) dedicated preventive diplomacy framework given its mandate to anticipate potential crisis situations and intervene in a timely fashion to prevent the escalation of a dispute or resolve existing tensions to reduce the likelihood of a return to violence.

This chapter will assess the establishment of the Panel as well as discuss its mandate and modalities of operation. It will also trace the cultural basis of the idea of a Panel of Wise third-party actors inherent in indigenous African culture. The chapter will further assess the collaboration between the United Nations (UN) and the AU on enhancing the work of the Panel as well as its framework of collaboration with Regional Economic Communities (RECs). The chapter will assess recent initiatives undertaken by the Panel, prior to concluding with some recommendations on how it can further strengthen its capacity for undertaking its preventive diplomacy mandate to prevent the prevalence of conflict in Africa.

The Panel of the Wise: Legal Basis and Modalities of Operation

From the outset, the architects of the AU recognized that the institution had to establish a framework for promoting peace and security that was qualitatively different from that of its predecessor, the Organization of African Unity (OAU). As discussed at length in the preceding chapters, following the inauguration of the AU in July 2002, in Durban, South Africa, the continental body promulgated a *Protocol Relating to the Establishment of the Peace and Security of the African Union* (hereafter PSC Protocol), at the First Ordinary Session of the Assembly of Heads of State and Government. The Protocol articulated a wide-ranging framework for implementing preventive diplomacy, peacemaking, and peacekeeping, as defined by the United Nations (UN) *Agenda for Peace*, which had been published ten years earlier, in 1992. The AU's peace and security architecture includes a Peace and Security Council (PSC); an African Standby Force (ASF); a Continental Early Warning System (CEWS); Panel of the Wise and the Peace Fund.

Constituted under the terms of Article 11 of the *PSC Protocol*, the Panel of the Wise has the mandate "to support the efforts of the Peace and Security Council and those of the Chairperson of the Commission, particularly in the area of conflict prevention" (African Union 2002, §11 (1)). Specifically, the Panel of the Wise has the mandate to "advise the Peace and Security Council and the Chairperson of the AU Commission on all issues pertaining to the promotion, and maintenance of peace, security and stability in Africa" (African Union 2002, §11 (3)). In addition, "at its own initiative, the Panel of the Wise shall undertake such action deemed appropriate to support the efforts of the Peace and Security Council and those of the Chairperson of the Commission for the prevention of conflict" (African Union 2002, §11 (4)). This endows the Panel of the Wise with the authority to facilitate and mediate potential or ongoing disputes on its own volition.

The *Modalities for the Functioning of the Panel of the Wise* were adopted by the AU Peace and Security Council at its 100th meeting, held on 12 November 2007, in Addis Ababa, Ethiopia (African Union 2007). These modalities stipulate that the Panel will be composed of five members "elected from among highly respected African personalities of high integrity and independence, who have made outstanding contributions to Africa in the areas of peace, security and development" (African Union 2007, 1). These individuals are selected by the Chairperson of the AU Commission based on consultations with the member states, but they are ultimately appointed through a decision of the Assembly of Heads of State and Government. The Panel Modalities are explicit on the requirement that members of the Panel should not be politically active at the time of their appointment and throughout their tenure. They can serve for a renewable term of three years. The Panel members appoint from amongst themselves a Chairperson who serves for only one year. In addition, "a member of the Panel may not be elected Chairperson more than once in any period of three years" (African Union 2007, IV-1). The Panel can meet as and when required, or at the request of the Council and Commission, but it has to meet at least three times a year.

Echoing the *PSC Protocol*, the *Panel Modalities* stipulate that its primary function is to "advise the [Peace and Security] Council and the Chairperson of the Commission on all issues pertaining to the promotion and maintenance of peace, security and stability in Africa" (African Union 2007, Mandate, 1). Therefore, its remit is clearly stipulated as a supportive one rather than as a parallel institution to the Council or the Commission. The Modalities, however, reiterate the independence of the Panel when they state that it "may, as and when necessary and in the form it considers most appropriate, pronounce itself on any issue relating to the promotion and maintenance of peace, security and stability in Africa […] may act […] at its own initiative" (African Union 2007, Mandate, 3). This endows the Panel with a very broad mandate to effectively comment, draw attention and intervene in virtually any situation on the continent that it deems worthy of attention.

Herein lies the added-value of the Panel of the Wise. The AU Peace and Security Council is more often than not constrained by the political considerations of its members and the wider AU membership when it comes to intervening in controversial situations such as Zimbabwe. Similarly, the AU Commission is, at least in theory, bound by the decisions of its member states, notably the Executive Council and Assembly, and is therefore not always at liberty to function independently. The mandate stipulated by the Panel Modalities is broad and unencumbered by the typical political considerations that undermine efforts to promote early warning and response. However, it is not sufficient to have such a mandate, the members of the Panel of the Wise have to be willing to use this broad mandate to act as the eyes and ears of the institution as far as preventing conflict is concerned. Furthermore, the Panel's independence needs to be assured by the provision of an adequate institutional support mechanism, one that enables close coordination with other pillars of the architecture (particularly the CEWS, to be discussed in the next chapter) to ensure that it has timely information and the ability to intervene, as the Modalities state, "on any issue" and "at its own initiative", as will be discussed further below. In addition, the Panel can also accept and receive proposals "from the Pan-African Parliament, the African Commission on Human and People's Rights and civil society groups" (African Union 2007, IV-7).

The Cultural and Philosophical Origins of the Panel of the Wise

Prior to assessing the practical arrangements that have been put in place to operationalize it, we should interrogate the very idea of a Panel of the Wise as part of the AU's peace and security architecture. Specifically, how did the idea of the Council of Elders translate into the contemporary manifestation of the Panel of the Wise? The notion for the establishment of the Panel did not emerge spontaneously or arbitrarily. The insights drawn from indigenous African culture provided a philosophical inspiration for the creation of the Panel of the Wise. Specifically, the wise counsel of leaders within the typical traditional African community was vital in intervening, resolving and sustaining peace (Murithi 2008, 16). In effect, one can argue that the AU Panel of the Wise is operating in a contemporary setting as the functional equivalent of a cultural council of indigenous leaders tasked with intervening and resolving disputes.

There is a wealth of knowledge within indigenous African culture on how to intervene and resolve disputes. Jannie Malan (1997, 16) reminds us that as far as conflict resolution approaches are concerned we should not "forget the time-proven methods which originated on African soil." Malan (1997, 20) argues that indigenous approaches to resolving a dispute in Africa emphasized taking into account "the history of preceding events which have led up to the conflict concerned" and taking the "possible implications for the future seriously." In this context, efforts to resolve disputes did not focus exclusively on the immediate disagreement but also sought to take into account the potential consequences for the social networks and the relationships within the community. Therefore, an emphasis was always placed on exploring the thoughts and intentions of others.

Malan (1997, 20) notes that "when an elder from a family, village or clan becomes involved in the talks, the traditional objectives are to move away from accusations and counter-accusations, to soothe hurt feelings and to reach a compromise that may help to improve the future relationships".

The role of councils of elders was (and in many communities still is) primarily to respond to the sentiments of the community as a whole. As illustrated by the role of the Council of Elders among the Tiv of Nigeria, as agents for resolving disputes within the community these councils can, in the first instance, play the role of a mediator. In some communities these councils had the authority to arbitrate and adjudicate on disputes and suggest decisions that the parties would need to respect (Murithi and Murphy-Ives 2007, 80). This is primarily because, in traditional communities, individuals deemed to potentially become members of the council of elders were distinguished by their moral probity and wisdom on matters affecting the community. This communally sanctioned moral authority gives their adjudicated and arbitrated decisions the normative imprimatur of a legal sanction.

An important dimension that is evident in the majority of traditional settings, for example among the Nguni ethnic groups of Southern Africa and the Somali, is that the rest of the community can participate in a mediation process (Murithi and Murphy-Ives 2007, 77). This is significantly different from contemporary approaches to international mediation. In this regard, it is important to recall that these traditional councils of elders are meant to mediate small-scale inter-personal and inter-group disputes. On the basis of a continental framework however, the sphere of operation for the AU Panel, it would not be feasible to include the masses of people in peacemaking processes (Murithi and Murphy-Ives 2007, 84). However, an important link does need to be retained with the grassroots communities through civil society interaction, which will be discussed later in this chapter.

The Panel of the Wise is a contemporary rendition of the traditional institution of the council of elders. However, the Panel is not a direct or an authentic replication of a traditional council format in its authority and remit. Specifically, the AU Panel diverges from traditional councils of elders in four respects, namely: it has no authority to impose a decision on state or non-state parties; mediation efforts are not conducted in public; it is constrained by limited human and financial resources; and, finally, it is composed of prominent and distinguished women and has therefore adopted a gender sensitive re-interpretation of the traditional council of elders.

These qualitative differences are a welcome departure from institutions that were, on the whole, patriarchal in their composition and could potentially be deployed as instruments for authoritarian rule. In any peacemaking and preventive diplomacy endeavor the threat of the use of coercion or force cannot feature in the range of tools available to mediators, since this would not produce an agreement that was achieved through the consent of the parties and a voluntary commitment towards respecting the interests of their interlocutors. The Panel though does require its privacy from the glare of the court of public opinion in order to achieve creative and innovative solutions to problems. The staff complement and the budget of the Panel are currently not unlimited, so it always has to deploy its efforts strategically. In the traditional setting, the council of elders was an integral part of the society and peacemaking could continue over a lengthy period of time.

The fact that the Panel currently includes two prominent women among its membership (see the next section) is the most significant departure from the model of the traditional council of elders. These councils were effectively dominated by men in the majority of traditional settings. There are of course an exceptionally small minority of cultures that ascribed a prominent role to women, particularly in matters of war and peace. This innovation of the Panel is important and upholds the AU's stated rhetoric on promoting gender parity. However, it is also vital in order to signify to African societies that there are women of all backgrounds and levels of expertise playing a vital role in the promotion of peace on the continent. These insights therefore indicate how the Panel of the Wise is, in effect, a contemporary rendition of the traditional notion of a council of elders. In effect, the function undertaken by these councils is mirrored by the Panel, which strives to anticipate situations and use innovative strategies for resolving disputes before they escalate. To reinforce this claim, in his statement during the inauguration of the Panel of the Wise, its Dean, Ahmed Ben Bella stated that wherever it is called to intervene it will endeavor "to lend its interlocutors the benefit of the ancestral African values of wisdom and dialogue, and ensure that peaceful solutions prevail, regardless of the nature of the crisis or conflict" (African Union Peace and Security Department 2008, 12).

The Launch of the Panel of the Wise

In January 2007 the AU Assembly appointed five distinguished African personalities to the Panel of the Wise for a period of three years. They include Salim Ahmed Salim, former OAU Secretary-General, representing the East African region; Brigalia Bam, Chairperson of the Independent Electoral Commission of South Africa, representing the Southern Africa region; Ahmed Ben Bella former President of Algeria, representing the North Africa region; Elisabeth Pognon, President of the Constitutional Court of Benin, representing West Africa; and Miguel Trovoada, former President of São Tomé and Príncipe, representing Central Africa.

On 18 December 2007, the Panel of the Wise was formally inaugurated at a meeting that included representatives of Member States of the AU as well as the diplomatic community. Later that day, the Panel held a meeting during which it elected Ben Bella as its Dean or chair, and exchanged views on the scope of its work as well as highlighting conflict and crisis situations affecting the continent. On 20 February 2008, the Panel convened its first meeting at the AU headquarters in Addis Ababa and adopted a broad outline of its program of work. At its second meeting on 17 July 2008, the Panel further enumerated its work program. Panel members agreed to devote that year's thematic reflection to the prevention of conflict emerging from disputed elections, influenced by the post-electoral violence that had afflicted Kenya in January and February 2008, as well as the crisis generated by the Zimbabwe elections.

As discussed above, the need for the Panel to have a dedicated and independent institutional support mechanism is vital for it to fulfill its broad mandate. The second meeting of the Panel addressed the issue of the resources needed to support the work of the Panel, including a dedicated Secretariat within the Conflict Management Division in the Peace and Security Department of the Commission on Peace and Security. However, the fact that the proposed Secretariat of the Panel of the Wise will be housed in the AU Commission means that it will inevitably face some of the political, bureaucratic, and logistical constraints that are typically found in any inter-governmental organization. The Panel Modalities stipulate that "the Commission shall provide administrative technical and logistical support as may be required to facilitate its work" and also provide "substantive services in support of the Panel's work, including information relating to specific situations, on mediation and negotiation processes" (African Union 2007, VIII-1). The Modalities also state that the Commission will provide the necessary research and advisory capacities to support the Panel's work. In this regard, the second meeting of the Panel also discussed the issue of how to complement the work of the Panel with specialized expertise as well as an annual budget.

According to the 2008 Work Program, the Secretariat of the Panel of the Wise will work in tandem with other relevant units of the AU Commission to, among other things, collect and analyze information on developments on the continent; conduct research on thematic issues relating to peace; produce policy papers; identify experts on peace issues; accompany Panel members on missions as required; produce and distribute Panel reports; facilitate coordination and communication between the Panel and other organs of the AU; organize Panel meetings; facilitate interaction with civil society and academic institutions; and contribute to raising the profile of the Panel and its program (African Union Peace and Security Department 2008, 25).

It is evident that in order to be effective the Panel of the Wise needs a robust mediation support unit within the AU Commission (Nathan 2004, 63). It also requires significant input from qualified political officers who have experience in bilateral and multilateral negotiation settings. These officers should ideally be cognizant and experienced in conflict analysis; have an understanding of the use of shuttle diplomacy; be knowledgeable about the components of a mediation process and how to generate options and effectively draft agreements (Field 2004). Without such a staff complement as well as close coordination with other components of the AU peace and security architecture, it will be difficult for the Panel to conduct its affairs of analyzing and mapping conflicts and determining who the key parties, secondary actors and spoilers are in a given situation (Assefa 1987, 94). In this sense, the Panel of the Wise needs a mediation support unit that can provide it with timely analysis of the positions, underlying interests, and options available to disputing parties. It is only on this basis that the Panel will be in a position to effectively pursue preventive diplomacy and peacemaking. In order to enhance its effectiveness, "if the Panel considers it necessary, it may invite resource persons, experts, institutions or individuals, to attend a meeting in order to assist the Panel in its deliberations on specific issues" (African Union 2007, IV-5). In this regard, the second meeting of the Panel noted that it would receive support from "ad hoc specialized expertise" (African Union Peace and Security Department 2008, 20).

In terms of the accountability of the Panel to the wider AU system, its members have to report to "the Chairperson of the Commission and, through him, the Chairperson of the Council" (African Union 2007, Modalities of Action, 3). This is vital to ensure that the Panel does not duplicate, but rather supports, the efforts of the Council or the Commission. The Chairperson of the Panel of the Wise can request to address the AU Assembly of Heads of State and Government. The Panel can submit its views and recommendations to the Council and to the Chairperson of the Commission "whenever it considers it appropriate" (African Union 2007, V-1). However, it has to submit regular reports on its activities to the Council and biannual reports to the AU Assembly of Heads of State and Government.

Preventive Diplomacy and the Panel of the Wise

The Panel of the Wise can "facilitate the establishment of channels of communication between the Council and the Chairperson of the Commission, on the one hand, and parties engaged in a dispute, on the other hand, in order to prevent such dispute from escalating into conflict" (African Union 2007, Modalities of Action, 1b). In addition, it can "carry out fact-finding missions as an instrument of conflict prevention [...] conduct shuttle diplomacy between parties to a conflict in cases where parties are not ready to engage in formal talks" (African Union 2007, Modalities of Action, 1c and 1d). When it deems it necessary the Panel is also mandated to issue a press release or a statement on any matter that it is considering. This, in effect, constitutes an array of tools for deploying preventive diplomacy.

However, the Panel's modalities of action also include the provision for its members to support AU mediation teams in their efforts. In cases where a dedicated AU Special Envoy or Representative has been appointed the Panel can provide support by undertaking additional shuttle diplomacy or behind the scenes confidence building between parties. In post-conflict situations the Panel can also "assist and advise parties on how to resolve disputes related to the implementation of peace agreements" and encourage parties to "carry out reconciliation processes" (African Union 2007, Modalities of Action, 1e).

The Panel of the Wise is also conscious of the fact that its engagement with situations has to add value to the overall promotion of conflict prevention and conflict reduction. In this regard, the Panel has adopted five criteria that will serve as a litmus test of when it should engage in crisis situations (African Union Peace and Security Department 2008, 23), including: (1) the degree to which a conflict situation already receives regional and international attention. Conflicts that have been neglected for lack of resources or other reasons may be especially appropriate cases for the Panel to engage with; (2) whether the PSC is already seized with a particular conflict situation and whether additional attention by the Panel may add further value to existing efforts; (3) whether a given situation has remained in conflict for a considerable amount of time or is in danger of descending into conflict, despite multiple mediation and negotiation efforts. In such a situation, the Panel may advise and strengthen existing efforts, inject new urgency to mediation processes, or take a fresh look at the conflict dynamics at play; (4) whether a conflict situation has experienced a sudden and speedy decline; and, finally, (5) whether a conflict situation has experienced difficulties in implementing a peace agreement and, therefore faces the risk of reverting to conflict.

The Panel of the Wise, the International Community, the Regional Economic Communities and Civil Society

Given its extensive experience in mediation over more than five decades, the United Nations is in a strong position to support the work of the Panel of the Wise. Indeed, it is mandated to do so through the UN 10-Year Capacity Building Program for the African Union to provide support in the area of peace and security. The UN has undertaken a proactive role in supporting the operationalization of the Panel of the Wise. In 2008, the UN Department for Political Affairs' (DPA) Mediation Support Unit (MSU) funded a short-term consultant to work with the African Union to undertake the necessary groundwork to define a framework for a Secretariat of the Panel of the Wise. The consultant reported to the Head of the Conflict Management Division and had the responsibility for identifying the needs and requirements for the establishment of the Secretariat; documenting lessons learned from other mediation support units of regional and international organizations; developing a framework for mediation tools and guidance; producing a communications strategy; and convening and participating in meetings that will enable the Panel to be operationalized. Throughout this period, this UN consultant in effect functioned as a one-person secretariat for the Panel, which is a situation that is being addressed by efforts to appoint additional staff. The consultant was nevertheless vital in providing technical support and institutional guidance to the work of the Panel and its interface with other structures of the AU.

In addition to the support that the UN is providing to the Panel, its members can also gain insights from the conflict prevention and preventive diplomacy frameworks of the European Union (EU) and the Organization for Security and Cooperation in Europe (OSCE). The EU has deployed a significant number of special envoys to a range of trouble spots around the world, and has acquired a significant degree of expertise in the politics of donor influence of peacemaking initiatives. The OSCE has established a relatively successful framework for preventive diplomacy in the form of the Office of the High Commissioner for

National Minorities (HCNM). In particular, the High Commissioner typically operates by undertaking discreet visits and assessing potential sources of tension or conflict in close collaboration with the host government. Where necessary, the High Commissioner has taken the initiative to make recommendations to amend legislation that was deemed detrimental to the welfare of minorities living in the host country. Both the EU and the OSCE therefore have vital experience to share with the Panel of the Wise.

The work of the Panel should also complement that of the mediation focal points in the Regional Economic Communities (RECs). The Economic Community of West African States (ECOWAS) Protocol on the Mechanism for Conflict Prevention, Management, Resolution, Peace-keeping and Security of 1999, established the ECOWAS Council of the Wise (previously the Council of Elders) as an institution that would work with the Mediation and Security Council. The Panel of the Wise can therefore gain a substantial amount of insight from the work of the ECOWAS Council of the Wise. The ECOWAS Mediation and Security Council has the authority to mandate the Council of the Wise to undertake third-party intervention in potential crisis situations. In a meeting convened in Addis Ababa, the Head of the Conflict Management Division within the AU Commission on Peace and Security, El-Ghassim Wane, noted that the establishment of the Panel of the Wise drew inspiration from the ECOWAS Council of the Wise (Institute for Security Studies 2008, 1). Therefore, the AU Panel of the Wise can gain insights by interfacing with the ECOWAS Council of the Wise and undertaking a regular exchange of strategy and experiences.

One of the objectives of the South African Development Community (SADC) is to ensure the undertaking of conflict prevention, management and resolution of disputes among its 14-members. In this regard, SADC operates through its Organ for Politics, Defense and Security, which has dedicated preventive diplomacy personnel to respond to early warnings on potential conflicts. Furthermore, through the SADC Ministerial Committee on Politics and Diplomacy, the body can undertake preventive action to mitigate escalating disputes. However, as with other RECs, while its peace and security architecture is well defined this does not translate to precipitous preventive action in practice. In the absence of any institutional interaction, the Panel has merely commented on some of the efforts of SADC. Specifically, at its second meeting in July 2008, the Panel reviewed the situation in Zimbabwe and expressed support of the efforts of SADC. In this regard, a more clearly defined interface between SADC and the AU Panel of the Wise would advance the cause of preventing conflict in Africa. This also applies to the relationship between the Panel of the Wise and the Inter-Governmental Authority on Development's (IGAD) Peace and Security Department as well as opposite units in the Common Market for East and Southern Africa (COMESA), the Economic Community of Central African States (ECCAS), the Community of Sahel-Saharan States (CEN-SAD), and the East African Community (EAC). This could be achieved through a series of regularized meetings perhaps on the sidelines of the AU conventions.

The *Constitutive Act* of the African Union states that one of the objectives of the Union is "to build a partnership between governments and all segments of civil society" and to promote the "participation of the African peoples in the activities of the Union" (African Union 2000, Preamble). The AU has, from the outset, expressed a commitment to engaging with civil society in the implementation of its objectives (Muchie et al. 2006, 5). As mentioned earlier, the Panel of the Wise can also accept and receive proposals from civil society organizations (CSOs) (African Union 2007, IV-7). In terms of the specific process of interaction with CSOs, its 2008 Work Program states that the Secretariat will "facilitate the Panel's outreach efforts to civil society, research and academic institutions, and other relevant organizations" (African Union Peace and Security Department 2008, 25). Some areas where CSOs can assist the work of the Panel is in providing information on conflict situations and their particular phases. With specific reference to early warning and considering the proximity of civil society to conflict areas, CSOs can undertake field missions to provide technical support in gathering and receiving information on political and other developments in specific countries or regions that the Panel is considering. Specifically, CSOs can undertake early warning reporting, conflict mapping, and situation analysis as well as assist in complementing the research and analysis capacity of the Panel. CSOs have already created several networks that can provide timely information to the CEWS and the Panel and consequently enhance the Council's ability to formulate well-informed political strategies to prevent or resolve conflicts. CSOs can also assist with supporting the mediation efforts of the Panel through sharing their practical peacemaking expertise.

When it becomes necessary to undertake thematic studies on issues that the Panel would like to examine, CSOs can convene, as requested, seminars to explore specific issues. CSOs can also provide training in preventive diplomacy for parties that the Panel may be working with through its field missions. In addition, the Panel can invite CSOs to assist it in its deliberations on specific issues. Where the Panel deems it necessary, CSOs can play a role in widely publicizing the peacemaking process so that the wider population is informed of the ongoing efforts to broker peace in the country. The important issue to factor in is for CSOs to explore areas of comparative advantage, strength, and synergies to avoid creating parallel processes that might undermine the work of the Panel.

The Panel of the Wise in Action

The Panel further discussed its work program during its second formal meeting held at the AU headquarters in Addis Ababa, on 17 July 2008, chaired by Ahmed Ben Bella. This meeting was also attended by the AU Commissioner of Peace and Security, Ramtane Lamamra and the Chair of the PSC for the month of July 2008 (African Union Peace and Security Department 2008, 20). The work program stipulated that the Panel would undertake four key activities, including:

deliberations among the Panel members, including formal meetings and informal consultations; collaboration and consultation with the relevant organs of the AU, including the Peace and Security Council and the Chairperson of the Commission; engagement with countries and regions affected by conflicts; and, consideration of key thematic issues related to conflict prevention and peace-building in Africa.

The meeting also considered how the Panel would engage with countries and regions affected by conflicts and its intention to consider key thematic issues related to conflict prevention and peacebuilding in Africa (African Union Peace and Security Department 2008, 20). The second meeting also committed the Panel to, on an ongoing basis, "consider developments in the countries and regions on its agenda" and to undertake "an overview of the current state of affairs on the continent in order to anticipate and identify any new conflict situations requiring the Panel's attention" (African Union Peace and Security Department 2008, 21). The work program recognized that "over the course of its tenure, the Panel may need to undertake a number of missions, and this may impose a heavy schedule on its members" and in this regard it may need "to devise guidelines regarding the situations in which partial representation (for example by 1 of its members) will be considered adequate" (African Union Peace and Security Department 2008, 21). The Panel held its third meeting in Algiers, Algeria, in October 2008 and its fourth meeting in Nairobi in November 2008.

Throughout 2008, the Panel undertook a number of fact-finding missions to several African countries (El Abdellaoui 2009). In July 2008, Ahmed Ben Bella—who was at the time the Dean of the Panel of the Wise—issued a statement expressing concern about the decision by the International Criminal Courts' (ICC) Chief Prosecutor, Luis Moreno-Ocampo, to seek an arrest warrant for Omar al-Bashir of Sudan for his government's atrocities committed in Darfur. Ben Bella's argument was that if the indictment was to be pursued it would lead to an unconstitutional removal of the government of Sudan (Kilner 2008). At that time, Ben Bella was not the only leader concerned with this issue. The challenge is that the issue of how to sequence peace and justice is emerging as a conundrum that may complicate efforts to stabilize African countries in the years to come. In this regard, Ben Bella's pronouncement does indicate that an internal dialogue among Panel members took place on how to balance the need for addressing the crisis in Darfur with ensuring justice for the victims of atrocities.

At its fourth meeting, held in Nairobi on 28 and 29 November 2008, the Panel undertook a review of the situation in Somalia through discussions with the Prime Minister of the Transitional Federal Government (TFG), Nur Hussein 'Adde' and the Chairman of the Central Committee of the Alliance for the Re-liberation of Somalia (ARS), Sharif Hassan Sheik Aden (African Union 2008, 1). The issue of the deployment of the AU Mission in Somalia (AMISOM) was discussed—with the recognition that the mission remains vulnerable and there is in effect a security vacuum in the country. The Panel issued a statement that "called on all the Somali parties that have not yet done so to join the peace and reconciliation process and demonstrate the much needed spirit of accommodation and tolerance in order to end the suffering of their people" (African Union 2008, 4). The Panel recognized the ongoing role of the Inter-Governmental Authority on Development (IGAD) in attempting to broker peace in Somalia, but concluded that it was necessary for "AU Member States to fully assume their responsibilities [...] by urgently providing troops" and "the much-needed financial and logistical support to AMISOM" (African Union 2008, 8). The Panel however also "strong urged the United Nations Security Council to fully assume its responsibilities, in particular by authorizing without any further delay the establishment of an international stabilization force" (African Union 2008, 7) to reinforce and ultimately replace AMISOM.

In November 2008, the Panel of the Wise convened a seminar on the theme of the nexus between elections and conflict management. It subsequently transmitted its recommendations on this theme to the AU Assembly for discussion during its Ordinary Session in June 2009. Salim Ahmed Salim undertook a Panel mission to South Africa where elections were due to be held on 22 April 2009. He met with government officials, civil society representatives and the media. Salim cautioned against parties generating tensions or fomenting violence in the lead up to the elections. In effect, Salim was fulfilling the Panel of the Wise's mandate to pre-empt potential crisis and to contribute effectively towards promoting a reduction of tension.

During a mission to the Central African Republic (CAR) in early 2007, the Panel of the Wise became involved in assessing the political situation in the country and the preparations for the convening of an inclusive political dialogue. The situation in the north-western and north-eastern parts of the country remained precarious and it was necessary to establish a confidence-building and problem-solving process. In this context, the Panel "conducted a series of consultations with national political parties, trade unions, civil society organizations and members of the diplomatic community accredited to the country" (United Nations 2007, 3). The Panel of the Wise received a mandate from the CAR's President François Bozizé to consult rebel groups and duly did so outside the country (United Nations 2007, 4). The Panel also met with CAR's former President Ange-Félix Patassé who has been living in exile since 2003. The Panel subsequently compiled and presented a report to President Bozizé. The Panel's report concluded and recommended that a national dialogue be convened in three stages, including preliminary consultations focusing on military and security areas; preliminary consultations among representatives of all the political parties and civil society organizations to define the content and procedures of the eventual inclusive national dialogue; and, an inclusive political conference bringing together all stakeholders and facilitated by an external mediator. Subsequently, the President forwarded the Panel's report to the CAR National Assembly and the Constitutional Court to seek their view on the document (United Nations 2007, 5). Essentially, the situation in CAR remains precarious and Bozizé continues to cite the importance of ensuring that the security situation in the country improves and that the legitimacy of the government and its institutions is respected. Despite this prevarication, the Panel of the Wise at the very least raised the importance of ensuring the momentum is geared towards national reconciliation.

On 5 and 6 March 2009, the Panel convened its fifth meeting in Addis Ababa, with Ben Bella, Elizabeth Pognon and Salim Ahmed Salim in attendance, to review conflict and crisis situations on the continent and discuss the implementation of its work program for the year. The Panel decided to adopt a thematic focus for 2009 on the issues of impunity, reconciliation and healing. Essentially, this is an attempt to bring to the fore the prevalent challenge of balancing the need for peace and the demand for justice. The Panel has commissioned a report and will convene a workshop to further explore this issue in mid-2009.

Challenges Facing the Panel of the Wise

The Panel will face the classic challenges that confront any early response and preventive diplomacy framework. Early warning will often not receive the political attention that it requires in order for an early response to be effective at preventing the escalation of violence. The second challenge that the Panel will face is the reception it will receive from countries in which it identifies a need for preventive diplomacy, including mediation. Typically, governments like to maintain the external perception that there are no internal problems until the situation has escalated to a point of social unrest or political violence. Therefore, the presence of the AU Panel of the Wise, particularly high profile members, will naturally make governments nervous. In the worst case scenario the Panel will be rebuffed even before it makes its intervention into a particular country, by the denial of the necessary protocol clearances that are vital to engage with a country's government and the wider society. In other instances the Panel may be given the authorization to travel to a particular country but will be met with obfuscation and non-compliance by the target government. In an ideal scenario the AU Panel of the Wise will undertake an intervention and hold productive discussions with the government, the political opposition, business leaders and civil society in order to ascertain the urgency of peacemaking efforts. Irrespective of which of these scenarios the Panel confronts, the important thing is for its members to recognize that it has the authority and mandate from the AU to undertake investigation and intervention. The extent to which it will succeed on making a genuine impact on the African continent will be based on its ability to operate and initiate interventions on its own volition, and its analyses of potential problematic situations that are under the radar of the AU Peace and Security Council as well as the AU Authority.

In terms of some of the key recommendations for enhancing and improving the efficacy of the Panel, the AU will need to ensure:

1. that the Panel has improved procedures for undertaking its work, with specific reference to ensuring the timely provision of logistical support to Panel members;

2. the establishment of a dynamic framework for continuously briefing of Panel members, its Secretariat and their staff;
3. the creation and management of a roster of experts to support Panel members in their mediation efforts;
4. the interplay and support between the various organs of the African Union and the RECs;
5. the Panel's engagement with civil society through regularized workshops and conflict prevention meetings;
6. a robust communication and outreach program to bring the work of the Panel to the attention of African people across the continent.

Conclusion

Since its inauguration in 2007, the Panel of the Wise is still at an early stage of its development and, on this basis, it is premature to make a critical judgment about its efficacy or salience. The Panel's relevance, however, is not in doubt. There is no question as to whether the Panel can add value to the initiatives of the AU Peace and Security Council or the Chairperson of the Commission and contribute effectively to conflict prevention and resolution. Unlike the PSC, the Panel is not politically encumbered and therefore has a remit to genuinely engage in preventive diplomacy at an early stage. The Panel Modalities clearly stipulate that it has the independence to pursue any conflict situation that it believes warrants its attention.

However, as noted above, the Panel will confront some political obstacles that typically affect the work of conflict prevention frameworks. Therefore, the importance of ensuring political buy-in from the rest of the AU peace and security architecture as well as AU Member States is absolutely vital for the efficacy of the Panel of the Wise. In the absence of system-wide coordination there is a very real danger that the activities of the Panel will be routinely undermined. Ultimately, a pragmatic appreciation of the nexus between preventing conflicts, making peace once conflicts have escalated, and keeping peace following agreements will determine how effective the Panel of the Wise will be. Specifically, the issue is whether the Panel will be empowered and appropriately staffed by the African Union and its partners to fulfill its mandate effectively. It goes without saying that the Panel of the Wise is a welcome innovation, as its initial pronouncements and its work program indicate. Wisdom will indeed be required to achieve the urgent aspiration for peace by the millions of Africans who remain affected and afflicted by the plague of violent conflict.

Chapter 6

The Continental Early Warning System: Methodology and Approach

El-Ghassim Wane, Charles Mwaura, Shewit Hailu, Simone Kopfmüller,
Doug Bond, Ulf Engel and João Gomes Porto

Introduction

This chapter documents and reflects on the development, operationalization and institutionalization of a pivotal pillar of the peace and security architecture, the Continental Early Warning System (CEWS). This structure is core to the fulfillment of the Union's conflict prevention, management and resolution mandates as without the capacity to monitor, analyze and develop tailored and timely response and policy options to threats to peace and security on the Continent, the African Union (AU) would be severely limited in its ability to address these appropriately.

As discussed at length in the chapters above, the *PSC Protocol* defines the PSC as "a collective security and early-warning arrangement to facilitate timely and efficient response to conflict and crisis situations in Africa". In conjunction with the Chairperson of the Commission, the PSC shall, inter alia, anticipate and prevent disputes and conflicts, undertake peace-making and peace-building functions and authorize the mounting and deployment of peace support missions (African Union 2002, §3 (a), (b), and §7. In these activities, the PSC shall be supported by among others, a Continental Early Warning System (African Union 2002, §2 (2)).

The PSC *Protocol* gives the CEWS a fundamental responsibility for which a carefully developed methodology and process are required: that of anticipating and preventing the occurrence of conflict through the provision of information and analysis to the Chairperson of the Commission. In the fulfillment of his responsibility to advise the PSC on potential threats to peace and security in Africa, as well as recommend best courses of action, the Chairperson relies therefore on a well-functioning, comprehensive and AU specific early warning system. Consequently, the CEWS assumes a critical role as regards the ability of key institutions of the Union and other pillars of the peace and security architecture to perform their responsibilities, particularly the PSC, other Departments within the Commission, the Panel of the Wise and the Pan-African Parliament among others.

Beginning with an overview of the legal rationale and operationalization of the CEWS to date, this chapter will document and reflect on the development of a conflict analysis and early warning methodology tailored to the specific needs of the AU. Although led by the AU's Conflict Management Division (CMD), this methodology, fully detailed in the *CEWS Handbook* (African Union, Conflict

Management Division 2008b), is the result of an extensive process of consultation with the Regional Economic Communities (RECs), the United Nations and other International Organizations, African Civil Society Organizations (including academia and research centers) as well as international experts. The chapter will conclude by reflecting on existing and future challenges to the functioning of the CEWS.

The CEWS: Legal Rationale and Operationalization

The establishment of the CEWS is a requisite of the *PSC Protocol* as detailed in Article 12, which states that, "in order to facilitate the anticipation and prevention of conflicts, a Continental Early Warning System to be known as the Early Warning System shall be established". The *PSC Protocol* notes that the information and analysis gathered through the EWS shall be used by the Chairperson of the Commission to "advise the PSC on potential threats to peace and security in Africa and recommend the best course of action" (African Union 2002, §12 (5)). The Chairperson is also called "to use this information for the execution of the responsibilities and functions entrusted to him/her under the present Protocol" (African Union 2002, §12 (5)).

The purpose of this continental early warning system is therefore the provision of timely advice on potential conflicts and threats to peace and security to enable the development of appropriate response strategies to principle decision-makers at the AU: the Chairperson of the Commission, the PSC and other Departments within the Commission. Others include various organs and structures of the AU, namely the Pan-African Parliament, the Panel of the Wise and the African Commission on Human and People's Rights.

According to the *PSC Protocol*, the CEWS is to consist of (1) an observation and monitoring center—the Situation Room—located at the Conflict Management Division (CMD) of the AU; and (2) observation and monitoring units of the Regional Mechanisms for Conflict Prevention, Management and Resolution, which shall "be linked directly" to the Situation Room (African Union 2002, §12 (2)). As will be elaborated below, this requirement clearly denotes the true continental nature of the CEWS in both structure and, perhaps more importantly, in operational terms—regarded as integral to the CEWS structure and functioning. Regional Mechanisms for Conflict Prevention, Management and Resolution (RMs) within the RECs play a vital role in the operationalization and functioning of this pillar of the African Peace and Security Architecture (APSA).

In order to analyze developments and recommend appropriate courses of action, the CEWS shall "develop an early warning module based on clearly defined and accepted political, economic, social, military and humanitarian indicators" (African Union 2002, §12 (4)). In addition, to facilitate the effective functioning of the CEWS, Article 12 (3) of the *PSC Protocol* requires the AU Commission to "collaborate with the United Nations and its agencies, other relevant international organizations, research centres, academic institutions and Non-Governmental Organizations (NGOs)", and Article 12 (7) stipulates that the Chairperson of the Commission "shall, in consultation with Member States, the Regional Mechanisms, the United Nations and other relevant institutions, work out the practical details for the establishment of the Early Warning System and take all the steps required for its effective functioning".

On sources of information, the CEWS is envisaged as an open-source system where information is gathered from a variety of different sources, including, inter alia, governmental and inter-governmental actors, international and non-governmental organizations, the media, academia and think-tanks. While key sources of data include those generated by the AU itself (Commission, AU Field Missions and liaison offices), the data generated at the level of the RECs/RMs and Member States or in collaboration with the United Nations, its agencies, other relevant international organizations, research centers, academic institutions and NGOs are clearly also requested by the PSC Protocol. In fact, it urges the Commission to undertake this collaboration in order to facilitate the effective functioning of the EWS as a whole (African Union 2002, §12 (3)). Additional relevant provisions of the *PSC Protocol*, to be discussed below, include Article 16 (Relationship with Regional Mechanisms for Conflict Prevention, Management and Resolution), Article 17 (Relationship with the United Nations and other International Organizations), Article 18 (Relationship with the Pan-African Parliament), Article 19 (Relationship with the African Commission on Human and People's Rights) and, finally, Article 20 (Relationship with Civil Society Organizations).

During the July 2003 Summit of the African Union in Maputo, Mozambique, the Heads of State and Government mandated the AU Commission to take the necessary steps for the establishment of the CEWS. Since then, the Commission has set in motion a series of activities with the aim of fulfilling this mandate, beginning with a series of workshops on the establishment of the CEWS with officials from the RECs, the United Nations (UN) and UN system organizations, civil society representatives and academic institutions, international organizations and African think tanks. In July 2005, and based on the series of recommendations that resulted from these consultations, the AU Commission developed a draft *Roadmap for the Operationalisation of the CEWS* with the purpose of developing an operational, cost-effective structure and determining the key steps and requirements necessary for the implementation of the early warning system. This draft roadmap contained a tentative concept and timeframe for the implementation and operationalization of the CEWS, covering the following areas: (1) information collection, (2) strategic analysis of the data collected and development of an indicators module, (3) early warning reports and engagement with decision-makers, and (4) coordination and collaboration between the AU, the RECs and other key stakeholders.

During the last three years, in consultation with Member States, the Regional Mechanisms, the United Nations and African civil society and research institutions, the Commission has put in place a process to explore the modalities for the development and operationalization of the CEWS. When, on 21 June 2006, at its 57th meeting, held in Addis Ababa, the PSC requested the AU Commission to hasten the operationalization of the continental peace and security architecture, including the CEWS, the Commission intensified its efforts to develop the relevant technical documentation in support of the draft *Roadmap* for consideration by representatives of Member States, RECs and other partners. In addition to an updated version of the draft *Roadmap* itself, the Commission prepared two issue papers of a technical nature—on the *Indicators Module* and on the *Participation of Civil Society*—and three background papers—on *Development of IT Technology*, on *Conceptual and Methodological Issues in the Development of Early Warning Indicators*, and on *Status of Implementation of Early Warning Systems in the RECs* (African Union, Conflict Management Division 2008a).

From 17 to 19 December 2006, the Commission convened a meeting of Governmental Experts on early warning and conflict prevention, bringing together experts from AU Member States and representatives of the RECs. Held in Kempton Park, South Africa, the meeting was also attended by representatives of African research centers and academic institutions, NGOs, as well as international organizations, including the United Nations, as observers. The meeting urged the AU Commission and the RECs, working together with the stakeholders identified in the *PSC Protocol*, to take all necessary steps to implement the observations and recommendations made in the draft Roadmap within a timeframe of three years, to ensure that the CEWS is fully operational by 2009. The meeting further urged Member States, as well as AU partners, to provide the necessary assistance to facilitate the timely operationalization of the CEWS. The *Framework for the Operationalisation of the Continental Early Warning System* and the timeframe for its implementation were then endorsed by the AU Executive Council, and included the mobilization of the financial and technical resources required from both AU Member States and partners, the speedy recruitment of the human resources needed and other relevant steps.

With the support expressed by the Assembly of Heads of State and Government of the AU, at its Eighth Ordinary Session held on 29–30 January 2007 in Addis Ababa, the implementation of the CEWS began in earnest.

Early Warning and Conflict Analysis: Overview and Synthesis

Every Early Warning System (EWS) requires an underlying methodology through which data and information are analyzed with the purpose of, if required, issuing warnings that enable decision-makers to take early action. In fact, the quality of the warning itself depends on the soundness of the analytical process. After all, early warning is a function rather than a method in and of itself. Underlying every EWS—whether designed to deal with refugee flows, human rights violations, ethno-political conflict, genocides, armed conflict, famine and food insecurity, minorities, terrorism etc.—is therefore a form of conflict analysis. The challenge for CEWS was precisely to devise a systematic approach to conflict analysis and early warning suited to the entire African continent. Following the approval of the Roadmap at the end of 2006, CMD staff began a process of exploring different early warning experiences as well as conflict analysis frameworks with the aim of developing the CEWS-specific methodology—this methodology is encapsulated in what has became known as the CEWS *Handbook* (African Union, Conflict Management Division 2008b).

In the last decade, our understanding and use of so-called "early warning systems" has deepened considerably through both theoretical and methodological development as well as the proliferation of EWS in a wide variety of fields. While these systems had their origins in national military and intelligence establishments, over the last three decades early warning has become increasingly associated with humanitarian action—particularly in the fields of food security and refugee flows. From a focus on the prevention of surprise nuclear attacks and other military incidents during the Cold War, early warning today is used in a wide range of phenomena, ranging from natural disasters, such as earthquakes, floods and drought, to the outbreak of epidemics and famines.

In the field of violent conflict, the call of former UN Secretary-General Boutros Boutros-Ghali in the 1992 *Agenda for Peace* for more systematic efforts directed at the prevention of conflict (specifically the adoption of EWS) gave initial impetus to the development and adoption of conflict early warning systems by an increasingly larger number of international organizations (governmental and non-governmental), academic and research institutes and national governments. The increase in the number, intensity and scope of violent internal conflict following the end of the Cold War, and the dramatic events in Somalia, Bosnia and Rwanda led to the realization of the need for strengthened mechanisms of conflict prevention—in particular preventive diplomacy, but not exclusively so. As Lund noted at the time, preventive diplomacy must be "concerned with efforts taken at the low end and incipient stages of a conflict and should be distinguished from action taken with regard to conflicts at higher levels of violence" (Lund 1994). The international community was beginning to realize that it had to address problems before they erupted, as the costs of inaction in the face of large-scale violence were too high in both human and material terms.

Early warning of conflict gradually became—or was seen to have the potential to become—the instrument of choice for the development of preventive options and the deployment of preventive action. Nevertheless, as a result of the variety of actors involved as well as the wide range of issues covered, the theoretical and practical evolution of EWS has resulted in a variety of definitions and methodologies. This is not surprising as "the development of a framework for operational conflict and policy assessment first and foremost asks for (theoretical) knowledge on the causes and dynamics of conflict" (van de Goor and Verstegen 1999, 4). And if there is an issue that divides academics and practitioners it is the causes (etiology) of violent conflict.

For instance, FEWER (1999, 3) suggests that early warning is "the systematic collection and analysis of information coming from areas of crises for the purposes of: (1) anticipating the escalation of violent conflict; (2) development of strategic response to these crises; and (3) the presentation of options to critical actors (national, regional and international) for the purposes of decision-making and preventive action." In one way or another, definitions of early warning attach considerable importance to the quality and timeliness of analysis, the identification of entry points for actions and the provision of sufficient time for the effective planning and implementation of a response as well the potential inherent in these systems to generate awareness and political will necessary for the mobilization of effective responses.

While the mainstreaming of early warning as an integral part of conflict prevention is widely recognized, two related issues remain contentious. The first relates to debates around methodologies and the resulting operational methods to be applied. Many different methodologies are used in early warning systems, ranging from purely quantitative to purely qualitative systems, to a profusion of hybrid systems in between. The early warning "field" is characterized by the existence of a great variety of disparate tools and often incompatible approaches. Yet, virtually no conflict or humanitarian EWS has operated in a sustainable manner over the time required to identify cyclical patterns of turmoil, conflict and disruptions. With the exception of a few data development projects that focus on a particular type of problem (for example, armed conflict or human rights abuses), no project has enjoyed the sustained institutional support required to build a sustainable capacity for early warning.

The second contentious issue regards "the manner in which early responses are produced", in particular the link between early warning and early action (see, for example, FEWER 2000). As emphasized by Adelman (1996), "the major point of early warning information gathering and analysis is not the information and analysis in itself of the crisis area, but the use of that information and analysis to gain the trust of the decision-makers and to provide them with effective options." In fact, as an essential element of conflict prevention, early response must include timely and targeted actions undertaken by actors on the basis of early warning. Such timely and targeted action should prevent the (re)emergence of violent conflicts and embrace "response measures to deal with root causes and risk factors in politically tense situations" (Adelman 1996). This approach to distinguishing root causes and risk factors pointing to "structural long-term and direct short-term preventive actions" is equally advocated by the Carnegie Commission on Preventing Deadly Conflict (1997) and adopted by the European Commission (1996, and reiterated 2001). Trying to define conflict prevention, Wallensteen and Möller (2003) consider that:

> There are two ways of understanding conflict prevention. One concerns the *direct* preventive actions: a crisis is judged to be in a dangerous phase of military escalation, intensification or diffusion. Thus, there is a need to act to prevent

> increasing dangers... A second concern is the *structural* prevention, where the idea is to create such conditions that conflicts and disputes hardly arise or do not threaten to escalate into militarized action... These two types of prevention are called light, direct or operational prevention on the one hand, and deep or structural, on the other hand, depending on the scholar. (Wallensteen and Möller 2003, 6, emphasis in the original)

Moreover, optimizing the linkage between early warning and early action has been a primary concern of scholars and practitioners engaged in the development and implementation of these systems. An often cited criticism of EWS points to the fact that, although there is a profusion of ever more sophisticated and timely warnings, there is a lack of political will, ability or capacity of actors to act in a preventative manner, rendering these systems' utility null. Nevertheless, the recognition that, although intimately linked, early warning and early action "have distinctively different dynamics" has been an important contribution, which has enabled the further development of both.

In addition, we should note that a wide number of processes and activities are part of an early warning system. In fact, the term is often used to describe a variety of activities that are not strictly early warning. These include conflict analysis and monitoring, data analysis, risk assessment and advocacy (Austin 2004). While early warning requires the ongoing and near real-time assessment of events that in a high risk situation are likely to accelerate or trigger the rapid escalation of conflict (Gurr 1996), analysis of these events in their specific context is critical as without it the response options developed may be unsuited to the situation and/or unrealistic as regards availability of means. A detailed understanding of the issue and its context is absolutely critical. This is why several authors have considered that purely quantitative systems are unable to identify the causes of conflict as they rely on "empirical causal relationships"— ultimately, as noted by Austin (2004, 21), "conflict analysis is where the researcher must draw the line himself". The importance of sound analytical tools is also emphasized by Carment and Schnabel (2003, 15) who posit that "a key concern in ensuring effective conflict prevention is how to ensure that the practitioner is equipped with the best available analytical skills to ensure valid and reliable evaluations of potential problems". More importantly, these authors note that "while some systems may rely on the monitoring of background factors and enabling conditions that are associated with the risk of conflict, others only provide information on the probability of specific events leading to conflict ... ideally, both approaches should be pursued simultaneously" (Carment and Schnabel 2003, 16).

In their review of existing theory and practice, the AU's CMD looked at several conflict analysis frameworks used by organizations operating in and/or around conflict. Within these, special attention was given to so-called conflict assessment frameworks widely used by operational agencies in an effort to minimize any potentially negative impacts of humanitarian assistance, post-conflict peace-building and, ultimately, development assistance. These conflict assessment frameworks aim at minimizing possible and unintended negative impacts by "understanding the underlying causes and consequences of violent conflicts, as well as the dynamics supporting or undermining peace efforts"—"conflict sensitivity" or "do no harm" (Anderson 1999).

Moreover, the development of conflict assessment frameworks has benefited significantly from the contributions of at least three very different fields: on the one hand, the contributions of conflict research and peace studies as regards our understanding of conflict, its prevention, management and resolution; secondly, the contributions of strategic studies and, in particular, those of strategic intelligence; and finally, the contributions from management science and organizational development—as regards a number of tools that have formed part of the "arsenal" of tools at the disposal of organizations to measure the impacts (positive as well as negative) of development policies and practices— conventional risk assessment methodologies or management-related tools such as program log frames.

Conflict assessment in international development assistance has advanced to levels that allow for a transfer of approaches and tools to other policy sectors, including conflict early warning. Four frameworks were reviewed in detail during the development of the CEWS methodology: the German Development Agency (GTZ)'s *Conflict Analysis Framework*, DFID's *Conflict Assessment Framework*, the World Bank's *Conflict Analysis Framework* (CAF), and the United Nation's *Inter-Agency Framework for Conflict Analysis in Transition Situations*. Several of the methodologies currently in use share a very similar approach to the stages or steps of conflict analysis. For example, both DFID's *Conflict Assessments* and the UN system's *Common Framework* are based on three analytical stages, combining the analysis of conflict causes with a scrutiny of responses, before going into the development of strategic options. In addition, these approaches share considerable common ground in terms of what they conceive to be the essential units of analysis. These four conflict analysis frameworks tend to emphasize that, because of the unique nature of each conflict situation, the design and conduct of conflict assessments will vary from case to case as regards the recommended method. One important recommendation stems from the UN's inter-agency framework (UNDG ECHA 2004: 4): that "the intention in applying this framework should therefore not be to 'fill in the boxes' but, in view of the specificities of each transition situation, to organize a process, which will help arrive at some common understanding of the key analytical components." Equally, the Department for International Development (DFID 2002, 7) warns that the methodology should not be seen as a formula and that it should (1) adapt according to the needs and objectives of the end-user; (2) develop according to the nature and phase of the conflict; (3) develop dynamic forms of analysis and, finally, (4) encourage "joined-up" analysis.

The CEWS: Methodology and Approach

During the various methodological working sessions held at AU CMD in 2007, the team concluded that a specifically tailored—or hybrid—Strategic Conflict Assessment (SCA) methodology could be a viable method underlying the CEWS early warning function. Yet, as practiced by development agencies, SCAs have been conducted to produce standalone analyses (usually in the form of SCA reports) that tend not to be part of a larger and regular cycle of reporting, assessment and policy/response options formulation. Usually, this type of SCA is carried out once a crisis situation has already arisen and the policy advice derived from such an exercise is singular, in the sense that there are no systematic follow-up assessments. CEWS requirements require that some degree of customization be undertaken as it must per force focus on ongoing monitoring of a large number of countries, issues and themes and aim at producing regular reports (with the associated feedback loops that link reporting to decision-making on emerging violent conflict). The specific challenge for CEWS was therefore how to integrate the processes of producing regular assessments based on a continuous process of data collection, on the basis of which early warnings could be generated.

The result of this review of best practice as regards early warning systems and conflict assessment frameworks resulted in a hybrid methodology, developed at length in the *CEWS Handbook* (African Union, Conflict Management Division 2008b). This methodology includes three iterative and concurrent phases, which can be seen in Figure 6.1. The three processes of (1) information collection and monitoring, (2) conflict and cooperation analysis, and (3) the formulation of response options are continuous, iterative and interactive. They are also integrated in the sense that each feeds into or may be triggered by the others. Because a detailed discussion of the Standard Operating Procedures (SOPs) that inform the various tasks and procedures to be undertaken by CMD staff (situation room staff, early warning officers and desk officers) is outside the scope of this chapter, a summary of each step of the CEWS methodology is provided below. For a more detailed elaboration of each step, the reader should refer to the *CEWS Handbook* (African Union, Conflict Management Division 2008b, Appendixes).

Information Collection and Monitoring

The first activity focuses on the continuous (and semi-automated) information gathering process, which ensures that CEWS fulfils the requirement of continuous monitoring of political, economic, humanitarian, social and military developments across the continent. As noted above, the Roadmap refers to the CEWS as an "an open-source system where information is gathered from a variety of different sources, including, *inter alia,* governmental and inter-governmental actors, international and non-governmental organisations, the media, academia and think-thanks" (African Union, Conflict Management Division 2008a). In addition to monitoring news data, the CEWS information gathering function must include key

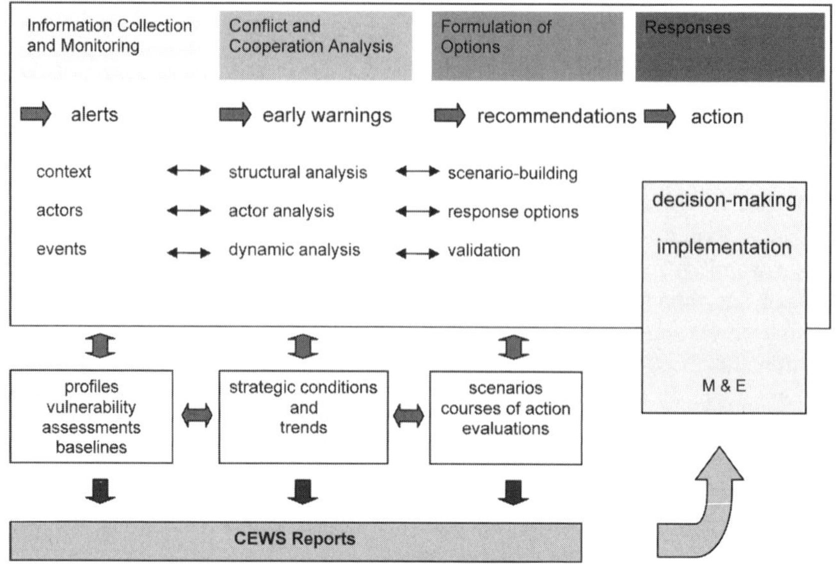

Figure 6.1   Summary of the CEWS methodology

sources of data such as the AU itself (Commission, AU Field Missions and Liaison Offices), as well as that generated at the level of the RECs and Member States, collaboration with the United Nations, its agencies, other relevant international organizations, research centers, academic institutions and NGOs.

Appropriate information collection, compilation, management and distribution systems are therefore critical for the functioning of the CEWS. Furthermore, several key recommendations of the participants at the various workshops that resulted in the *Roadmap* contributed to the design of this particular set of processes. These recommendations included: the introduction of an automated data gathering and processing system (including but not limited to news clippings); the introduction of an internal news trends tracking service; the development of a system of grading sources and reports to diminish information overflow and to increase efficiency; greater use of African information sources, particularly in indigenous languages; and, finally, the strengthening of the existing system of internal country profiles through the introduction of sub-national detail.

Yet, the continuous monitoring of political, economic, social, environmental, military and humanitarian indicators at multiple levels of analysis and for a large number of countries and regions is a complex undertaking. To enable this, the specification of the framework of variables, indicators and parameters guiding these activities was conducted jointly by CEWS staff (the Situation Room, Early Warning Unit and the Desk Officers). This range of parameters established for the entire continent has allowed for regular information collection, monitoring and management around three generic clusters: Context and Structural Information on Countries and Regions; Actor Attribute Information on key Individuals and Groups; and, Information on Behaviors and Events as they evolve over time. In order to assure that the CEWS methodology is anchored upon data driven analysis, the information collection and monitoring function is designed to enable the development of base line information (including country and actor profiles, vulnerabilities propensities and baselines upon which alerts are initiated). The results of data driven analysis are presented in a baseline or time series measure of the indicators as they evolve. These data driven baselines represent both the slowly changing structural indicators of countries and the more rapidly changing dynamic indicators of human action and behavior.

Data driven analysis begins with the specification of indicators followed by continuous monitoring for changes over time. As noted in the pages above, the PSC Protocol underlies that the collection and analysis of data should be based on the development of an early warning module with clearly defined and accepted political, social, military and humanitarian indicators. International best practice as well as African experiences on structural indicator development were taken into account in the development by the CEWS of a structural indicator module—the result was a further elaboration on each of these indicator "baskets" resulting in a detailed list of indicators of structural conditions.

The CEWS has begun the compilation of three data sets of structural indicators (the expectation being that these indicators required updating annually). First, many Member States offer their own datasets across a number of domains—these public data are surveyed annually and compiled by CEWS as an official data source for structural indicators. Second, various time series data based on numerous indicators are publicly available from a wide range of international organizations (IGOs) such as the United Nations or the World Bank. These time series data are also surveyed annually and compiled by CEWS; they are most useful for analyses where cross-national, temporal data are required. Third, certain supplemental data, typically based on a smaller but focused set of indicators, are also surveyed periodically; the supplemental data collected on these supplemental indicators are compiled by both IGOs and NGOs. They focus on human rights, governance and other indicators that may not be as well established as the global structural indicators compiled by IGOs on a regular basis, and are used to supplement analyses as appropriate.

Complementing the structural indicators, dynamic or behavioral indicators embody the basic event parameters of who did what to/with whom, when where, why and how. Behavior baselines are extremely useful due to their short-term, rapidly changing character, representing the interaction of dynamic events. They may be generated from field or news reports, with a typical temporal interval ranging from daily to weekly. The CEWS methodology has been developed to enable the continuous monitoring of a set of behavioral indicators.

Field reporting is carried out by AU Missions and regional offices, but the bulk of the burden for field data collection is likely to be carried by the RMs at the RECs. As noted above, both IGAD and ECOWAS have already developed operational frameworks for indicators relevant to their respective mandates and/or areas of interest. These include pastoral conflict, the media and peace-building, state collapse, elections, forced migration, human rights and judicial reform, small arms proliferation and environmental degradation. Furthermore, these two RECs are already operational in their field reporting, with field data streams that extend four and two years respectively.

In addition to Incident Reports, or "IncReps," the integration of Situation Reports, or "SitReps", to the information collection framework is important. SitReps enable observers to provide contextual information and narratives on a regular (typically weekly) basis; thus ensuring continuity in the data stream collected at the field level. More importantly, SitReps monitor pre-cursors to conflict and cooperation.

As noted above, another source of event baselines is news reports. Within this approach, a software application automatically monitors and analyses numerous international news service feeds as well as regional and local news sources to develop the baselines similar to the field data baselines discussed above. The African Union has partnered with the European Commission's Joint Research Centre to design and deploy an Africa-specific news tracking system for exclusive use by CEWS and its partners. This application, the *Africa Media Monitor*, has begun tracking news reports in real time using the same basic events data parameters.

Whether tracking event parameters or topics, this events data approach yields a measurable baseline for the full range of social, political, economic and environmental events reported in the news. From these events data, dynamic baselines are compiled from which subtle inflections and anomalies in their incidence may be visualized. In other words, the inflections in the baseline of reported activities can be flagged prior to their escalation into a volatile situation and possible violence. When inflections over time indicate a possible escalation, especially when the deviation is large relative to historical patterns, an alert is generated. This alert in turn is examined by an analyst and/or early warning expert on the basis of conflict and cooperation assessment frameworks (to be discussed below) to determine whether the deviation has surpassed a threshold that may call for action or at least further analysis. CEWS thus can conduct near real-time baseline monitoring and communicate timely alerts to relevant parties. Alerts then may be considered the analytic product of the information collection and monitoring step.

Such data driven analysis is also usefully considered a pre-requisite for effective early warning and response. With both types of indicators (structural as well as dynamic), baseline analysis of the changes over time is a pre-requisite for effective early warning and early response. By continuously tracking the evolution of both structural conditions and events (behavior), CEWS early warning officers are able to compare baselines over time, assess risk potential and anticipate subtle changes that may lead to escalations in a conflict situation, instability or disruption. Structural baselines reveal slowly changing, structural issues that may exacerbate a conflict. On the other hand, and stemming from the continuous monitoring of ongoing behavior and interaction by actors, events baselines are critical as they relate to the immediate timeframe, revealing a stable situation, with relatively little change, or an escalation (or de-escalation) of conflict. The approach of using data driven baselines applies to the structural data of a country context, the attribute data of actors and their networks, as well as to the dynamic data of interactions and behavior.

Conflict and Cooperation Analysis

The second step of the CEWS methodology is that of *Conflict and Cooperation Analysis*, a phase that corresponds more closely to the traditional understanding of SCAs as discussed above. As part of the analytical framework with which events and structural baseline deviations referred to above are interpreted, SCAs help to contextualize the alert against the specific nature and background of the situation in question, possibly resulting in the production of early warnings and other types of reports. Yet, different from the traditional undertaking of a SCA, the CEWS strategic conflict and cooperation analysis stage is wholly integrated with the development of baseline data and information as detailed above. Indeed, strategic conflict and cooperation analysis as performed by the CEWS would normally be developed as an ongoing process rather than just undertaken prior or during the production of early warning reports.

Conflict and cooperation analysis begins with an understanding of structural sources of conflict—requiring the identification of key sources of tension that have led to or are likely to lead to conflict. These key structural sources may be found in political, economic, security, social, and religious structures; they may also be found at local, regional, national and international levels. Defined broadly, "structures" are considered the "long term factors underlying violent conflict". They are regarded as "cleavages" in the political, economic and social realms upon which the mobilization of individuals and groups for violent conflict is often undertaken. They are regarded as "pervasive and long standing factors and differences that become built into the policies, structures and culture of a society and may create the conditions for violent conflict" (UNDG ECHA 2004, 5). It is also useful to differentiate between different geographical levels (local, regional national, international), on the one hand, and different arenas (political, security, economic, social), on the other. Some weighting (in terms of relative importance) of the sources of tension and conflict needs to be undertaken—a task made easier by the structural risk assessments discussed above—as do the linkages and connections between sources of tension in different sectors and levels. The benefit of structural country profiles as well as structural risk assessments maintained by the Situation Room as part of its information collection, monitoring and management function for structural analysis should therefore not be underestimated. Indeed, the analyst conducting the SCA or writing the early warning report has at his or her disposal a considerable repository of relevant and up-to-date structural data.

As part of the SCA, the CEWS methodology requires that actors—main protagonists (groups, institutions, individuals) who influence (positively or negatively) the situation under analysis—be analyzed. Actor analysis assesses their interests and motivations, and also looks into their relationships. The interest is on both the actor's potential for conflict and for cooperation. Actor analysis is meant to focus on shorter term issues and dynamics and be comprehensive in the sense of including as many internal and external relevant actors as possible. Possible actors include: governments (and within them government departments and ministries), armed and security forces, political leaders, non-state armed groups, traditional and community leaders, trade unions, political parties, businesses, other interested governments, MNCs, humanitarian and human rights organizations, etc. At a later stage, the formulation of policy and response options also depends on knowledge of the "capacities for peace" of different actors. These may refer to structures, mechanisms, processes and institutions that exist in society to manage conflict peacefully (practical examples being: a strong civil society, role of traditional authorities, informal approaches to conflict resolution, etc.). On a macro-level, understanding existing and potential capacities for peace can help us understand a country's "peace-building capacity".

Once structural causes and actors are analyzed and identified, the next step is dynamic analysis: identifying possible aggravating, inhibiting and triggering events and behavior will allow for scenario development and a prognosis. In addition to proximate causes of conflict, it takes a case-specific trigger to turn a constellation of structural and agency-related facts into a situation where violent conflict actually is breaking out. *Triggers* are understood as single acts, events or their anticipation that may set off or escalate violent conflict (examples could include coup attempts, sudden changes of government, a forthcoming election, assassinations, sudden movements of large numbers of people, spill-over effects from neighboring countries or the anticipation of such effects, the discovery of new mineral resources, etc.). However, sometimes a conflict might not be triggered by a single identifiable act, but just start on the basis of aggravating factors. In addition, certain aggravators can act as triggers. Likewise, certain activities, events or perceptions can work against the escalation of conflict or the occurrence of violence—these factors are called *inhibitors*. These can be incentives to the conflicting parties (like the prospect of becoming part of a power-sharing arrangement), strong non-conflict interests of a third-party to the conflict, the threat of an intervention, etc.

Finally, this analysis also takes into account the responses of other international actors. In a first instance, responses of international actors in a variety of fields is investigated—including in areas such as humanitarian relief, development assistance, political cooperation, security, etc. Both aggravators and inhibitors can be summarized at different geographical levels and in different fields or arenas.

Policy and Response Formulation

In the final step, *Policy and Response Formulation*, the focus is on the development of possible scenarios and actionable options. As noted by Clark (2004, 173),

> Scenarios are used primarily for planning and decision-making. Scenario
> planning is normally used to explore possible future conditions given a set of
> assumptions. Each scenario represents a distinct, plausible picture of a segment
> of the future. Because it is impossible to know the future precisely, the solution is
> to create several scenarios. These scenarios are, essentially, specially constructed
> stories about the future, each one modelling a distinct, plausible outcome.

Scenario development enables the CEWS to come up with recommendations for action to AU decision makers. Recall that the process of information collection and monitoring "begins" with continuously observing events and actors in their unique contexts. However, the process also "ends" with these observations. In other words, the information collection and monitoring process is continuous, and it merges into the regular analysis of the data driven baselines, keying off of the alerts that represent deviations and inflections from the past. Likewise, the analytic process is continuous and feeds into the process of formulating response options. Ideally, of course, the formulation process anticipates conditions in a proactive mode as opposed to simply offering reactive responses.

It is the contextualized and actor specific negative and positive scenarios that drive the formulation of response options. Thus, the formulation process begins with the specification of alternative scenarios representing a worse (to be avoided) and best (desired) case, and the default status quo condition that marks the starting point or conditions as described in the strategic analysis. Is the conflict likely to escalate, de-escalate or remain at the same level of intensity? And what needs to be done if these things happen?

A basic type scenario is called the *demonstration scenario*, pioneered by Herman Kahn, Harvey DeVeerd and others at RAND in the early days of systems analysis. As noted by Robert Clark (2004, emphasis in the original), "in this scenario, the writer first imagines a particular end state in the future and then describes a plausible path of events that could lead to that state. The *branch-point* version of this type of scenario identifies decisive events along the path (events that represent points at which key choices determine the outcome)". This notion of branch points is very important for the purposes of scenario building as part of the CEWS methodology. By mapping out all the possible paths by which a specific situation (scenario) can materialize, the early warning officer/analyst becomes sensitive to these key moments—as they ultimately provide opportunities for preventing, diverting or facilitating a particular set of processes.

In order to structure policy and response options around *demonstration scenarios* it is useful to focus on three basic scenarios: (1) a worst case scenario, (2) the continuation of the status quo and (3) a best case scenario. The worst case scenario refers to a feared state of affairs, a deterioration of the present situation; the status quo describes the situation as identified through the conflict and cooperation analysis detailed above; and the best case scenario outlines a desired, but also attainable situation. The case-description then has to be matched with a preliminary outline of goals or strategies—what kind of activities, by whom, would contribute towards the realization or achievement of the described scenario? Finally, recommended courses of action (COAs) which are based on actual mandate, instruments and political will should be attached to each of the three scenarios.

The primary utility of scenario building for the formulation of response options lies in the specification of the key or decisive events along the paths that shape the outcomes. The specification of these paths represents the range of response options for courses of action to be considered in any given situation. The process of specifying these alternative paths helps illuminates opportunities in terms of timing as well as in terms of the key networks or nodes of influence that can help achieve the desired outcomes. And these can only be fully understood on the basis of a prior SCA, as detailed above, whereby the analyst has identified the structural root causes, key actors, conflict dynamics etc.

Once scenarios of desired and undesired developments have been built, the formulation of response options can begin. This process of formulation links the present to the desired (or undesired) scenarios and is informed by the data driven analysis. Alternative paths are specified that begin with the current conditions and highlight the choice points along the way. These points serve as markers of progress and can guide the formulation of response options. The formulation of options is also based on past experience and a wide range of principle courses of action, as detailed in the *PSC Protocol* and discussed in several chapters in this volume.

Validation of the dynamic analyses described above ideally entails testing of the recommended response option in a similar past situation. To the extent that the historical conditions are analogous to the present, such validations can lend insight into likely levels of future success for alternative COAs. In other words, the process of validation can help illuminate the lessons learned, both positive and negative, from past interventions. For example, if the baselines for pastoral conflict reveal seasonal fluctuations in the raiding at a particular time of year, one can assess the prior attempts to address these raids to identify the most efficacious response option under similar conditions in subsequent seasons. To formalize this validation procedure, analysts should track each course of action taken and its outcome as well as the conflicts themselves. This approach offers feedback to the entire process beyond the basic data quality control procedures that are typically associated with validation. To be sure, validation certainly includes ongoing quality control of the data collection process.

Conclusion

This chapter has focused on the process of development of the CEWS from an institutional as well as methodological point of view. Although the CEWS in and of itself is not mandated to undertake response actions (a responsibility given to several of the institutions discussed above) it plays a vital role at the centre of the African Peace and Security Architecture. As discussed above, the purpose of the CEWS is the provision of timely advice on potential conflicts and threats to peace and security in Africa to several key institutions of the Africa Union. The analysis and advice to be provided by the CEWS have a very specific purpose, namely to enable the development of appropriate response strategies by the African Union and its institutions.

The ability of CEWS to carry out this very specific mandate by successfully implementing the methodology and set of procedures outlined above will ultimately determine its usefulness and validity. Yet, a fundamental part of this is, of course, the ability of the CEWS to engage AU decision-makers appropriately and influence decision-making. The extent to which the various "outputs" produced by the CEWS under the methodology outline above will achieve this goal must therefore be the subject of ongoing evaluation as the link between analysis and response must be a fundamental underpinning of CEWS operations.

The implementation of the CEWS, now in its third and final stage, is well advanced, even in the face of constraints of a varied nature, as discussed below. The technical ICT applications necessary for running the CEWS are at an advanced implementation stage. In July 2008, cooperation with the EU Joint Research Centre in Milan was started, which led to the joint development and implementation of a number of important technical tools, among them the *Africa News Brief* (online-based search engine and dynamic data bank-generating tool modeled around the Europe Media Monitor which has been vastly enhanced with regard to coverage and language, violent event extraction, dynamic indicators); a country profile database (*Country Profile*); an Indicators' Module; storage modules; visualization tools etc. These applications, plus a variety of relevant AU and REC documents, have been integrated into a *CEWS Portal*, which is also accessible for the RECs.

The development of the CEWS methodological framework during 2007, which resulted in the *CEWS Handbook* discussed above, has been a key achievement. Since then, the focus has been on AU CMD staff development and training on the basis of the analytical tools contained in the *Handbook*. As a result of this methodology which builds on comprehensive and real-time monitoring function, the CEWS has developed a new type of report, the *Early Warning Report*. This type of report will serve as an instrument on the basis of which, and through the appropriate channels, a specific issue or incident is tabled for discussion by the PSC—by communicating to other Divisions, to the Commissioner on Peace and Security and to the Chairperson the urgency of a specific issue or event. The AU CMD has, since early 2009, begun testing the production of early warning reports on the basis of this methodology. Of note is the fact that in the development of these tools, early warning analysts, situation room staff as well as the desk officers, have played a lead role and develop the highest level of ownership.

As emphasized above, the development of appropriate modes of engagement by the CEWS with the Chairperson of the Commission is key to the fulfillment of the CEWS primary functions. The Chairperson's pivotal role in efforts and initiatives to prevent, manage and resolve conflicts—by bringing to the attention of the PSC any matter that may threaten peace and security in the Continent—requires the CEWS to contribute in an efficient and timely manner to the formal as well as informal communication between both institutions on peace and security matters. In this regard, the CEWS role in contributing to the Chairperson's reports to the PSC as well as to the Assembly of Heads of State plays a critical role.

The implementation of additional strategies for engaging decision-makers and, in particular, the development of an effective outreach strategy in support of key AU structures as well as other stakeholders outside the AU is also a critical priority. In this regard, the ability to simultaneously reach as well as integrate the views, policy initiatives and recommendations of a number of key AU institutions is critical (systematic feedback loop). These institutions include the Pan-African Parliament, the African Commission on Human and People's Rights, the Regional Mechanisms for Conflict Prevention, Management and Resolution, the United Nations and other international organizations, and Civil Society Organizations.

Other types of interaction with decision-makers, such as on-demand briefings and unstructured interaction—but not in prejudice of formal lines of communication—constitute also an ongoing priority. In this regard, the Situation Room, in its role as "Point-of-Contact", must increasingly play the role of "point of contact" between the AU and its various field missions, Member States as well as other Organizations; answering requests for information and inquiries from a wide variety of stakeholders as well as serving as the main point of contact between the CMD and the UN Department of Peacekeeping Operations (UNDPKO).

As was noted above, RECs are a constituent part of the overall security architecture of the AU and, in particular, the CEWS, where they are given an important and specific role. Not only are the monitoring and observation units to be linked directly to the situation room in Addis Ababa, but Regional Mechanisms are urged to continuously inform the PSC on their activities and, when necessary, brief the PSC—a request that is based on reciprocity. Harmonization and coordination are therefore key and will largely be a function of an effective partnership between the Regional Mechanisms and the PSC. We recall the *Roadmap*'s recommendation to the effect that "rather than attempt to create a single, unified system applicable to all early warning systems involved, and following closely the recommendations of the RECs, this Roadmap proposes the development of a 'continental framework' of information and analysis sharing able to build and supplement the efforts already developed by Regional Mechanisms" (African Union, Conflict Management Division 2008a).

The conclusion of the *Memorandum of Understanding* between the African Union and the RECs in January 2008, and the series of quarterly meetings which, since then, have brought the AU and the RECs early warning teams together have played a critical role, as detailed in the chapter by Gomes Porto and Engel later. This MoU was signed by representatives from the African Union and the following RECs: CEN-SAD (Community of Sahel-Saharan States), COMESA (Common Market for Eastern and Southern Africa), EAC (East African Community), ECCAS

(Economic Community of Central African States), ECOWAS, IGAD, SADC and UMA (Maghreb Arab Union).

Once fully operational, CEWS will fulfill a number of functional roles and, in the very practice of doing so, will set standards for the African continent (and beyond). These standards will be both of a technical and of a methodological nature, and they will cover mainly information collection, information sharing and processing. Partly, the standard setting role of the AU will be due to the fact that the AU is the first African institution to introduce a fully-fledged EWS (i.e. covering all aspects of violent conflict and all geographical areas of the continent); and partly it is because of a specific division of labor evolving between the AU and the RECs. For instance, when it comes to data collection from open sources, the AU, by default, not only takes a continental, but also a transnational perspective. On the other hand, the RECs currently enjoy a different advantage, i.e. access to and analysis of sub-national or sub-regional information. Hence, a particular modus of sharing information can be foreseen for the CEWS, one that involves an optimum division of labor and resources between the AU and the RECs. In addition and because of its mandate to liaise with other institutions—such as the United Nations, its agencies, other relevant international organizations as well as continental and international research centers, academic institutions and NGOs— the CEWS will become a standard setting hub for the collection and exchange of open-source based information on early warning with relevance to Africa.

In processing this information, the CEWS is making use of state-of-the-art technology, which places it in a unique position not only vis-à-vis other EWS on the continent, but also internationally. And, finally, in the analysis of the information collected, the CEWS utilizes a set of indicators that is continent wide and Africa-specific. Against this background, the CEWS framework is set to play an important role in setting harmonizing standards and procedures in African early warning.

For CEWS to set meaningful and useful standards however, it will require interoperability and a division of labor among the RECs. Although the RECs have been engaged throughout the CEWS formation process, the details of system (AU-RECs) interoperability have yet to be jointly resolved, as such interoperability affects all aspects of communicating on early warning between the AU and the RECs, including—in the case of information collection and monitoring—the question of applications, data, formats, indicators, etc. Thus, this is a critical issue on the CEWS agenda in the immediate period, being addressed through periodic consultations with the RECs, both bilaterally and as a group. The optimal division of labor, however, is likely to involve policy considerations that transcend the technical issues.

One plausible scenario is to build upon existing strengths and resources among the RECs, specifically their proximity to the conflicts within their respective regions. Such a scenario might draw upon the RECs to continue their field information collection and monitoring while CEWS coordinates the sharing of data summaries among them. Meanwhile, the CEWS Situation Room can take primary responsibility for information collection and monitoring of news reports—given that it is a more centralized activity—the results of which can be readily distributed to the RECs. Another area where the CEWS may take a central role is with the development and maintenance of an indicator module as specified in the *PSC Protocol*. The CEWS SitRoom can manage a "basket" of indicators to which RECs may contribute and which the RECs may use for their information collection and monitoring activities in the field. Such a division of labor with respect to the indicators module would facilitate interoperability and data sharing among the RECs. It would also support the setting of common standards while encouraging region-specific in-depth analysis.

During this stage of implementation of the CEWS, a number of questions need to be addressed concerning the sharing, exchange and ownership of data. Specifically, protocols for collaboration and measures to insure confidentiality of sensitive information will be paramount. In addition, procedures for controlling the dissemination of information and the harmonization of a common indicator framework jointly used by the AU and the RECs will need to be detailed. In the future, it will be crucial to systematically address questions of operational development and sustainability of the CEWS. Among others, this includes, finance and staffing, training, monitoring and evaluation. In addition, the organizational interactions with external partners need to be assessed regularly with a view to further integrating and harmonizing the CEWS.

Chapter 7
The African Standby Force

Jakkie Cilliers and Johann Pottgieter[1]

Introduction

The purpose of the African Standby Force (ASF) is to provide the African Union with capabilities to respond to conflicts through the deployment of peacekeeping forces and to undertake interventions pursuant to Articles 4(h) and (j) of the *Constitutive Act* of the African Union (AU) (African Union 2002). The ASF is intended for rapid deployment for a multiplicity of peace support operations that may include, inter alia, preventive deployment, peacekeeping, peace building, post-conflict disarmament, demobilization, reintegration and humanitarian assistance.

As discussed at length in the chapters above, the transformation of the Organization of African Unity into the AU and the adoption and entering into force of the Protocol establishing the Peace and Security Council on 26 December 2003 demonstrated an invigorated commitment by the organization to conflict prevention, management and resolution. In their reflection on the creation of the PSC and associated structures above, Sturman and Hayatou provided the historical and political background underpinning the gradual movement by OAU member states from a firm rejection of the idea of an Inter-African peacekeeping force capable of dealing with military aspects of conflict to accepting, in principle and in practice, the need for a more robust role for the organization in the maintenance and enforcement of peace. The creation of the ASF demonstrates that, to some extent, the idea of an African army suggested by Kwame Nkrumah in the early days of the OAU—and in later years often put forward by Gaddafi of Libya—has retained some of its appeal.

This evolution has taken some time to take shape. As we noted elsewhere and with particular relevance for African peacekeeping, the creation of the OAU's Mechanism for Conflict Prevention, Management and Resolution (henceforth referred to as the Mechanism) in 1993 represented a true watershed moment, the "beginning of the organisation's second generation peace and security agenda" (Cilliers and Malan 2005, 1). By the time the Mechanism was formerly adopted at the OAU Summit in Cairo in June 1993, the OAU's pivotal experience with the military observation operations in Rwanda—NMOG I and NMOG II—had convinced member States that limited observer missions and small operations

---

1   An earlier version of this chapter was published by the Institute for Security Studies in 2008. See Cilliers, J. (2008).

were indeed possible. These missions contributed to the gradual acceptance by member States of a more robust role for the organization, and, partly as a result, the newly created Central Organ of the Mechanism was able to approve a series of small peacekeeping operations. These included OMIB in Burundi; OMIC I, II and III in the Comoros; the JMC in the DRC and OLMEE in Ethiopia-Eritrea. In many regards, these operations were substantially more complex than the largely ad hoc monitoring missions and peace support undertakings that the organization was used to, with the possible exception of the operation in Chad from 1979 to 1982 (see Cilliers and Malan 2005 as well as Berman and Sams 2000).

In support of the work of the Peace and Security Council, the *PSC Protocol* calls upon the Commission as well as a new set of institutions, namely a Panel of the Wise, a Continental Early Warning System, a Special Fund and an African Stand-by Force (African Union 2002, §2 (2)). Article 13 of the same Protocol is devoted to defining the ASF in more detail, focusing on composition, mandate, chain of command, the military staff committee, training and, finally, the role of member states. It defines the ASF as follows:

> In order to enable the Peace and Security Council [to] perform its responsibilities with respect to the deployment of peace support missions and interventions pursuant to article 4(h) and (j) of the Constitutive Act, an African Standby Force shall be established. Such Force shall be composed of standby multidisciplinary contingents, with civilian and military components in their countries of origin and ready for rapid deployment at appropriate notice. (African Union 2002, §13 (1))

Based on the authors' professional engagement and various documents developed by the AU and the Regional Economic Communities (RECs), extensive interviews and available research, this chapter provides a critical commentary and update on the remarkable progress that has been achieved in recent years on the establishment of the ASF—an ambitious scheme to enable Africa to play a greater role in, and assume more responsibility for, continental conflict management.

The ASF Concept

During May 2003, the African Chiefs of Defense and Security (ACDS) adopted a document entitled 'The policy framework document on the establishment of the African Standby Force (ASF) and of the Military Staff Committee (MSC)'. During a meeting a few days later, African ministers of foreign affairs recommended regular consultations to consolidate the proposals contained in the framework document. AU Heads of State and Government endorsed this recommendation during their summit meeting two months later and, after two key meetings of the ACDS in May 2003 and January 2004, adopted an amended framework document in July 2004.

The final concept for the ASF provides for five standby brigade level forces, one in each of Africa's five regions, supported by civilian police (CivPol) and other groups. When fully established, the ASF will consist of standby multidisciplinary contingents, with civilian and military components located in their countries of origin and ready for rapid deployment anywhere in Africa, and possibly even outside the continent.

Effective command and control of the ASF requires the installation of an appropriate Africa-wide, integrated and interoperable command, control, communication and information system (C3IS) infrastructure, to link deployed units with mission headquarters, as well as the AU, planning elements (PLANELMs) and regions. Much of this was set out in the March 2005 document entitled *Roadmap for the Operationalisation of the African Standby Force*, which was adopted at an AU experts meeting in Addis Ababa. The Peace Support Operations Division (PSOD) developed an internal follow-on roadmap document in November 2006, although this document has no formal status. A recent development is the conceptualization of an ASF rapid deployment capability, which will be discussed in the pages below.

ASF missions are mandated by the AU's Peace and Security Council (PSC) within the framework of the Charter of the United Nations. Once mandated, missions are placed under the command and control of a Special Representative of the Chairperson of the AU Commission (SRCC). The Chairperson also appoints a force commander, commissioner of police and head of the civilian components. As discussed in Chapter Four, mandates are approved by the PSC and, once deployed, ASF forces come under AU command and control. Thereafter, the Chairperson submits periodic progress reports to the PSC on the implementation of the mandates and relies on the Commissioner for Peace and Security to perform these tasks. The primary role of the five regional mechanisms, in each of Africa's five regions, is that of force generation and preparation (that is, pre-deployment activities) and the provision of planning, logistic and other support during ASF deployment.[2] The overarching structure of the ASF is set out in Figure 7.1.

The military brigade is the largest and most resource-heavy component of each of the five regional standby forces, as Table 7.1, the composition of key resources within one of the regional brigades, demonstrates.[3] These numbers can vary depending on the specific task and subsequent configuration.

---

2   Article 3(f) of the Constitutive Act of the AU clearly states that the AU has primary responsibility for the promotion of peace, security and stability in Africa while article 7.2 makes it clear that the PSC acts on behalf of its member states when carrying out duties relating to peace and security. Articles 7(j) and 16(9) of the PSC protocol are explicit in tasking the PSC and the chairperson of the commission of the AU with harmonization and coordination of the activities of the regional mechanisms in the area of peace and security.

3   Adapted from the log concept, par 26. These figures do not fully correspond with those in the 2003 roadmap and in certain instances, for example armoured vehicles, would be insufficient for deployment in a mission that requires more robust capabilities.

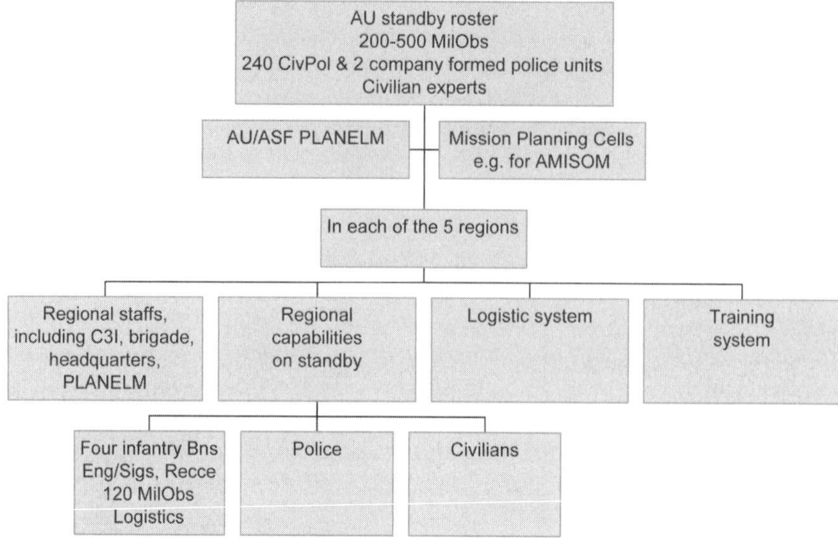

Figure 7.1   ASF approved order of battle

The ASF structure—with its associated deployment timelines—is determined by six missions and scenarios. Scenario 1 is characterized by an AU/regional military advice to a political mission with deployment required within 30 days of an AU mandate provided by the PSC. In scenario 2, an AU/regional observer mission is co-deployed with a UN mission and deployment is required within 30 days of an AU mandate. Scenario 3 sees a standalone AU/regional observer mission also deployed within 30 days of an AU mandate. Scenario 4 sees the deployment (also within 30 days) of an AU/regional peacekeeping force under UN Chapter VI and preventive deployment missions (and peace building). In scenario 5, an AU peacekeeping force for complex multidimensional peacekeeping missions, including those involving low-level spoilers, is deployed within 90 days of an AU mandate, with the military component being able to deploy in 30 days. And, finally, scenario 6 is characterized by an AU intervention, for example in genocide situations where the international community does not act promptly. Here, it is envisaged that the AU would have the capability to deploy a robust military force within 14 days.

The deployment timelines, already ambitious by any standard, are made particularly demanding by the multinational and standby character of the ASF. As a general rule, the more multinational a force, the more difficult it is to train and operate. Multinational forces also take longer to deploy if not pre-assembled at a staging area. Forces based on a single lead (or framework) nation, or forces largely consisting of one country's armed forces, are much easier to maintain at high readiness than multinational forces that require substantial periods of

Table 7.1   Composition of key resources in a regional brigade

Unit	Personnel	Light vehicles	Armoured vehicles	Light recce	Helicopters
Brigade headquarters	85	15	As required		
4 x infantry battalions	3,000	280	As required		
Helicopter unit	80	10			4
Recce company	150		15	13	
HQ sp company	65	16			
Military police unit	48	17			
Light signals unit	135	47			
Field engineer unit	505	65			
Logistic specialization unit	190	40			
Level 2 hospital	35	10			
Total	**4,293**	**500**	**15**	**13**	**4**

collaboration and joint exercises over several years, but they do not enjoy the legitimacy and trust that multinational forces engender. For example, the Scenario 6 deployment of a military component within 14 days can only be performed by forces that are ready, assembled, fully equipped and exercised with transport available on immediate call and with logistic supplies pre-packed and ready for delivery by air. A force at such a state of readiness cannot take leave or be used for other duties, with the result that it cannot be maintained at this level for very long and so has to be rotated at regular intervals. That being said, it is important to recognize that the intention is not to maintain a force at such a high level of readiness, but rather to use the early warning systems and mechanisms, such as the Peace and Security Department's PSOD, to place troops on the appropriate level of readiness for emerging eventualities.

It is also quite likely that the levels of readiness between different regions and national contingents will differ from one another, implying that the AU will have to institute a continental system of validation to ensure that national/ regional forces comply with the stated requirements. During one of the AU training and evaluation workshops, experts finalized an evaluation and validation system that would confirm the operational readiness of the various components of the ASF at three levels: (1) assessment of the state of readiness of the entire force; (2) validation of the training instructions and organizations with a focus on headquarters at AU, regional brigade and unit level as well as coordination between the various components and humanitarian organizations/agencies; and, (3) application of lessons learnt during operations, and training at all levels.[4]

The rapid deployment of ASF components requires an ongoing planning function (provided at AU and regional levels by the proposed 15 person PLANELM[5] at all levels), a mission planning cell at the level of the AU (such as the AU Mission to Somalia planning and management cell and previously the Darfur Integrated Task Force) and an effective field level mission headquarters (provided by the region upon deployment). The ASF concept does not provide for an AU-level field headquarters capability. In other words, the AU depends on the various regions for the provision and deployment of a headquarters at short notice.[6]

The AU had agreed that the ASF be established in two phases, although delays in implementation have marked the process. In phase one, which lasted up to 30 June 2006, the AU's key objective was to establish a strategic level management capacity. At the same time, the regions would complement the AU by establishing forces up to brigade level strength for scenario 4. In phase one the priority was the military and police aspects of the ASF, since it was deemed that UN humanitarian, development and human rights elements, which do not require a UN Security Council mandate, would be able to deploy in tandem with ASF missions. In addition, scenarios 1 to 3 entailed less complex structures, minimal management effort and fewer resources for deployment and sustainability compared with the other scenarios. The ASF has not been able to meet this milestone fully, although Western and Southern Africa have made substantial progress and Eastern Africa progressed substantially towards this requirement by the end of 2008.

---

4   In West Africa, Ghana—a major troop contributing country—is already under tremendous strain because of the deployment of four battalions and preparation of an additional battalion for deployment in the UN–AU Mission in Darfur. With all its infantry units either on deployment or preparing for deployment, Ghana has committed a level-two field hospital and company of engineers to the ECOWAS Standby Force (ESF) and is lobbying for a system whereby it guarantees a particular capacity, and then rotates the commitment internally in accordance with its own troop deployment schedule. By implication, Ghana will therefore not be providing a dedicated and named capacity as part of the ESF/ASF, and will furthermore rotate the capacity according to its internal operational schedules. If adopted by a region or a number of countries, such an approach could result in an ASF capacity that cannot be verified and tested at any point in time. (Information based on an interview with Odetei 2008.)

5   The original concept of a 15 person PLANELM, based on the SHIRBRIG model, has been adjusted and the posts have been absorbed into different organization configurations.

6   In the case of ECOWAS and SADC the regional brigade headquarters and PLANELM are co-located in Abuja and Gaborone. In the case of Eastern Africa, member states have agreed on the establishment of a standing brigade headquarters element in Addis Ababa that is separate from the PLANELM and EASBRICOM secretariats in Nairobi. Technically, the latter arrangement is contrary to AU guidelines but it resulted from the concern amongst the other members of the region about the concentration of EASF resources in Kenya.

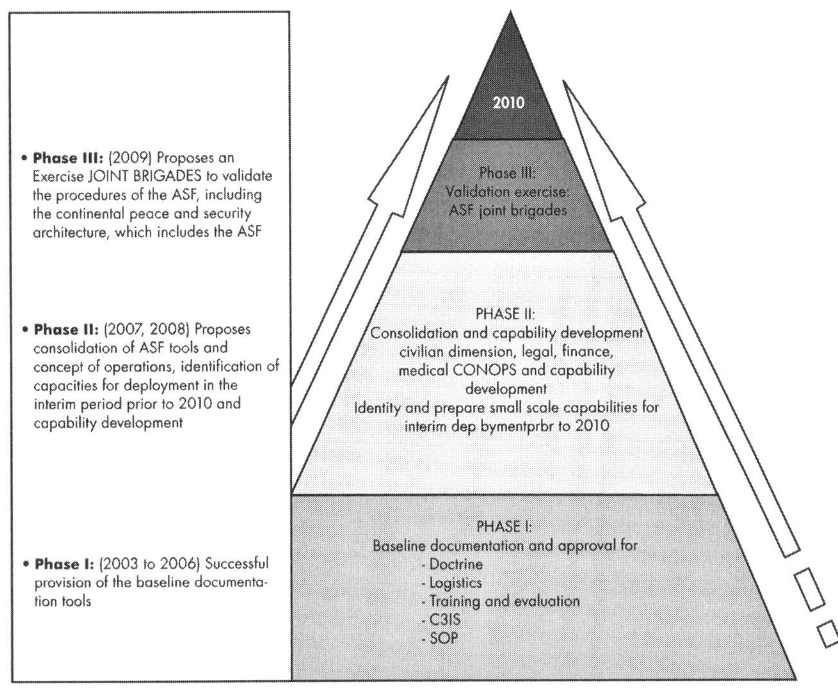

Figure 7.2   Progress with the ASF at the end of 2006

Phase two, to end by 30 June 2010, requires the AU to have developed full scenario 5 and 6 capacities. These missions entail enormous management effort, as well as considerable resources for the deployment and sustainability of missions. At the time of writing this chapter, it is unlikely that the AU will be able to meet more than the nominal targets, in the time that remains, without a change in the capacities that member states are prepared to devote to the ASF and much greater leadership and action at AU level.

After having finalized the March 2005 roadmap, the AU hosted a meeting of experts in Addis Ababa during November/December 2005 to finalize the arrangements for a series of workshops to develop the appropriate concepts relating to doctrine; standard operating procedures (SOPs); guidelines on C3IS; logistics and training and evaluation. It was agreed that different regions lead on separate aspects—the Southern African Development Community (SADC), for example, took responsibility for the development of ASF doctrine, Eastern Africa for logistics, etc.[7] In addition, the AU recognized the importance of dedicated work

---

7   From the executive summary on the meeting of experts on the workshops for the formulation of African standby force policies, held in Addis Ababa between 28 November and 2 December 2005.

on four additional areas not listed separately in the roadmap, namely legal aspects, the civilian component of the ASF, finances and medical issues.

These key policy documents were developed through the conducting of some 16 workshops in 2006 alone. During the following year there was further progress but at a less hurried pace, consisting of the consolidation of the ASF tools and concept of operations, the identification of capabilities for deployment in the period up to 2010 and progress with regard to the inclusion of the civilian dimensions of peace operations, legal matters and medical planning. Most of these were considered by the African Chiefs of Defense Staff and approved by the Ministers of Defense and Security in March 2008. The member states and RECs/RMs must now implement these policies, which will be reviewed in 2010.

Schematically the level of progress, as presented to the Commissioner of Peace and Security early in 2007, was as shown in Figure 7.2.[8]

The ASF training policy,[9] which was adopted during the ACDS meeting in March 2008, defines the objectives of training as the provision of all ASF personnel with the technical, tactical and specialized knowledge in a multinational environment and identifies basic training, basic PSO training, staff training and specialized training as the four levels of ASF training. ASF training must also be in accordance with UN Standard Training Modules. A number of regions have also been designated centers of training excellence to conduct tactical, operational and strategic training. However, in accordance with the policy, the AU will develop an accreditation process for these centers, coordinate training, establish an ASF database to which the centers are to contribute data of trained beneficiaries to enhance the AU's list of resource persons and ASF roster, and coordinate the establishment of training evaluation teams.[10] The continental training plan provides for various workshops, an annual exercise for the AU PLANELM and one major exercise involving three regions in the lead-up to 2010. Apart from

---

8   Adapted from D. Baly, Presentation on the development of the African Standby Force, Roadmap ll, slide 20.

9   The ASF Training Policy, was adopted by 5th meeting of the ACDS and Heads of Security, and approved by the 2nd ordinary meeting of Ministers of Defence and Security on 28 March 2008.

10   ASF Training Policy adopted at the 5th meeting of the ACDS and Heads of Security, and approved by the 2nd ordinary meeting of Ministers of Defence and Security on 28 March 2008. The list of instruction that could be provided by the centres of excellence include courses on train-the-trainer; the four types of training areas (individual, collective, command and staff, and specialist); public information and media operations; joint operational planning for staff; crisis management and contingency planning; intelligence analysis and management; negotiation; disarmament, demobilization and reintegration; CIMIC; humanitarian, international human rights and child protection legislation; sexual exploitation and abuse; cultural awareness; gender awareness; stress management; senior management and leadership; the role of civilian police in PSOs; election monitoring/ observers; HIV/AIDS; military observers (MILOBs); and land mine awareness and de-mining.

various workshops, regional training is expected to include a map exercise and two interregional deployment exercises.[11] The AU is now planning to host a field exercise of the regional forces in 2009, to validate the procedures for the ASF and a command post exercise early in 2010, with a continental ASF exercise later in 2010.[12]

While Africa has seen good progress with regard to the development of the majority of policies, the issue of ASF logistics remains problematic. The policy framework proposed a system of AU military logistic depots, consisting of the AU military logistic depot in Addis Ababa and regional logistic bases, was aimed at rapid deployment and mission sustainability. Anticipating the need for technical, and not political, considerations to inform the potential location of substantial logistic assets in particular countries, the 2005 roadmap proposed that the AU PLANELM "initiate and complete a study to present a costed continental logistic system for the ASF that outlines the appropriate concepts and plans for preparing, deploying and sustaining the ASF."[13]

If the ASF were to be able to deploy within the timelines for the various conflict scenarios, it would require that mission-ready units and headquarters, with equipment that includes vehicles and communications, be held either at a centralized regional logistic base or be provided on an 'on-call' basis by international partners or private contractors under clear terms of commitment. To launch the ASF elements into mission areas, these pre-deployment arrangements would have to be backed by standing arrangements for strategic sea- and airlift.

At present, the UN has contracted out most of its logistic requirements to commercial companies. For example, the Los Angeles-based Pacific Architects & Engineers (now part of Lockheed Martin) that provided the logistics backbone for the AU Mission in the Sudan (AMIS) (and recently DynCorp) provides 34 base camps in Darfur as well as vehicle maintenance and telecommunications equipment based on a series of contracts, the most recent of which was valued at $21 million (Cole 2007). Logistic arrangements for the ASF would be particularly onerous when one considers the complexity of funding arrangements for ASF deployment, reimbursement mechanisms, government-to-government arrangements and outsourcing requirements.[14] A final ASF logistic plan will have to include equipment procurement and preparation, finalization of a memorandum of understanding on reimbursement, and plans for mounting and strategic lift. Each

---

11   ASF Training Policy adopted at the fifth meeting of the ACDS and Heads of Security, and approved by the second ordinary meeting of Ministers of Defence and Security on 28 March 2008, par 4.

12   D. Baly, Presentation on the development of the African standby force, slides 7 and 8.

13   Roadmap for the Operationalisation of the African Standby Force, 22–23 March 2005, par 23 (EXP/AU-RECs/ASF/4(I)).

14   Planning multi-dimensional peace support operations. Amended draft, November 2006, chapter 7, par 47.

regional PLANELM will therefore have to decide what equipment is to be held in depots and how to procure supplies from commercial sources at short notice. Each will furthermore have to develop plans and prepare draft contracts for rapid procurement of equipment, conclude draft status of forces and status of mission agreements, draft memorandums of understanding covering partner support, and prepare budgets and conclude financial arrangements.

Figure 7.3 provides an illustrative schematic for mounting an ASF operation.[15]

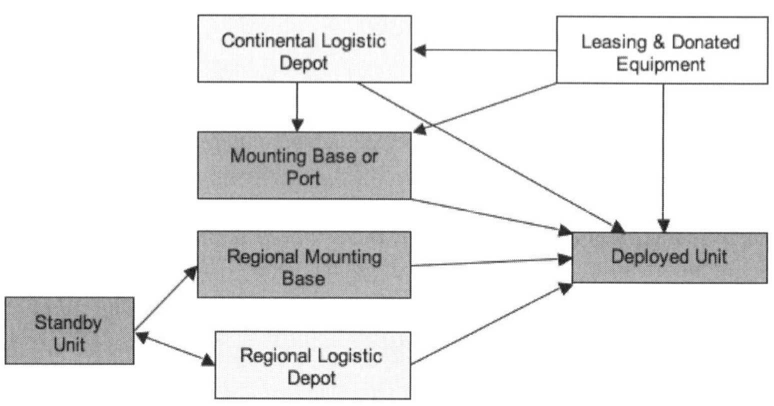

Figure 7.3   Schematic diagram to illustrate logistic concepts

To some, the implication of the policy framework requirement was straightforward—a continental depot (probably in Addis Ababa) and a regional logistic base in each of the five regions. Others argue in favor of a more flexible arrangement consisting of a single continental depot at the most appropriate location (generally accepted to be either at a deep-sea port and/or co-located at an international air base) with the ability to forward deploy stores to regional depots or mounting bases, depending on the operational plan. The UN has also offered the use of its Brindisi logistic facilities in Italy—either as a continental logistic base or for use by the North Africa Standby Force. A logistic depot study was conducted to determine the most viable placing of the continental logistic depot; whether it can be collocated with regional depots, and if so what are the resulting implications. The ACDS considered the options and recommended that the initial concept of one continental depot and five regional depots should be retained, pending the outcome of further consultations on the issue with the regions and member states.

---

15   Mudave, DSL, Draft support concept for African Standby Force (ASF) peace support operations, 7 August 2007, par 22.

The Policy Framework[16] requires that the forces pledged by member states "comply with UN standards"—this means fully equipped and ready for utilization. However, many ASF countries do not provide fully equipped units and the question is how much additional capacity should be provided for at the logistic depots and who should take ownership of the various logistic bases—international partners, the region, the AU or the UN? Or should it be outsourced? In practice, troops cannot be provided with equipment from a depot only upon deployment, as they need to train with the same equipment that they will use operationally.[17]

In summary, it can be said that the AU has made substantial progress in meeting its 2005 roadmap goals for phase one, although the different regions progressed at uneven rates (as will become clear from the discussion below), which has affected the extent of progress at the continental level. Disappointing as this may be when measured against the ambitious goals of the original 2005 roadmap, this period at least served to bring about greater clarity about the roles of the UN and the AU.

Mandates: The UN and the AU

In a reversal of thinking at international level, it has now become accepted that the AU can and should deploy in advance of the UN—demonstrated both during AMIS in Darfur and subsequently with the AU Mission to Somalia. Originally, the purpose of the ASF was premised on the need for quick response capabilities and the capability to mount a mission to cover the early days, while the ponderous UN peacekeeping system lumbered into operational mode. Today, it is accepted that the AU will deploy first, opening up the possibility for a UN follow-on multi-dimensional peace support operation.

In this scenario, ASF forces will therefore be deployed into a situation as part of the peacemaking process at an earlier stage than UN forces would be allowed to engage. They would thereby help to create the conditions on the ground that could lead to a comprehensive peace agreement and the deployment of UN forces. This was indeed the situation in Burundi with the AU and UN, and the relationship between the Economic Community of West African States (ECOWAS) and the UN in Liberia, Sierra Leone and Côte d'Ivoire. The exit strategy for ASF operations is therefore a transition to the UN—which could include the re-designation of substantial ASF resources as UN contingents.

There are two practical challenges with this idea, however. The first concerns the relationship between UN and ASF operations, which could lead to a severe and

---

16   Policy Framework for the Establishment of the African Standby Force and Military Staff Committee—EXP/ASF-MSC/2(I)

17   In terms of the draft logistic concept of August 2007 (par 27): 'Until the ASF stand-by brigades are able to provide the required level of logistic support organically, there will be a need for innovative solutions to be developed. One such solution might be to develop a Lead Nation Concept for specific Logistic capabilities, such as Strategic Lift, medical services, Mission HQ provision, etc.'

early depletion of ASF forces available for deployment elsewhere. This could be alleviated by using forces from countries such as Pakistan, Bangladesh and India, which have emerged as major peacekeeping force providers in Africa. While the potential full standby strength of the ASF would come to 25,000 troops and up to 980 military observers, the UN had 70,285 troops, 1,528 military observers and 11,041 police deployed on peacekeeping missions by 31 January of 2008, of which the six key missions in Africa account for 48,043 troops, 1,941 military observers and 6,520 police.[18] As these numbers indicate, the re-designation of ASF forces as part of UN operations would quickly deplete the available ASF capacity. This could be exacerbated by the fact that although Africa provides substantial numbers of troops to UN missions, African troop contributors appear to choose between deployment on UN missions and a commitment to the ASF. Given the disparities in resources available to the two types of missions, the ASF does not generally receive the same level of support as that of UN missions. Clearly, the relationship between the UN and ASF operations is something that will require attention in the future, as will the envisaged size of the ASF.

The second is the challenge of handing over control to the UN with its more restrictive entry criteria than the AU. In the aftermath of a slew of challenging missions, the 2000 Brahimi report on peacekeeping emphasized the importance of 'there being a peace to keep' and set as a benchmark that the UN should not deploy forces unless a binding and overarching peace agreement was in place.[19] The result is a marked UN reluctance to assume a peacekeeping responsibility before a comprehensive agreement is in place. In addition, once the UN has accepted such a role there are often extremely long delays in effecting the transition from an AU to a UN mission, as occurred in Burundi and Darfur.

Despite the apparent differences between ASF and UN peacekeeping, a close reading of the PSC protocol makes it clear that the ASF was established, and should develop and deploy, in close collaboration with the UN. Indeed, the prologue to the protocol reiterates the primary responsibility of the UN Security Council (UNSC) for the maintenance of international peace and security. It subsequently mandates the chairperson of the AU and the PSC to promote and develop a strong partnership for peace and security between the AU, the UN and its agencies. Although dedicated to Africa, the ASF is part and parcel of a global system. This close relationship between the AU and the UN is evident in the references to the use of international standards, codes and treaties and general cooperation where appropriate, but also in the roles envisaged for the UN in

---

18   Calculated from data provided at http://www.un.org/Depts/dpko/dpko/bnote.htm (accessed 9 March 2008).

19   The Brahimi Panel on UN Peace Operations was convened by the UN Secretary General in March 2000 to 'assess the shortcomings of the existing [UN] system and make frank, specific and realistic recommendations for change'. The report of the panel, which was led by Lakhdar Brahimi, a former Algerian foreign minister, was submitted on 21 August 2000 (United Nations 2000).

assessments of African peace support capacities and coordination of external initiatives in support of the ASF.[20] Hence, Article 17 on the relationship with the UN and other international organizations makes it obligatory for the PSC to cooperate and work closely with the UNSC as well as with other relevant UN agencies. The protocol makes specific reference to Chapter VIII of the Charter of the UN and the provision of financial, logistical and military support from the UN. This is also a position evident in the 2003 policy framework document that underpins the ASF.

As discussed above, the *PSC Protocol* determines that the PSC, in conjunction with Chairperson of the AU Commission, "shall authorize the mounting and deployment of peace support operations; lay down general guidelines for the conduct of such missions including the mandate thereof, and undertake periodic reviews of these guidelines; recommend to the Assembly [...] intervention, on behalf of the Union, in a Member State in respect of grace circumstances, namely war crimes, genocide and crimes against humanity [...]; [and] approve the modalities for intervention by the Union in a Member State" (African Union 2002, §7). Since the PSC protocol has been ratified by all AU members, it follows that only the AU/PSC can authorize the use of the ASF and that the PSC, acting in conjunction with the chairperson of the AU, is the sole authority for mandating and terminating AU peace missions and operations. The AU's Assembly of Heads of State and Government does so in the case of interventions in a member state.

As a rule, the AU has sought the support of the UNSC for all missions, in part as this is a requirement for access to the financial resources from the African Peace Facility provided by the European Union. Or, put differently, should Eastern Africa decide to undertake a peace mission in Somalia without an AU mandate, this could not legally be undertaken as part of the ASF nor would a donor such as the EU readily agree to fund it except if mandated by the UNSC. This does not, of course, preclude regions from undertaking peacekeeping missions under their own auspices, provided they comply with the relevant provisions in the Charter of the UN (SADC 2007, §7 (1)).

---

20   For example, article 12.5 of the memorandum of understanding that established the SADC standby brigade states: 'The SADC Summit shall appoint a Force Commander, Commissioner of Police and Head of the Civilian Component for each specific mission from the Personnel Contributing State Parties. These appointed officers shall report to the Special Representative, while the Military Contingent Commanders shall report to the Force Commander.' According to the PSC protocol, ratified by all SADC members, the chairperson of the commission appoints these key staff in the case of ASF missions. SADC also requires that '[t]he SADCBRIG shall only be deployed on the authority of the SADC Summit'. See articles 7.1(k),13.13, 13.4, 13.15 and 13.16.

Command and Control

In recent years, the term 'integrated mission' has been used increasingly to describe the set of management principles and practices that support unity of effort in post-conflict settings that feature multiple international actors. It is a term that has also become widely accepted within the ASF and the "Integrated Mission Planning Process" has been incorporated in doctrine, SOPs and related policy documents. More an approach than a template, an integrated mission approach implies that the military effort is fully integrated with other components and that all keep in mind the long-term strategic objective of the mission.

As is clear from ASF documents, integration does not necessarily require or imply unity of command, an approach that would seek to make all international assets within a mission work towards a single plan, answerable to a single source of authority. Rather, an integrated mission is one in which divergent political, humanitarian, developmental and security components all have common strategic objectives. Such an approach implies a shared understanding of the priorities and types of program interventions to be undertaken at each stage of a peace process by numerous actors, some of whom may not be part of the AU's direct planning process.

Military staffs often assume an important role in this process. Normally, the military 'campaign plan' is the most formal and stylized of the various functional planning components that inform and constitute the integrated plan, and may influence the latter to a large extent. Often, the military will be the first formal representation of a peace mission in a country in crisis and, in the early stages of planning, the military may have to assume a leading role, interfacing directly with UN agencies and non-government organizations that are already on the ground. Until such time as a Special Representative of the Chairperson of the Commission (SRCC) is appointed, the commander of the military component may also have to act as the head of mission and in this role commence with a draft mission plan.

Having learnt from UN practice, a PSC mandate will be preceded by a technical assessment to the mission area and the development of a concept of operations. Once the mandate has been approved, the doctrine calls for the Chairperson of the AU Commission to issue a directive and finalize the rules of engagement. This directive provides the basis on which the AU Peace and Security Operations Division (PSOD) planning staffs develop an integrated mission plan.[21] Depending on when mission personnel are appointed, the PSOD is likely to retain the lead in planning until such time as there is a viable mission headquarters in place, after which the head of mission or SRCC will gradually assume the lead in the further development and eventual implementation of the plan.

In the event that the majority of capacities that are deployed come from one region alone, the PSOD will typically look towards that region and not individual

---

21   In Chapter 7 the ASF doctrine refers to a comprehensive peace support operations plan.

troop contributing countries to sustain the forces in the field, and to that end negotiate a memorandum of understanding with the region. The region will then be expected to sustain its forces through various individual agreements with the different troop contributing countries. In this manner, the AU will rely upon the regions for force provision.

Alternatively, if an ASF mission consists of troops from all over the continent, the PSOD mission staff may have to negotiate agreements with individual countries, rather than with one or more regions. This was the situation with AMIS troop deployments, where troops from different regions were deployed in adjacent sectors in Darfur. Some RECs/RMs have already, as was required in the Policy Framework document, certified their readiness to deploy regional standby forces, and the PSOD should verify the readiness of these forces and mobilize them according to the existing SOPs. The practice, where the AU negotiates directly with member states for forces, will stop once the RECs/RMs are able to coordinate and mobilize the forces as required.

In all instances the regions or individual troop contributing countries will be expected to maintain their forces in the mission area indefinitely, for which they will ideally be compensated after the initial 90-day period. This command and control status is reflected in Figure 7.4 based on "The African Standby Force Command and Control System".

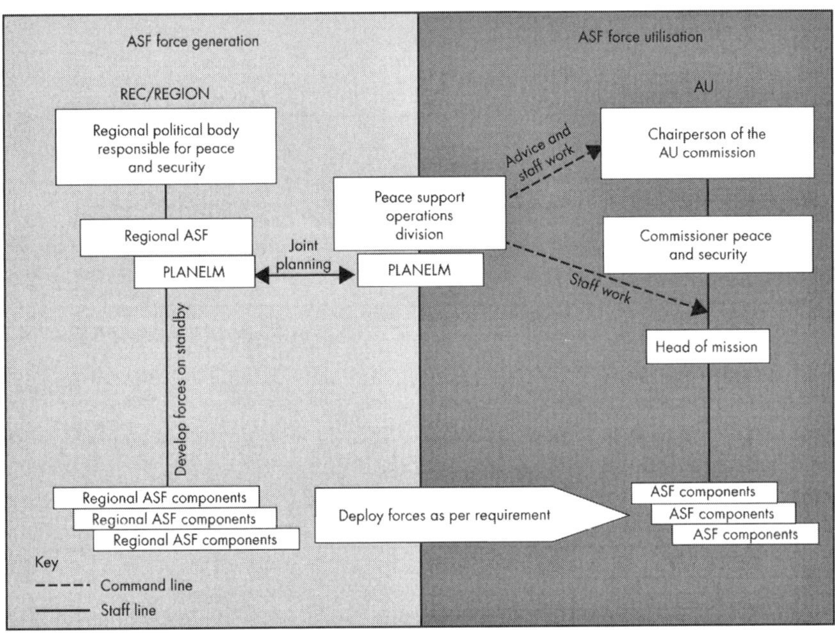

Figure 7.4   **The relationship between force generation and force utilization**

Rapid Deployment Concept

The ASF concept calls for the ability to intervene within 14 days from the provision of a mandate by the PSC in the case of genocide, for urgent assistance to a peacekeeping force, and as an early intervention presence in the case of imminent conflict.[22] This is set out as follows in the 2003 policy framework: "In an emergency situation, the OAU [now AU] should undertake preliminary preventive action while preparing for more comprehensive action which may include the UN involvement." The emphasis here is for speed of action and deployment. As a principle, the OAU should take the first initiative in approaching the UN to deploy a peace operation in response to an emergency in the continent. If the UN is unresponsive, the OAU must take preliminary action whilst continuing its efforts to elicit a positive response from the world body.[23] In considering these requirements it is important to recognize that a number of preparations will precede a mandate, including a fact-finding mission, development of a concept of operations and various warning orders to troops on standby to improve levels of readiness.

Purpose of the RDC

The early intervention during a crisis to stop violent conflict and/or atrocities and stabilize the situation, or to render emergency assistance in cases of natural or human disasters

Tasks

Rapid deployment under scenario 6
Rapid deployment to start-up a scenario 4 or 5 mission
Rapid intervention to support stabilization of a situation
Rapid deployment in support of existing mission
Rapid support to provide humanitarian relief

Roles

Secure point of entry; Separate belligerents; Guard key installations; Active and, if necessary, aggressive patrolling; Provide protection to civilians; Assist with the return to rule of law; Assist with humanitarian relief

Figure 7.5   The Rapid Deployment Capacity (RDC)[24]

---

22   Policy framework for the establishment of the African Standby Force and Military Staff Committee, par 5.2c.

23   Policy framework for the establishment of the African Standby Force and Military Staff Committee, par 1.4a, as quoted in par 4 of a concept paper delivered at the workshop on the development of the ASF's rapid deployment capability, held in June 2007

24   Source: Presentation, Rapid deployment capability, 29 November 2007.

The results of a first meeting of experts on a The Rapid Deployment Capacity (RDC—see Figure 7.5) in July 2007 in Addis ended inconclusively. The workshop did quantify the RDC requirement as the ability to deploy around 2,500 or more troops in two phases (see Tables 7.2 and 7.3). The requirements are that during the first phase 1,000 personnel (including mostly infantry, police and civilians) must be ready to deploy within 14 days and a follow-on force (second phase) of 1,500 or more must be ready within the next 14 days see Figure 7.6).[25] This would mean that the AU would, within 30 days, have half a brigade size force on the ground. Since the force has to be logistically self-sustainable for at least a month, it would have to deploy fully equipped. During a third phase, the "normal" ASF deployment would take place and the RDC would either be integrated into the force or rotate back to its base(s).

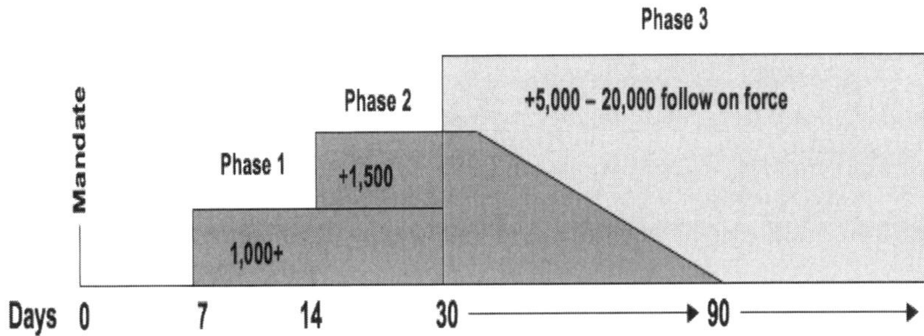

Figure 7.6   RDC deployment concept

During the July 2007 meeting, no agreement could be reached on the nature, location and command/control relationship of the RDC. Key officials within the AU argued in favor of a standing high-readiness capability, pre-assembled at a permanent base and ready for deployment to stabilize a situation under the mandate of the PSC. This would constitute an early entry force that would hand over to the follow-on ASF forces provided, by regions, after which the RDC could regroup and return to its base, ready for the next task. In terms of this approach, the RDC would serve as a force on call to the chairperson of the AU commission.

During their meeting in March 2008, the African Ministers of Defense and Security agreed that the RDC should be a standby capacity under regional command and control during peacetime, either as part of or in addition to the regional ASF capacities. RDC capabilities would therefore only come under the command and control of the AU upon deployment and the Chairperson of the AU would have to negotiate their release for deployment with the region. It will

25   Presentation on the rapid deployment capability on 29 November 2007.

Table 7.2   RDC illustrative deployment (Phase 1)

Unit	Personnel	Light vehicles	Armoured vehicles	Helicopters
HQ and support	67	16		
Reconnaissance	22	2	6	
Light infantry battalion	700	49		
Mechanised infantry company	120	8	15	
Air support	20	6		8
Engineers	30	6		
Logistics, medical and military police	66	20		
Police and civilians	32	12		
Total	**1,057**	**119**	**21**	**8**

Table 7.3   RDC illustrative deployment (Phase 2)

Unit	Personnel	Light vehicles	Armoured vehicles	Helicopters
HQ and support				
Reconnaissance	22	2	6	
Light infantry battalion	700	49		
Mechanised infantry battalion	570	31	45	
Air support	15			2
Engineers	30	6		
Logistics	60	15		
Police and civilians	46	10		
Total	**1,443**	**113**	**51**	**2**

remain the responsibility of the region to negotiate for the release of the forces from individual troop contributing countries. The AU commission was tasked to develop further the concept in close collaboration with the regions—the modalities around the release/activation of regional RDC needs to be properly developed and formalized in order to avoid unnecessary delays when a RDC is required.

Each regional standby force will thus develop its own high readiness combat group, either as part of, or in addition to, the regional standby force, and possibly structured around a lead nation concept. The AU will then develop a continental roster whereby the ASF rapid response capability will be shared between the five regions.

Prior to the March 2008 meeting, the West African standby force (ECOWAS Standby Force—ESF) and the SADC Standby Force had both advanced substantially in their preparations for such a capacity through the ESF task force (with a Nigerian and a composite/Senegal battle group) and the SADC early entry rapid reaction force. In neither region does the RDC apparently form part of the main brigade, but is it rather an addition that provides an added deployable capacity.[26] In the case of Eastern Africa, the United Kingdom proposed that Ethiopia, Uganda, Rwanda and Kenya each consider a single nation standby high readiness battle group, and has subsequently committed £1 million to establish a Kenyan battle group command structure with an enhanced headquarters in 2008 (Ward 2008).

While the separation between the location of the standing brigade element in Ethiopia and the PLANELM in Kenya may complicate or delay the deployment of an Eastern Africa standby force headquarters, this could be overcome if the region agrees on the deployment of a leading nation battle group as the RDC. In Southern Africa, current thinking appears to be that the core RDC will be provided on a rotational basis by the more capable countries, such as South Africa, Angola and Zimbabwe, but that it would still have a multinational character.

The RDC concept is ambitious given the requirement that units come fully equipped and that regions supply some additional operational requirements, while the AU coordinates strategic support such as airlift as well as logistics after the initial period of self-sufficiency. In this approach, the AU could trigger the deployment of the RDC to a mounting base as a prelude to possible deployment pending a final mandate from the PSC or place the RDC on shorter deployment notice within the respective countries. Whatever the choice, the operationalization of the RDC would require a strict regime of training and evaluation in preparation for a period on standby as well as various protocols and agreements that would govern deployment.

Funding

An earlier paper by Cilliers and Malan (2005) had explored seven options for external support to African peacekeeping, ranging from the unlikely scenario of AU missions funded by means of assessed UN contributions to 'burden sharing' in which specific countries provide dedicated support to African partners, and included a range of intermediate options. The AU has come around to the view that relying on external partners alone is not a feasible option. Accordingly, the AU Commission now emphasizes the need for greater efficiency of program budgeting, effective allocation of current externally generated resources and mobilization of additional resources from within Africa.[27] What is unclear is the

---

26   This was not the original intention, in which the task force was seen as part and parcel of the ESF.

27   Background and concept paper (par 35) for the brainstorming retreat between the AU and the regional mechanisms for conflict prevention, management and resolution, at

extent to which African troop contributors share that view, since they, and not the AU Commission, are the ones who would have to provide the money.[28]

Thus far, the AU has not seen fit to implement the provisions of Article 21 of the *PSC Protocol*, which provides that when required, and following a decision by the relevant policy organs of the Union, the cost of ASF missions can be allocated to member states on the basis of their contributions to the regular budget of the Union. Following the adoption of a new scale of assessment during the AU summit in Sirté, Libya, in 2005, South Africa, Algeria, Nigeria, Egypt and Libya each contribute 15 per cent of the total budget of the AU while the other 48 member states contribute the remaining 25 per cent.[29]

In 2003, the EU established the Africa Peace Facility, which had provided the AU with almost €300 million for peacekeeping and related capacity building by 2006.[30] The instrument became operational with the first Africa Peace Facility grant for the AMIS I operation in July 2004. These funds made a significant contribution to the African peacekeeping efforts in Burundi, Darfur, the Central African Republic and the Comoros. By March 2007 EU member states had contributed €400 million for Darfur, the USA $350 million and various international partners such as the UK and Canada significant additional amounts through various bilateral arrangements. In fact, without the Africa Peace Facility, it is unlikely that the AU would have been able to undertake any of these missions. Since the implementation of the Africa Peace Facility, the relationship between the AU and EU has developed quite strongly, resulting in the EU strategy for Africa and recently the extension of the joint EU–Africa strategy in December 2007. The EU is currently considering topping up the fund with an additional €300 million for 2008 to 2011 under the tenth Economic Development Fund (EDF).

At the Kananaskis summit in 2002, the G8 adopted an Africa action plan that contained a detailed list of commitments, including the provision of "technical and financial assistance so that, by 2010, African countries and regional and sub-regional organizations are able to engage more effectively to prevent and resolve violent conflict on the continent, and undertake peace support operations in accordance with the UN Charter". At the Evian (2003), Sea Island (2004) and Gleneagles (2005) summits, the G8 reiterated and developed this commitment. The Evian summit adopted a more specific joint Africa/G8 action plan that provided for the establishment, equipment and training of coherent, multinational, multidisciplinary standby capabilities at the AU and regional levels. The Sea

---

Algiers, Algeria on 5 and 6 January 2008.

28   Five percent of AU members' contributions go to the peace fund, which would have totalled $4,350,000 in 2007 if all members had paid their contributions (26 out of 53 have not).

29   In 2005/6, South Africa contributed R105 million in membership fees to the AU (South Africa Department of Foreign Affairs 2005/6:65).

30   Consisting of an initial amount of €250 million, replenished by €50 million in 2006.

Island summit adopted an action plan on the expansion of global capability for peace support operations with a particular focus on Africa. It consists of several elements, including training and equipping 75,000 troops by 2010, developing transportation and logistic support arrangements, increasing efforts to train *carabinieri/gendarme*-type forces, and establishing G8 expert level meetings to exchange information and to coordinate efforts. The Gleneagles summit called for action in the UN to boost peace building, improve the effectiveness of sanction regimes, improve international controls on arms transfers, and combat the role of 'conflict resources'. It also committed the G8 to focus more attention on humanitarian emergencies and financing for post-conflict countries.

After the Sea Island summit, a system of six-monthly consultation meetings between the AU, African peace and security institutions, G8 member countries and other partners was established.[31] The first two meetings were held in April and October 2005 and, provided that they are held regularly, they serve as an important mechanism for ensuring the necessary coordination between the AU, sub-regional organizations and development partners as a whole (both G8 and non-G8), and for tracking the implementation of commitments.

In the absence of a consolidated strategic plan on peace and security, or indeed for any specific component of it such as the ASF, external partners tend to have separate channels of engagement with the AU and with regional mechanisms. Some, and particularly the UK and France, also engage on a bilateral basis with individual countries to build national capacity outside either the AU or regional context. Generally there has been something of a donor scramble for support to the various training institutions as the most politically attractive mode of engagement with the ASF.

During a brainstorming retreat between the AU and the regional mechanisms for conflict prevention, management and resolution, the AU made the following comment:

> This pattern of engagement is not limited to the levels of the AU or the Regional Mechanisms. Even within the AU or in any one Regional Mechanism, there is a tendency to have multiple channels of engagement with external partners rather than deal with them on the basis of one consolidated strategic plan on peace and security [...] Coordination is not only an issue for the AU and the Regional Mechanisms, but also for external partners, who tend to operate bilaterally with each organisation or programme within an organisation and at times appearing to compete for an opportunity to fund specific initiatives.[32]

---

31 Communiqué on the consultation between the AU, the member countries of the G8 and other partners and African peace and security institutions at Addis Ababa on 4 April 2005.

32 Background and concept paper, op. cit. (pars 39 and 40).

At the same retreat, the UK and Denmark attempted to address this lack of coordination by encouraging the AU to develop an annual plan, to which international partners could provide support without duplication of efforts and resources (par. 42 of the background and concept paper):

> Notwithstanding the efforts by external actors, it is, however, clear that external support and engagement with the AU and the Regional Mechanisms will only be as organised and as coordinated as these organisations allow it to be. Without coordination of their agenda and resource requirements, it will be difficult to achieve or demand coordination by external actors in the way they engage with the AU and the Regional Mechanisms. External partners can only build on the framework and practice established and on the agenda and principles set by African organisations themselves.[33]

All of this reinforces the requirement to establish a single point of entry for international partners at AU and regional level to coordinate and harmonize funding.

Progress at Regional Level

The African Chiefs of Defense and Security (ACDS) have acknowledged that the term "force" primarily represents the military and have tasked the AU Commissions to find appropriate terminology to reflect the multidimensional and multifunctional nature of the ASF—the term African Standby Capability (ASC) was used in certain discussions and seems to have general acceptance. ASF membership is as shown in Table 7.4.

West Africa   The main brigade (ECOBRIG) of the ECOWAS Standby Force (ESF) will comprised 6,500 soldiers within pre-determined units, which will be ready to deploy within 90 days. Also in existence is the ESF task force, a high readiness component of the ESF consisting of 2,773 soldiers at 30 days' readiness. The latter is based on Nigeria as lead nation. West Africa has appointed a task force chief of staff, established a task force headquarters (in Abuja) and has an operational PLANELM. It has also completed its concept of operations, doctrine and SOPs. The region has also undertaken a training needs analysis and designated Hastings, in Sierra Leone, as its regional logistic base, although some other options are under consideration. All countries have pledged their support and the commission has undertaken a verification mission to confirm the levels of readiness among member states and has also conducted a number of command post exercises. The intention is that all contributions on standby in member states be ready and available for deployment by the end of 2008.

---

33   Brainstorming retreat between the AU and the regional mechanisms, op. cit., par 42.

Table 7.4   ASF membership

Central region (FOMAC)	Southern region (SADCBRIG)	Eastern region (EASF)	Northern region (NASBRIG)	Western region (ESF)
Angola		Sudan	Western Sahara	Mali
Democratic Republic of Congo		Ethiopia	Mauritania	Cape Verde
São Tomé and Príncipe	Malawi	Eritrea	Algeria	Senegal
Equatorial Guinea	Zambia	Djibouti	Tunisia	Gambia
Cameroon	Zimbabwe	Somalia	Libya	Guinea Bissau
CAR	Namibia	Kenya	Egypt	Guinea
Gabon	Swaziland	Uganda		Sierra Leone
Chad	Lesotho	Rwanda		Liberia
Congo (Brazzaville)	Botswana	Tanzania		Côte d'Ivoire
	South Africa	Burundi		Ghana
	Mozambique	Comoros		Togo
	Madagascar			Benin
	Mauritius			Nigeria
	Tanzania			Niger
				Burkina Faso

Note: Those countries with an uncertain status or active in more than one region are indicated as such. Angola has separate forces earmarked for the Southern Africa Standby Force as well as the Central Africa Standby Force, which is not the case with the Democratic Republic of Congo. Madagascar and Mauritius are both SADC members but still nominally part of EASF. They are not very active in either.

There are three centers of training excellence, namely the National Defense College in Abuja for strategic level, the Kofi Annan International Peacekeeping Training Centre in Accra for operational level and the Ecole de Maintien de la Paix Alioune Blondin Beye in Bamako, Mali, for tactical level training. A fourth center, for police, has also recently been announced.

Southern Africa[34]   The SADC Chiefs of Defense Staff and Police Chiefs approved the modalities regarding the formation of a SADC Standby Brigade (SADCBRIG), which includes police, in July 2004 in Maseru, Lesotho, and received the blessing of Ministers of Defense and Security and the SADC Heads of State shortly

---

34   Brig. Gen. G.M. Yekelo, Presentation Status and Way Forward for the SADCSF, 14 July 2007.

thereafter. SADCBRIG was officially launched in August 2007 and the region has made steady progress with its operationalization.

Following protracted negotiations, the memorandum of understanding that underpins the associated arrangements between its member states that "the command structure of any SADCBRIG headquarters shall strictly be representative of all contributing State Parties" (SADC 2007, §12 (2)). The SADCBRIG PLANELM is functional and co-located with the SADC secretariat in Gaborone, it has a centre of training excellence (consisting of the Regional Peacekeeping Training Centre in Harare), and pledged forces and elements are in place, as is the brigade headquarters.[35] The region has also had a number of peacekeeping exercises (the most recent was in Botswana), but has not yet finalized the civilian component or the details around the establishment of a logistic concept and depot.

Having completed its doctrine, operational guidelines, SOPs and logistic concept and verified the various countries' pledges, the SADCBRIG lists the following remaining challenges: (1) additional forces on standby are required (because some pledged forces/elements are still committed elsewhere); (2) finalization of the standby concept and roster; (3) funding; (4) logistic support and location of the depot; (5) operationalization of an early warning system; (6) interoperability (equipment, etc.); (6) effective coordination and communication; and, (7) capacity building, especially in a civilian environment.

Eastern Africa The absence of an appropriate regional mechanism within which to anchor the Eastern African Standby Force has delayed progress in this region. In 2004, Eastern Africa first mandated the Intergovernmental Authority on Development (IGAD), consisting of only seven Eastern Africa troop contributing countries, to coordinate the Eastern African Standby Brigade (EASBRIG). When non-IGAD members protested against this role, the council of ministers approved the creation of an "independent EASBRIG Coordination Mechanism" (EASBRICOM) to assume coordination from IGAD. The mechanism was to be co-located with the PLANELM in Nairobi but agreement on its location was only reached in 2007, after intervention by the heads of state. The members of the Eastern Africa Standby Force now include Comoros, Djibouti, Eritrea, Ethiopia, Kenya, Rwanda, Seychelles, Somalia, Sudan and Uganda. Burundi has asked to join Eastern Africa and is therefore no longer considered to be a member of the central area. Tanzania, Madagascar and Mauritius, who had previously been members, are active in Southern Africa. Eritrea is not currently engaged with EASBRICOM and Seychelles has rejoined SADC.

35　The SADC standby brigade, which can list eight helicopters and six medium lift transport aircraft, is perhaps better off than most other regions. South Africa has also pledged substantial naval assets (five harbor patrol boats and a large ship) and Angola has also pledged a marine platoon. Various countries have pledged 137 military observers and Zambia 200 civilian police.

EASBRICOM has proposed that it will anchor the Eastern African standby force within a regional peace and security mechanism to provide the political oversight and appropriate strategic decision-making system for multidimensional peace support operations. This, it is proposed, will serve as a regional mechanism for conflict prevention, management and resolution for Eastern Africa in accordance with Article 16 of the *PSC Protocol.*

The proposed Eastern Africa Peace and Security Mechanism (EAPSM) provides, amongst others, for the reconfiguration of EASBRICOM as an Eastern Africa Peace and Security Secretariat (EAPSS) to coordinate the mechanism. This would make it possible to include the military and other PLANELMs in the peace and security directorate.

The proposed subsidiary structures and systems of the EAPSM consist of a standing brigade headquarters element (located in Ethiopia) responsible for a deployable military headquarters, an integrated logistic system, integrated training system and military, police and civilian standby components in member states. The EAPSS will also manage the Eastern Africa peace fund. The region has agreed on the establishment of a logistic base in Ethiopia (as part of the logistic system) and will shortly undertake a study of the EASBRIG logistic system. EASBRICOM currently operates on the basis of a memorandum of understanding. These recommendations do not, however, enjoy the support of all EASBRICOM member states. EASBRIG has also identified training centers of excellence, in Rwanda, Kenya and Uganda, although there is not complete unanimity in the region on this matter, either.

Central Africa   The Economic Community of Central African States (ECCAS) is composed of 11 member states, namely Angola, Burundi, Cameroon, Central African Republic, Chad, Congo (Brazzaville), Democratic Republic of Congo, Equatorial Guinea, Gabon, Rwanda and São Tomé and Príncipe. Rwanda has been a member of the EASF (from the beginning and recently Burundi has also applied to join the EASF. Angola and the DRC are members of both the central and southern standby forces and the former has designated different units on standby for Central and Southern Africa.

The standing orders of the Council for Peace and Security in Central Africa (COPAX), including the Defense and Security Commission (DSC) Multinational Force of Central Africa (FOMAC) and the Early Warning Mechanism of Central Africa (MARAC), were adopted at the Tenth Ordinary Session of Heads of State and Government in Malabo in June 2002. The protocol relating to the establishment of a mutual security pact in Central Africa (COPAX) entered into force two years later. Substantial progress regarding the ECCAS Standby Force dates from 2006.

In terms of force levels, FOMAC—which will include sufficient air and naval assets and multinational general staff appointed by consensus—will be comprised of one major brigade at a low degree of notice of deployment; two major brigades at a medium degree of notice of deployment; and, three major brigades at the highest degree of notice of deployment. ECCAS has now approved a structure for the regional headquarters and the ECCAS PLANELM. By 2008, the regional PLANELM in Libreville had 13 staff members, consisting of six from the region and seven from Gabon, as well as the structure and equipment for the ECCAS standby brigade with a strength of 2,177. Although a national division of labor between individual countries of the region has been made, the effective realization of the regional stand-by brigade as well as the Rapid Deployment Force still faces many technical challenges.

The proposed centers of excellence for ECCAS are CSID (Cours Superieur Inter-Armees de Defense, created in 2005 and funded by France) in Youndé, Cameroon, for the strategic level, EEML (Ecole d'Etat-Major de Libreville, created in 2003 and also funded by France) in Libreville, Gabon, for operational training and EFOFAA (in Luanda, Angola, for tactical level training. There are also plans to develop a school in Cameroon into an international police training centre of excellence. In addition, the region has a number of smaller national centers including one for medical training (Libreville) and engineers (Congo) that could play a regional role in due course. The region has agreed to locate the logistic base for the ECCAS Standby Force in Doula, Cameroon.

The region conducts multinational training exercises known as Exercise Barh El Ghazel every two years. The most recent exercise took place in November 2007 in N'Djamena, Chad, and its purpose was to determine the operational capabilities of ECCAS and to test the capacities of national commands for operating within the framework of the regional standby brigade. An assessment of the exercise will be conducted in 2008 to identify lessons that could be learned from it.

Since most of the ECCAS troop contributing countries are former French colonies, the intention is that CivPol would be supplied by gendarmerie for robust missions and may include civilian police where the mission allows this. France generally plays an important role in the building of military capacities of Central African States, particularly in terms of logistics, finance and, more importantly, training. Yet, before it will be able to carry out multidimensional peace operations, ECCAS will have to address a number of challenges. The first concerns the chronic lack of resources of the secretariat and the over-reliance on external support (especially the peace facility) for almost all activities of the ECCASSF. Major pillars of the ECCASSF, such as centers of excellence, the logistic base and training program are at a standstill, partly because of non-existing endogenous resources and competing donor initiatives. The second challenge concerns the weak harmonization with the AU. Prior consultation would have eased the implementation of the rapid deployment force and the identification of logistic bases. Structural challenges such as the weak managerial capacity of the department of peace and security, the slow decision-making procedures of the COPAX and the inadequate skills of many officers attached to the regional PLANELM (especially the strategic planning) further hinder the development of an integrated regional peacekeeping force.

North Africa   The Arab Maghreb Union (AMU) was originally nominated to coordinate the Northern Region but its members are divided over Western Sahara. Its problems were compounded by the fact that Egypt, potentially a major contributor, is not a member of AMU. Libya eventually emerged as the coordinator and the region established the North Africa Regional Capability (NARC) that now includes Egypt, with the exclusive responsibility of developing the North Africa standby force. The focus is still very much on the military component. A memorandum of understanding has been signed at ministerial level and by a number of heads of state and government. The brigade headquarters and PLANELM are to be located in Libya and Egypt respectively. Each country will provide training but only Egypt has offered to designate the Cairo peacekeeping training school as a regional centre of training excellence.

Conclusion

In reviewing the progress with the development and operationalization of the ASF, Africa has admittedly not met the ambitious milestones that it set for itself. Nevertheless, the progress made has been impressive if uneven. Strategically, the lack of adequate financial resources to meet the demands of peacekeeping in Africa remains the most obvious hurdle. With regard to finances, the commission of the AU has undergone a very steep learning curve on how to handle the massive budgets relating to the African peacekeeping function. For example, the African Union's first peacekeeping operation, AMIB, had an approved budget of approximately $130 million per year—at a time when the annual budget of the entire AU was about $32 million. The second mission, AMIS, was even larger with close to 8,000 personnel and an annual budget of approximately $466 million.[36]

While the lack of predictable financing for operations has undoubtedly been an important consideration, perhaps a more important factor in the halting progress compared with the original timeline has been a lack of capacity at the level of the AU. A competent command and control structure is required at the strategic level in order to effectively employ the resources of the ASF as envisaged. Member states and regions will be reluctant to release forces/capabilities if the application/utilization thereof does not comply with the highest professional standards. The Peace Support Operations Division (PSOD) is central to the organizing and employment of ASF capabilities, but cannot perform the tasks as required if not properly structured. An organization study, which was completed in May 2008, recommended a reorganization of the division and an expansion of the current post structure. The recommendations were favorable accepted, a 'roadmap' for implementations was developed, but progress was halted to await another study for the reorganization/restructuring of the Conflict Management Division (CMD), within the Peace and Security Department. The staffing of the recommended

---

36   Background and concept paper, op. cit., par 34.

PSOD structure is thus of critical importance if the target dates for 2010 for the operationalization of the ASF are to be achieved.

Add to this that the AU PLANELM has had only four staff members for several years, and the lack of capacity translates into an absence of leadership. Whereas the 2005 roadmap had emphasized the need for the early secondment of five experienced offices from African member states as a first step towards the expansion of the AU PLANELM to its required key staff of 15, this has not taken place. Tragically, the appointed chief of staff of the ASF and head of the AU PLANELM, Major Gen Hassan from Nigeria, passed away only 13 months after assuming his position. The AU PLANELM has had to make do with a severely limited staff complement for several years—outnumbered at all times by the military staffs attached to embassies in Addis Ababa from donor countries and AU member states, who are all eager to assist but often overwhelm the AU staffs (who also have had to deal with a much more immediate crises in Darfur, Somalia, Comoros and others). In this vacuum, and in the absence of guidance from Addis Ababa, regions have applied their own interpretation to the roadmap.

In preparation for a recent experts working session in Algiers, the commission of the AU listed the following challenges about the key roles in future African peace operations:[37]

1. The likelihood that the UN will stage robust operations or enforcement missions under Chapter VII of the UN Charter remains small for the foreseeable future. The AU and the regional mechanisms will, therefore, continue to face the challenge of summoning the political will as well as the capacity to plan and execute robust missions.

2. While some of the ongoing situations of armed conflict will remain a challenge for some time to come, emerging trends suggest that such incidents of large-scale armed conflict will gradually decline in Africa. However, situations of low intensity conflict are likely to remain a challenge. While these situations do not necessarily pose significant threats to international peace and security, they do constitute a threat to stability and sustainable development in the affected countries. As such, situations of this nature will occupy the attention of the AU and the regional mechanisms and will be the focus of conflict prevention and management.

3. An operational African peace and security architecture will therefore need to develop effective early response systems and effective support for mediation efforts through, for example, preventive deployment.

4. A standby force implies that it consists of several components, including, for example, military, police and civilian dimensions. However, there has been more focus and attention on the military components. Although the AU has recognized this lack, there is a need for more targeted attention to rectify this shortcoming.

---

37   Ibid., par 31.

5. Training of future peace operations personnel (i.e. the ASF) must of necessity address the different dimensions of the challenges of conflict and post-conflict environments in which such persons will operate. This means that more attention should be given to the civilian dimension, including child protection, gender issues, human rights, civil affairs, economic recovery and HIV/AIDS issues, in addition to disarmament, demobilization and reintegration and security sector reform programs.

6. African organizations have not demonstrated the ability to mobilize the financial resources required to address post-conflict, reconstruction, and development needs on their own. However, they can nonetheless set the agenda for external and other partners in terms of articulating priority approaches to peculiar needs of the targeted post-conflict environments. The AU policy on post-conflict, reconstruction, and development needs does articulate the principles and approaches, and the ongoing process of developing operational guidelines will be particularly relevant in guiding the training of ASF personnel for future missions.

The standby force concept adopted by Africa is complex and ambitious, but very necessary. Implementation inevitably presents numerous practical challenges, particularly given the time constraints for the realization of this vision. The original concept presented to African Chiefs of Defense and Security at their 2003 meeting in Addis Ababa was for a single on-call standby brigade level force that would be available to the AU as a first priority and was modeled on the UN Standby High Readiness Brigade (SHIRBRIG). This arrangement would have allowed for direct agreements between the AU and member states, but force levels would clearly have been inadequate for anything but the most modest commitments.

The insertion of an additional level of regional political control between the AU and its member states necessarily complicated matters and it has taken some time to come to the realization that the primary role of the regions is force preparation on behalf of the continental structure, and that of the AU is force employment—and this is still not a commonly accepted view. These structural problems have been compounded by the requirement for focus in Darfur and Somalia at the continental level and at times also by a lack of coordination and engagement between the AU and regions. The result is that the development of the different ASF components has not adhered to a single coherent concept. Instead of a continental logistic system able to support the deployment of any component of the ASF elsewhere on the continent, the ASF has the beginnings of regional logistic systems based on political considerations. The same challenges inform various components of the training, command, control and other systems. The requirement that components of the ASF in each region be parceled out between countries, based on political and not practical considerations, will continue to present many problems in the future.

A second, perhaps less tangible, problem is that of ownership. Some African partners have seized on the ASF concept to such a degree that it sometimes undermines African ownership. This is most pronounced in West and East

Africa, where the number of officers seconded from donor countries to training institutions, PLANELM and regional structures are rapidly outnumbering their African compatriots. Often these embedded 'advisors' control significantly more resources than the African commanders they nominally report to, are paid several times the salaries that accrue to the former and can play a decisive role through their direct access to even larger purses located in their capitals, or under the control of regional embassies in African capitals. It is therefore not uncommon to find middle ranking expatriate officers from European countries effectively in control of key aspects of ASF preparations, and exerting considerable influence on the concepts, standards and decisions taken at every level. Only SADC has resisted such an infiltration.

While Africans often have the greater political acumen, these advisors are often technically more capable than their African counterparts (apart from the fact that they are subject to less oversight and have access to more resources). For their part, the Africans sometimes deliberately take a back seat, engaging in an old game of extracting the maximum benefit from their benefactors. This may take the form of providing the absolute minimum of funds and resources to a PLANELM, training institution or facility in the knowledge that it is only a question of time before a donor, frustrated by the lack of progress, will step in to pick up the tab. There is also considerable competition between Africa's international partners for a demonstrable impact, which they hope will translate into influence, which leads to insufficient information sharing between, for example, the UK/France and Scandinavian partners, as well as with and between countries such as the Netherlands and Canada. Conversely, a concerted effort by the UK and Denmark has resulted in a considerable improvement in donor coordination in recent years, although the AU could improve on the use that it makes of regular meetings and briefings.

In all this maneuvering for influence and funding, the most important aspect is that the AU and the various regions should ensure that they assume ownership and drive donor support and not the reverse. For example, there should be mutual accountability between the friends of EASBRIG and the EASBRIG development support committee, which were launched in Nairobi during December 2007. Whereas the current practice is often that the Africans brief their international partners on progress, planning and requirements, these mechanisms should provide for sharing of all information on bilateral and multilateral support efforts that impact upon ASF capabilities.

Finally, African peacekeeping will at some point have to be placed on a more sustainable basis. Arguably, the way forward in all of this is that a more integrated concept of peace and security should be developed between the AU and the UN. In effect, the degree of support and succor that the UN has provided to the ASF has been a disappointment. Instead of leading, the UN has indeed followed. Thus far, the discussions regarding the future way in which the UN can respond to the challenges of peace and security on the African continent have revolved around the expanded use of Chapter VIII of the Charter of the UN. In Articles 52 to 54, the drafters made provision for the complementary role of regional organizations in the maintenance of international peace and security, on condition that such arrangements and activities are consistent with the purposes and principles of the UN, that the UN security council is kept fully informed of such activities and with the clear proviso that enforcement action requires the (prior) authorization of the UN Security Council. Perhaps it is time that the UN play a more forceful and meaningful role in the ASF. Although the UN established a peacekeeping support cell within the Peace and Security Operations Division (PSOD) in mid-2007, much more can and should be done if we are to move towards an integrated system that will play a meaningful part in keeping peace on the African continent.

Chapter 8

The African Peace and Security Architecture: An Evolving Security Regime?

João Gomes Porto and Ulf Engel

Introduction

The aim of this edited volume is to provide students, academics and practitioners with an informed and critical analysis of the operationalization and institutionalization of the African Union's Peace and Security Architecture (APSA). The previous chapters have provided critical points for reflection on the architecture as a whole as well as on each of the structures currently under implementation.

Common to all authors is the recognition that the political, institutional and normative processes that underpin the transformation of the Organization of African Unity (OAU) into the African Union (AU) have the potential to transform the way the continent addresses the mutually constituted challenges of peace, security and development with potentially significant consequences to the lives and livelihoods of millions of Africans who remain affected by war and armed conflict. Yet, permeating these pages is also the acknowledgement that in creating the APSA, the AU is treading new, uncharted waters for which there are no templates, no proven recipes, no off-the-shelf roadmaps. The risks are therefore many and the implementation and the successful actualization of this complex architecture are not assured. Building on the main findings of the previous chapters, this chapter will conclude the volume by discussing the principles underlying the architecture's design and reflecting on some of the conditions of its actualization.

Initial Reflection on Findings

Söderbaum and Hettne firmly situate the diverse and increasing phenomena of African security regionalism(s) and ensuing conflict prevention, management and resolution institutions and mechanisms in the context of globalization. Their discussion of the growing importance of regions and regionalism processes in an increasing globalized world acknowledges that these may not necessarily be contradictory but potentially complementary processes. In an earlier paper, Hettne had in fact proposed a modified approach to the study of contemporary regionalism— an approach requiring, in his words, "an understanding of contemporary regionalism both from an endogenous perspective, according to which regionalization is shaped from within the region by a large number of different actors, and an exogenous perspective, according to which regionalization and globalization are intertwined articulations, contradictory as well as complementary, of global transformation" (Hettne 2003, 24). Indeed, the careful consideration of what Bøås et al. (2003, 201) have termed the globalization/regionalization nexus as it applies to the various dimensions of security in Africa and therefore directly to the APSA is, in our view, a fruitful line of enquiry. In this regard, the authors' delineation in the pages above of the interlinked concepts of "regionness" and "actorness" in the security field are indispensable, as in our view is an understanding of the conditions for the gradual development of security communities. Looking at the provisions of the *PSC Protocol* through theoretical lenses, one would be hard pressed not to deduce that what is implied is a vision of the continent as a security community of the pluralistic variety (Adler and Barnett 1998).

The multi-dimensionality and pluralism of new regionalism raises a series of additional points for further reflection and further research. In a situation where the African state is often the main threat to the security of its citizens as well as its neighbors, a perspective on security which transcends the traditionalist view of security as the business of the state and the state alone is surely called for. The profound linkages between security and development should indeed underlie the steering of the architecture towards a human security perspective, where the responsibility to protect is taken seriously, while the pluralism of new regionalism suggests, to borrow again from Bøås et al. (2003, 198) that "we should not only analyse the interplay and various roles played by the [...] states, firms and civil societies (NGOs, social movements, etc) in processes of formal regionalization, but also the intersection between the same set of actors within processes of informal regionalization". As will be highlighted below, the normative provisions of the AU's *Solemn Declaration on a Common African Defence and Security Policy* give us some indication that, indeed, such steering may be possible.

Klaas van Walraven's historical perspective on the evolution the OAU/AU's conflict management role contributes to a more nuanced understanding of the possibilities as well as limitations of the APSA. Reflecting on the creation and institutionalization of the continental body, this author clarifies the underlying reasons for the OAU's inter-governmental cooperation approach, based on sovereign equality, respect of territorial integrity and non-interference in the affairs of member states. Furthermore, and specifically related to conflict management, this author notes that with the creation of the continental organization member states implicitly confirmed their aspiration to settle conflicts in an African framework first, in an attempt to discourage external interference (so-called *competence of initial concern*).

The author's reflection on the decision-making culture of the African Union's predecessor is particularly informative in light of the organization's current challenges, and in particular the fact that the Assembly remains the highest decision-making body of the Union, where Article 4 (h) interventions are to be decided. A diplomatic practice marked by circumspect handling of fellow heads of state, the tendency to keep disputes in camera to avoid public criticism, and caution in addressing rule violations or controversies, as well as a cumbersome decision-making process that required two third majorities, characterized the OAU's decision making. This organizational culture was marked by the predominance of plenary organs, with a largely administrative Assembly Bureau (the precursor to today's Commission-come-Authority) until the 1990s. Van Walraven points to two interlinked reasons for this: (1) lacking a hegemonic state or group of states for much of its existence, the OAU had no other choice but to negotiate to arrive at Pan-African decisions rather than imposing them—partly explaining the centrality of the Assembly of Heads of State over time; and (2) the nature of Africa's domestic politics (often characterized by personal despotism, escalating cultures of corruption, absence of the rule of law and political freedom) undoubtedly played a part in the decisions taken as regards the institutional features of the organization.

Nevertheless, even with such an organizational culture, individual OAU decision makers played important roles throughout the organizations' history, in particular Administrative Secretary-Generals who headed the General Secretariat. In the specific case of mediation and management of intra-African conflicts, although the Commission of Mediation, Conciliation and Arbitration was never seized with any dispute, several other OAU organs played important roles. These included the General Secretariat, but more importantly the Council of Ministers and the Assembly—often acting behind the scenes to provide communication between belligerents, offering good offices or mediation, even if in an ad hoc fashion. Van Walraven makes a critical point when he notes that member states of the organization considered it more important that a conflict be managed with the OAU's institutional framework than by it—which explains why it was often heads of state who got involved in conflict management activities. Yet, the combination of lack of continental leadership and Africa's internal domestic orders contributed to an approach which the author describes as minimalist, concentrating on persuasion and containment, in an ad hoc decentralized basis. Nevertheless, and against general perceptions on this matters, Van Walraven considers these approaches has having been averagely successful—a conclusion based on a qualitative assessment of mediation efforts between 1963 and 1993. Furthermore, his analysis points to several cases of OAU's concern with internal conflicts, especially cases where external interference was a prominent feature or conflicts that resulted in consequences for Africa's international relations.

More crucially perhaps, Van Walraven's chapter explores the complex ways in which the normative and institutional changes that took place in the period 1990–1993—pivotal to the transformation of the OAU into the AU a decade later—were a function of these accumulated experiences. The Assembly's adoption of the *Declaration on the Political and Socio-Economic Situation in Africa and the Fundamental Changes Taking Place in the World* in 1990 heralded a fundamentally new direction—henceforth, the organization would concern itself with the settlement of all conflicts on the continent. The reform of the General

Secretariat, the creation of a Conflict Management Division, the adoption of the Mechanism for Conflict Prevention, Management and Resolution and the so-called Central Organ in 1993, under the direction of the then new Secretary-General Salim Ahmed Salim, were visible institutional dimensions of this transformation.

These developments represent the early beginnings of a continental system of conflict prevention, management and resolution, what Cilliers and Pottgieter term, in their chapter, the organization's "second generation peace and security agenda". These developments also concern Sturman and Hayatou, who in their contribution to this volume explore the multiple ways in which the OAU's *ad hoc* conflict resolution ability was tested to the limit during the period. The end of the Cold War and the ensuing withdrawal of super power patronage to a number of regimes coupled with the increase in number and intensity of intra-state conflicts with significant regional dimensions created additional exogenous and endogenous pressures for change. And, echoing Van Walraven's focus on understanding the importance of the OAU's experiences over the years, Cilliers and Pottgieter discuss how the OAU's pivotal experiences with limited military observations had contributed to convincing member states that small operations were indeed possible—partly explaining the series of small but increasingly more complex peacekeeping operations approved by the Central Organ.

As noted in Chapter 1 by the editors above, the OAU finally took a series of decisive steps when on 9 September 1999 in Sirte, Libya, African Heads of State and Government declared their commitment to transform the organization and on 11 July 2000 in Lomé, Togo, the legal-institutional framework for the AU was adopted in the form of the *Constitutive Act*. Furthermore, as discussed above, the ratification of the *PSC Protocol* by AU member states and its entry into force on 26 December 2003 provided the articulation of the series of new institutions and decision making procedures (also known as *pillars*) that form the new peace and security architecture: the Peace and Security Council (PSC); the Panel of the Wise; the Continental Early Warning System (CEWS); the African Standby Force (ASF) and the Peace Fund. Furthermore, as we noted above, because the Regional Mechanisms are considered part of the overall security architecture of the Union, they too form an integral pillar of the APSA. Indeed, in his report to the special session of the Assembly dedicated to a "Consideration and Resolution of Conflicts in Africa", held in Tripoli on 30–31 August 2009, the Chairperson of the Commission considers the *MoU on Cooperation in the Area of Peace and Security between the AU and the Regional Mechanisms for Conflict Prevention, Management and Resolution* as one of the pillars of the APSA (Afican Union 2008).

In their review of the Peace and Security Council since its launch in May 2004, Sturman and Hayatou consider that the PSC has been central to the reforms of the OAU into the AU, changing both procedures and norms. The PSC can recommend interventions with or without the consent of the member state in which a conflict takes place and approve the modalities for such interventions. Furthermore, it may recommend sanctions against unconstitutional changes of government. In what Van Walraven would have probably termed a *heritage* factor, the PSC is based on the principle of equality between member states as all 15 members have equal rights, no veto power and the preferred method of decision-making is that of consensus. Moreover, the authors consider that some of the best performers in the PSC have been smaller member states such as Botswana, Senegal and Ghana. Able to act more decisively than the Assembly, the authors conclude that the PSC has gained clout and authority not only on the continent, but also in the global arena. Its decisions have been respected by the international community in a number of cases (such as the conflict in Côte d'Ivoire) and also implemented by actors such as private companies (e.g. the sanctions imposed on the Comoros Island in Anjouan). It has approved several peace-keeping interventions and imposed sanctions, it has sent diplomatic and observer missions to several situations and it has used its meetings to pronounce African positions on several issues.

However, Sturman and Hayatou also note that this is an institution in the early stages of its existence, which depends on the commitment of member states— indeed, national interests of member states have remained a countervailing force within the institution, often shielded by the same diplomatic culture and posturing that characterized the OAU. The PSC fell short of its primary role in the resolution of a number of situations such as the post-electoral violence in Kenya in 2007 and in Zimbabwe in 2008 or the resurgence of violence in the DRC in 2008. In sum, cases such as these undermine the PSC's image as the premier institution for the prevention and management of conflicts on the continent. For these authors, the fact that the PSC has not defined any current conflict situations as "grave circumstances, such as war crimes, genocide or crimes against humanity" is evidence that the PSC has not yet institutionalized the norm of "humanitarian intervention". Yet they also note that the PSC is part of a larger conflict prevention and management regime—and, as a result, where it fails to act, other institutions, and the Assembly in particular, should take up the task, as was the case regarding the situations in Zimbabwe, Kenya, and the tensions between Ethiopia and Eritrea. Sturman and Hayatou consider that an important step would be the formalization of a sanctions committee for the PSC, which would give it the ability to more appropriately operationalize part of its enforcement mechanisms. In conclusion, Sturman and Hayatou argue that the PSC is certainly important, but still only one element of a larger evolving architecture.

In functional terms, the APSA is designed to address the various stages of conflict—its *pillars* conceived to address prevention, management and resolution (including post-conflict peacebuilding) challenges. The overall rationale is that of preventing conflict before it turns violent. The costs (humanitarian, political, economic but also to the organization, financial) of acting once conflict escalates mitigate against a purely conflict management approach through, for example, an approach based exclusively on peace enforcement and peacekeeping operations. In fact, in addition to the inordinate severity of direct and indirect human costs of conflicts on the Continent, the consequences of armed conflict to Africa's socio-economic development are pervasive. As noted by the Chairperson of the Commission these costs include direct costs (medical/rehabilitation costs due to casualties, injuries, disability, military expenditure, care for refugees and displaced people, physical destruction leading to loss/depletion of infrastructure and assets); indirect costs from lost opportunities such as reduced economic activity due to insecurity, reduced mobility and workforce, capital flight and macroeconomic impacts, loss of development aid and ecological degradation (African Union 2009, 3).

Indeed, the imperative of conflict prevention is clearly contained in the design of the PSC itself, as its primary functions are to anticipate and prevent conflicts. In this function, the PSC is to be supported by several other mechanisms, and in particular the Continental Early Warning System (as regards monitoring and analysis) and the Panel of the Wise (preventive diplomacy and other related activities).

Tim Murithi and Charles Mwaura focus on this important preventive diplomacy tool, making the point that since its inauguration in 2007, the Panel of the Wise has already added value to the initiatives of the AU Peace and Security Council and the Chairperson of the Commission (especially because it is not politically encumbered and therefore can genuinely engage in preventive diplomacy at an early stage). From the editors' perspective, it is interesting to note the extent to which the creation of such a Panel gives concrete form to one of the strengths of the organization (OAU/AU) over its existence. As noted above, and so clearly demonstrated by Van Walraven, the OAU's record of mediation, good offices and conciliation, even if *ad hoc* in nature, contributed positively to the containment and resolution of several instances of conflict on the Continent. In many regards, the Panel formalizes this practice by centering its activities on the facilitation and mediation of potential and ongoing disputes and being constituted by eminent African personalities, capable of carrying these through. Murithi and Mwaura also explore some of the normative and socio-cultural dimensions underlying the creation of a Panel of the Wise, by discussing at length the role and function of council of elders in traditional African societies and noting similarities and differences between them and the African Union's panel. The extent to which the approach and methodology to be used by members of the Panel in their mediation and related forms of intervention will reflect so-called African principles of conflict resolution—or indeed, as seems to be the case, a combination of different methods—constitutes, to the editors, an important avenue for further research.

Reviewing the Panel's activities to date, Murithi and Mwaura finally reflect on some of the obstacles likely to be experienced by the Panel. To the authors, buy-in from the rest of the AU peace and security architecture as well as AU member states and the ability of the Panel to navigate difficult entry points and engagement with certain countries are critical. In the absence of system-wide coordination, they furthermore argue, there is a very real danger that the activities of the Panel will be routinely undermined.

Crucial to the ability of the AU to act preventively, manage as well as mitigate against the escalation of violent conflicts, is its ability to monitor continuously and analyze developments on the Continent. The group of AU Conflict Management Division professionals and academics responsible for the development and implementation of this *pillar* of the architecture provide us with a reflection on the process of development of the CEWS from an institutional as well as methodological point of view. They remind us that because every early warning system requires an underlying analysis methodology through which data and information are analyzed with the purpose of, if required, issuing warnings, the challenge for the CEWS was to devise a systematic approach to conflict analysis suited for the entire African continent. The authors discuss in detail the approach developed and reflect on some of the conditions for its successful implementation, not least the need to strengthen the CEWS' ability to influence decisions on early action by the continuous improvement of policy options and response formulation.

Reviewing the implementation of CEWS to date, the authors consider that although a series of critical processes and tools have been developed, areas such as the quality of analysis, or the division of labor with the RECs with regard to information collection, information sharing and processing still required a considerable effort. They argue that although the CEWS will gradually play a vital role at the center of the APSA, its ability to carry out its very specific and complex mandate and therefore demonstrate its validity depends on the successful implementation of the methodology and set of procedures. Ultimately, the authors note, the validity of CEWS will depend on its ability to systematically provide good quality analysis and response options that will strengthen its engagement with decision-makers and influence decision-making.

On the conflict management side of the spectrum, the African Standby Force (ASF) is designed for rapid deployment in a multiplicity of different scenarios, and may include preventive deployment, peacekeeping, peace-building, as well as post-conflict disarmament, demobilization and re-integration and humanitarian assistance related activities. In their review of the development and operationalization of the ASF, Jakkie Cilliers and Johan Pottgieter allude to some of the operational challenges likely to be faced by such a force. The multinational and standby character of the ASF means that deployment timelines, joint training, collaboration and operation are critical. Scenario 6 deployments, which would apply to grave circumstances of genocide or crimes against humanity, require the African Union to act promptly, deploying within 14 days—and this deployment can only be done by forces that are ready and fully equipped and exercised. In their conclusions, the authors argue that although the ASF has not met the ambitious milestones that it set for itself, progress made has been impressive if uneven.

A common theme across several of the chapters above focuses on the question raised by Söderbaum and Hettne at the outset of this volume: what is the optimal relationship between global bodies and regional security agencies? Seen as simultaneously a cause (regional security complexes), the means (regional security management) and the solution (regional development)—all three with significant international dimensions—Söderbaum and Hettne consider that a region-centered approach may often be more relevant as a result of factors such as proximity, commitment, being better tuned to understanding the specifics of particular cases, and so on. Yet, because at present security regionalism in Africa cannot afford to ignore multilateralism (witness the cases of the AMIB/ONUB and AMIS/UNAMID as examples), further exploration and understanding of the vertical linkages between the APSA and global peace and security institutions, mechanisms and norms is called for. Indeed, a loosely defined relationship with the United Nations (UN) may challenge the effectiveness of collaboration, and therefore compromise a complementary multilateral-regional strategy. In fact, the debate between the UN and regional organizations has resurfaced as one of the most important issues in the global security architecture, with regard to various emerging regional security architectures, their respective mandates and responsibilities.

As AU practice has already demonstrated, it is not simply subordinated to the UN under the provisions of Chapter VIII of the *UN Charter*, at different junctures seeking UN "blessing" after the fact. As Cilliers and Pottgieter note in their chapter above, it has now become accepted that the AU can and should deploy in advance of the UN so that the conditions on the ground can be made appropriate for a follow-on multidimensional peace support operation (where substantial African Standby Force resources could then be re-designated). Exploring the vertical linkages between the AU and global peace and security mechanisms but also horizontal linkages as a result of the fact that African Regional Economic Communities' are integral parts of the APSA seems therefore an important focus of both policy and research.

Finally, all authors provide their thoughts on the challenges that may hinder the efficacy of the APSA. Looking at the experience of African security mechanisms to date, Söderbaum and Hettne highlight the potential for the instrumentalization of regional mechanisms by states to pursue narrowly defined interests (which in effect compromise regional agendas) as well as the lack of neutrality often evidenced by regional institutions. Several of the authors emphasize the lack of commitment of African leaders to providing the AU with the necessary resources—resulting in over-dependence on external development assistance, which in and of itself questions the very sustainability of the APSA and the conditions for its successful implementation. Van Walraven notes that although the five major African powers agreed to shoulder 75 per cent of the regular budget of the organization, free-rider behavior still persists. Cilliers and Pottgieter discuss at length the details of APSA funding, and in particular the serious constraints posed by lack of predictable funding for the ASF.

In addition, staff resources and capacity are highlighted by all contributors to the volume. As Sturman and Hayatou point out, staff limitations is a particular challenge to the operations of the PSC, which has seen its workload increase rapidly since its inception. Likewise, Murithi and Mwaura make the point that, without a staff complement, which will form the core of a mediation support unit, it will be difficult for the Panel to conduct its affairs. As regards CEWS, the authors also note the need for the recruitment of specialized staff to fulfill the analysis and early warning reporting as a critical immediate priority. Cilliers and Pottgieter emphasize that while funding has undoubtedly contributed to slowing down the progress of ASF implementation, a more important factor in their opinion is the lack of capacity at the level of the AU. Finally, in his concluding remarks, Van Walraven makes a critical point when he alerts us to the perils of continuous *soul-searching* in the institutional realm—the example here being the debates around a Pan-African government—which may divert attention from political commitment to the Union as it is and the imperative of effective leadership.

From Security Architecture to Security Regime

The discussion above reveals that the African Union's Peace and Security Architecture (APSA) began as a vision, expressed and underscored in the series of agreements (the *Constitutive Act*, the *PSC Protocol*, the CADSP, and so on) which are now gradually being implemented, and, in certain important regards, institutionalized. And yet "architecture", as a qualifier to the African Union's peace and security vision, itself requires reflection and explanation. In our view, more than simply a convenient term to encapsulate what in practice is a complex set of arrangements and institutions, the narratives around a peace and security "architecture" may in fact reveal the fundamental direction underlying the transformation of that vision into reality. A transformation which, as was pointed to above, does not rely simply on a commitment to implementation by the AU Commission itself but depends on a much wider set of actors, and therefore will inextricably be a result of the way those actors (ranging from RECs, to member States, to civil society organizations) and the AU as a whole continue to navigate, to negotiate, indeed to agree on the way forward.

In this sense, while steering the institutionalization of the architecture (expressed often in terms such as coordination, harmonization, standard setting), the African Union has rightly shied away from a directive, controlling approach, opting for a more cooperative stance where at each stage of the process relevant actors are involved in its co-development (witness for example the process of development and implementation of both the CEWS and the ASF). To the AU Commission's credit, its politico-diplomatic strategy of involving all relevant actors as a way of increasing "ownership", "participation" and a deeper sense of collaboration has resulted in a series of interesting developments—even if it has inevitably led to some delays in implementation. A good example of this was the much needed and finally agreed upon *Memorandum of Understanding* between the AU and the RECs in the field of peace and security of January 2008.[1] From a conceptual perspective, as will be discussed below, what seems to underlie this

---

1 This document was signed by representatives from the African Union and the following RECs: CEN-SAD (Community of Sahel-Saharan States), COMESA (Common Market for Eastern and Southern Africa), EAC (East African Community), ECCAS (Economic Community of Central African States), ECOWAS Economic Community of West African States), IGAD, SADC and UMA (Maghreb Arab Union).

approach is the development of an African peace and security regime—needed precisely due to the "architecture's" dependence on a variety of different actors for its actualization.

It is true that, on the surface, "architecture" is a convenient term, conjuring images of a coherent relationship between form and function, best achieved when the design of the structure and choice of components of a particular system (form) are developed to ensure and indeed maximize purpose (function). In this perhaps parochial sense—notice how in the world of physical architecture, the strict observance of the once ruling maxim "form follows function" has lost part of its appeal—"architecture" expresses a structured approach, envelops a concern with systems' functional adequacy, hints at the way the various structures and processes of the APSA will ultimately deliver on a more peaceful and secure continent. "Architecture" therefore sounds good.

Yet, "architecture" also possesses a normative dimension as it remains the space where essential principles underlying the design and organization of a particular system are reflected upon, debated, defined and ultimately practiced. Whether subject to the confines imposed by function or, perhaps more likely, the result of a compromise between function, available means and the challenges of the surrounding environment, "architecture" should ultimately reveal a set of inter-subjectively shared expectations about appropriate role behavior and norms (Finnemore and Sikkink 1998, 891). And while these norms may find expression in decisions as regards APSA's structure, design and purpose, choice of components and organization, as well as some degree of clarity in terms of their interrelationships and implementation, there is still a long way to go in terms of institutionalized behavior based on the standards agreed upon. Outlining the structure of Africa's New Peace and Security Architecture, its components, their implementation and nascent interrelationships is perhaps the least controversial part of this discussion, as hopefully became clear in the pages above. While many of the *pillars* of the APSA are currently under implementation, there is some degree of clarity (at least on a legal basis) on their roles and mandates, as well as on the way they are expected to interact with each other. What seems to be particularly challenging is identifying the multiple (often contradictory) ways by which the principles underlying the creation of the APSA may affect (positively as well as negatively) the conditions for its actualization in a sustainable manner.

While there seems to be considerable legal agreement on many of the principles that underlie the architecture, the same cannot be said as regards practice according to many of the standards of behavior (norms) agreed upon. This is particularly the case as regards respect for fundamental human rights and freedoms, sanctity of human life, as well as respect for democratic principles, good governance and the rule of law, as well as the place of core principles such as "human security" and the "responsibility to protect". Furthermore, there has been some reluctance by Member States in using, indeed contemplating the use of, Article 4 (h) in several cases where it could presumably have been invoked. In fact, the PSC is often accused of ignoring serious situations because of political and other motives (the case of Zimbabwe is very often used in this regard). Thus, a perception of the African Union's continued inability to take concrete action seems to be taking hold in some circles, perhaps a function of the concern that not only will Article 4 (h) always be open to interpretation but there is always the possibility of circumventing it via the non-interference norm. This conundrum has become known in academic and policy circles as *the policy of non-indifference*.

In some important ways, the difficulties experienced in the implementation of several of the pillars of the architecture and the need to obtain the green light from Member States at every stage reveals that to a large extent the momentum that characterized the transformation of the OAU at the turn of the millennium may no longer be as strong, with states wavering on their support to regional integration in matters of peace and security. A substantial number of states continue not to meet their contributions to the organization, increasing its dependency on external aid—raising issues of sustainability and ownership. In addition, the escalation of conflicts in the Horn and Central Africa, coupled with election-related disputes and violence, have substantially increased the demands on the organization. In a context where the capacities of the Commission are stretched to the limit (see African Union High-Level Panel 2007), and where organizational development, training, and additional recruitment of staff are urgent, the questions on the sustainability of the APSA are many. The operational and logistical challenges for AU missions and the ASF are well known and discussed at length by Cilliers and Pottgieter in Chapter 7 (see also Schümer 2004; Kinzel 2007).[2] Yet, the intervention on the Comoros where an African Union-led force, on 25 March 2008, ended the illegal secession of Anjouan (although it was primarily symbolic) managed to demonstrate renewed commitment to the very norms agreed upon.

How then to reflect on the actualization of an architecture that depends on such a variety of actors for its implementation, effectiveness and resilience? In our view, such a reflection may benefit from the use of the concept of regime, developed within the field of International Relations in part to understand the conditions upon which institutionalized international cooperation develops and is sustained. And in this vast literature, for some years characterized by intense debates on the nature, function, creation and demise of international regimes—pitting realist, neo-liberal institutionalist and cognitivist authors against one another[3]—we combine the "implicit or explicit principles, norms, rules, and decision-making procedures around which actors' expectations converge in a given area of international relations" of Krasner's (1983, 2) often cited definition, with Rittberger's (2002,

---

2   Including the fact that capacities of Member States are already over-stretched with the operations in Sudan (AMIS-cum-UNAMID) and Somalia (AMISOM); air transport capacities are severely limited; the African Union is heavily dependent, for intelligence, on the USA or the information shared by European services; the mandate for peace-keeping operations is not robust enough; deployment is delayed; Member States did not provide enough troops; command structures are far from clear.

3   See in this regard the excellent review in Hasenclever et al. (1997).

9) concern in believing that at the heart of regime analysis is "the institutionalized co-operation of states for managing conflicts and interdependence problems, instead of relying on self-help strategies, either individually or collectively (alliance), even though self-help action may seem to produce greater individual benefits or less individual costs in the short-term". We should note that this notion of regime incorporates the element of practice—borrowed from Wolf and Zürn's (1986) emphasis on the "observable behavioural elements" of regimes as their litmus test—highlighting the importance of institutionalized practice, which is characterized by effectiveness and durability.

At this point a caveat is needed. We are cognizant of Keohane's (2002, 27) warnings on avoiding the perils of circular reasoning: "to identify regimes on the basis of observed behavior, and then to use them to 'explain' observed behavior". In line with Krasner, an emphasis on the requirement of converging expectations as a precondition for the existence of a regime is indeed critical—and Keohane acknowledges Kratochwil and Ruggie's contributions to the effect: "principled and shared understandings of desirable and acceptable forms of social behavior" as being on the basis of regime formation. Yet, Rittberger's definition of regime departs in some fundamental ways from that of Keohane—particularly as the latter considers that agreements become regimes when states recognize that they have continuing validity and refer to them in "an affirmative manner, even if they are not scrupulously observed" (Keohane 2002, 28). The more complicated issues regarding regime compliant behavior are regarded by this author as belonging to the issue of effectiveness.

However, although the affirmation of an agreement's validity may go some way to creating the conditions by which a regime becomes, de facto, actualized, it would seem reductionist, perhaps even legalistic to ignore behavioral aspects as critical evidence of actualization (including of course effectiveness and also resilience). In this regard, Haufler (2002, 98) notes that "Rittberger and Zurn add another dimension to the debate over regimes by arguing that some minimal level of effectiveness and durability is essential for a useful definition of regimes".

This is particularly important when reflecting on the conditions affecting the evolution of the APSA towards a *de facto* regime—it is partly because of this that we regard institutionalized cooperation (which partly stems from a degree of expectations' convergence) as being critical. Note that Rittberger carefully chooses the term "institutionalized" to refer to the type of cooperation that better characterizes a regime—to distinguish it from mere legal regimes. That is because a regime is not simply the product of explicit and agreed upon rules, but requires behavior, practice. If so, then the legal foundations of the APSA represent but a legal regime (one built on the agreement by member states on principles, norms and rules) but will only become a regime once behavior follows through. It is furthermore important to recognize that regimes by and of themselves do not act—although true international institutions, they require organizations and/or states to act.

Yet, is the state centricity of Rittberger's definition counter-sensical to an analysis of the APSA—which after all depends to such a large extent on other types of actors? In our view, far from restrictive, such an approach allows us to have a more dynamic and perhaps nuanced approach to reflecting on the conditions for the successful actualization of this particular regime and, as a consequence, the architecture itself.

Conclusion: Norms, Interests and the Conditions of Regime Building

The on-going process of implementation of the APSA reveals a set of at least three interrelated challenges. First, although the AU Commission has risen as a new actor, it is not free of the influence of member states, which as a result of the institutional frameworks bring their individual interests to bear—interests that may reveal 'self-help' strategies which directly contradict the norms agreed upon. At this important juncture of institutional development and implementation, member states have played and continue to play a very important role (witness how at each and every stage of APSA's institutional development the support of Member States has been critical). In several important ways, this dimension also applies to the RECs, and, in particular, those that are venturing into the field of peace and security for the first time and therefore rely on member State approval at every stage of the process (the example of the East African Community is a case in point).

Perhaps more importantly, in a number of ways—particularly at the higher end of the spectrum of the intervention of the AU, i.e. the grave circumstances of genocide, war crimes, crimes against humanity and unconstitutional changes of government—member states retain the ultimate decision-making power at the level of the AU through the General Assembly. Indeed, as was noted above, decisions on an Article 4(h) intervention require at least a two-thirds majority of member States.[4] In addition, on the ASF, member states enjoy considerable latitude when it is up to them to provide standby peacekeeping troops to sub-regional brigades.

While the Constitutive Act strengthened, in very important regards, the powers of the AU Commission, clarifying its areas of exclusive competence, it stops short of a fully blown executive and legislative Commission à la European Commission—the last Heads of State and Government Summit in Addis Ababa at the end of January 2009 once again shying away from adopting outright the proposal for an Authority, suggesting instead that a special committee of Member States should further investigate it. Even in areas where agreement has been reached, the translation into practice of those powers and functions has continued to require patient negotiation with Member States. This is particularly the case in the field of peace and security, where the workings of the PSC have shown the need for such an approach, one based on consensus building and buy-in of Member States.

Secondly, institutionalized behavior on the basis of the norms agreed upon has often been compromised by Member States who openly pursue 'self-help'

---

4   See in this regard Sturman and Hayatou, Chapter 4 of this book.

strategies, often in direct contravention to those norms (a group that includes Sudan, Zimbabwe and others), and who exert considerable leverage at several levels (including RECs as well as the AU). The continuing violation by several Member States of fundamental principles such as the sanctity of human life and respect of human rights, democratic practices and good governance, rule of law and protection of fundamental freedoms, raises the question of whose security is actually being, in practice, protected. Normatively, APSA subscribes to a multi-dimensional concept of security—so clearly elucidated in the *Solemn Declaration on a Common African Defence and Security Policy* (§I, 6). While we agree with Rittberger that prescriptive rules need not be honored at all times to qualify as a regime, the multitude of questions raised by non-compliance by such important constituents of the architecture will certainly require constant monitoring and further research.

Thirdly, the institutionalization of APSA has revealed serious capacity deficits. A substantial number of Member States—a fifth to a quarter—continue not to meet their financial obligations, thus increasing the organization's dependency on external aid and raising issues of sustainability and ownership. Moreover, the escalation of conflicts in the Horn and Central Africa, coupled with election-related disputes, has substantially increased the demands on the organization. The operational and logistical challenges for African Union missions and the ASF are well known. In a context where capacities are stretched to the limit (see African Union High-Level Panel 2007), and where organizational development, training, and additional recruitment of staff are urgent, the questions on the sustainability of APSA are many.

Having made these points, we should note that we have no doubt that the success, indeed efficacy and resilience of the APSA, will depend to a very large extent on the African Union, its organs and the institutions put in place within it to deal with the prevention, management and resolution of conflicts—but particularly so the Commission. In important regards, it is up to the Commission to steer the institutionalization process, to harness the required support from Member States as well as partners, to promote the participation, collaboration and inclusion of the eight RECs as integral parts of the APSA. As a continent-wide architecture, the legal agreements, roadmaps and the creation of new institutions at AU headquarters and the RECs form the initial necessary steps for this regime to begin to take shape—yet, over and above this, the success of the various pillars will depend on the internalization, by all actors involved, of the set of principles, norms and rules that underpin the architecture. If the APSA is to become a *de facto* regime and not just a series of formal legal agreements from time to time positively reinforced by AU Member States, it must pass the test of institutionalized behavior. If norms and rules are systematically disregarded at the discretion of member states, following Wolf and Zürn (1986) a regime is not, in fact, in existence.

What this implies is that some form of internalization of the norms and rules of the legal regime has to occur within the drivers of such a regime. It is precisely the conditions for such processes of internalization that should be used when inquiring whether particular forms of international cooperation (at the very least through the agreement on a certain set of norms and rules) have become or will become an international regime. The factors and conditions that explain the complex process by which participants realize over time that they are better off in the long run by cooperating—even though acting alone may produce a greater pay-off or represent a less costly alternative—gives us precisely the necessary tools to reflect upon the future of the APSA. This internalization by AU member states is even more important if we recall that, although reached by consensus, the transformation of the OAU into the AU and the new roles assigned to the AU in matters of peace and security were driven by specific (at times contradictory but ultimately aligned) foreign policy objectives of a core number of states (in particular Nigeria, South Africa but also Libya) as clearly demonstrated by Tieku (2004). If this is so, does this mean that the success or failure of the regime solely depends on whether dominant powers are willing to enforce treaty provisions which they themselves have signed—as concluded by Krasner's study of four historical human rights regimes? This, after all, is the neo-realist argument. As noted by Haas (2002), neo-realists predict that "regimes are only likely to emerge when a systemic concentration of material power resources exists and will persist only so long as such a power concentration exists (neo-realism and follow the leader thesis). An hegemon creates the regime and then others try to emulate its behavior or are compelled by it and it persists while the hegemon's control over resources persists".

Is there a possibility that the reduction in power and interest of these leading states may lead to a weakening of the regime, as anticipated by realist and neo-liberalist theories of regimes and so emphatically criticized by Haufler (2002, 95)? What of Krasner's (2002, 141) point that "if all states were prepared to accept the principles and norms of the regime, there would not be any need for a regime in the first place"? This author's analysis of human rights regimes is a warning on the role of power. In his words: "the question of whether states adhere to such regimes is not a function of the extent to which a regime enhances information and discourages cheating by other actors; rather it is a function of the extent to which more powerful states in the system are willing to enforce the principles and norms of the regime" (Krasner 2002, 141).

In the context of African inter-governmental politics, the transformation of the OAU into the AU through the adoption of the *Constitutive Act* and the adoption of the *PSC Protocol* stand as landmark achievements, forming the legal—one could say contractual—context upon which the APSA emerges. Yet, as noted above, legal agreements and even the institutions (in the sense of organizations) that may or may not ensue are not regimes. Effectiveness and durability are as important as principles, norms, rules and decision-making processes. It is here that the promotion of learning and the transmission of knowledge and information become important. In this regard, Hurrell (2002, 59) notes that "an essential element is the legitimacy of rules which derives from the common sense of being part of a legal community and which serves as the crucial link between the procedural rules of state behavior and the structural principles which define the character of the system and the identity of the players".

It is also interesting to note, following Kratochwil (2002, 74) that "when 'regimes' need formal organisations for their implementation, their establishment is not possible without a high degree of domain consensus defining the mission of these organisations". Cognition and learning, as a political process through which collective behavior is modified in light of new collective understanding (Haas 2002, 175), will play a fundamental role in the future effectiveness of the APSA as a peace and security regime.

Against this background, the relationship(s) between the AU Commission, the RECs and member states, and their impact on the behavioral institutionalization of the APSA will be critical. Future research could benefit from Haas's concept of "epistemic communities", a cognitivist approach to the study of regimes with a focus on "networks of knowledge-based communities with an authoritative claim to policy-relevant knowledge within their domain of expertise" where "members share knowledge about the causation of social or physical phenomena in an area for which they have a reputation for competence, and a common set of normative beliefs about what actions will benefit human welfare in such a domain" (Haas 2002, 179). Note that, for this author, epistemic communities share the following set of characteristics: (1) shared values or principled beliefs (these provide a value-based rationale for social action of the members of the community); (2) shared causal beliefs or professional judgment: these provide analytic reasons and explanations of behavior, offering causal explanations for multiple linkages between policy actions and desired outcomes; (3) common notions of validity: intersubjective, internally defined criteria for validating knowledge; (4) common policy enterprise: set of practices associated with a central set of problems that have to be tackled (Haas 2002, 179).

In this sense, while "the regime would still be created through the intercession of the hegemon[s], but its substance would reflect epistemic consensus" and "learning may occur through persuasion and bureaucratic clout exercised by members of the epistemic community in countries where they have consolidated their bureaucratic influence, and by emulation and other patterns in other countries" (Haas 2002: 188). That this author highlights the importance of international organizations' secretariats as sources for new policy ideas and information seems to resonate with the role of the AU Commission, and particularly its Peace and Security Department.

Thus, further research on the conditions for the gradual development of epistemic communities around the various pillars of APSA, at all levels of this evolving regime, seems needed. A very promising point of entry, from our perspective, relates very specifically to the implementation of the CEWS. As participant observers in a series of meetings between the AU and the RECs regarding the design and implementation of the CEWS, the authors observed first hand the importance of not disregarding cognitivists' concern with the importance of knowledge-based communities as core to the development and sustainability of regimes. Although a comprehensive reflection on this issue is outside the scope of this volume, further research could be conducted on the possible gradual development of an epistemic community (at this stage, to be sure, proto-community) bringing together the officials tasked with conflict analysis and early warning functions at both the AU (Conflict management Division) and the RECs (particularly CEWARN and ECOWARN but also EAC, ECCAS and SADC). It should be recalled that there had been some level of discomfort from some of the RECs with the prospect of an AU that would attempt to dominate, indeed take over, some of their early warning functions. Organizations such as IGAD and ECOWAS, which had been engaged in the design and implementation of early warning systems for several years (CEWARN and ECOWARN respectively) approached the CEWS process with some caution, perhaps believing that if someone should drive it, it should naturally be them.

What this discussion highlights is an approach to thinking about the development of the APSA as an evolving peace and security regime. To be sure, while resources are critical (in all their variety, from human to financial), looking at the APSA within a regime perspective brings to light above all the importance of internalization of norms leading to institutionalized behavior. And for this to have any chance of gradually taking shape, albeit in a longer time frame than most are prepared to accept, the role of fundamental drivers—or potential norm entrepreneurs (see Finnemore and Sikkink 1998)—such as the AU Commission, individual member states and in many regards the RECs at the centre of nascent epistemic communities, is critical. Even considering the slow pace of progress in some areas, member state's continuing disregard for many of the norms that underpin the APSA, and the AU's unwillingness or inability to act in several situations that would require it, the evidence points to a nascent regime.

Bibliography

Acharya, A. (2001), *Constructing a Security Community in Southeast Asia: ASEAN and the Problem of Regional Order* (London: Routledge).

Adelman, H. (1996), "Defining humanitarian early warning," in S. Schmeidl and A. Adelman (eds.), *Early Warning and Early Response* (Columbia International Affairs Online).

Adibe, C.E. (1997), "The Liberian Conflict and the ECOWAS-UN Partnership," *Third World Quarterly* 18:3, 471–88.

Adibe, C.E. (2002), "Peace-Building in ECOWAS," paper presented at the Norwegian Institute of International Affairs (NUPI), Oslo, Norway, 29 August (mimeo).

Adler, E. and Barnett, M. (eds.) (1998), *Security Communities* (Cambridge: Cambridge University Press).

African Union (2000), *Constitutive Act of the African Union* (Addis Ababa: African Union).

African Union (2002), *The Protocol Relating to the Establishment of the Peace and Security Council of the African Union* (Durban: African Union, 2002).

African Union (2003), *Policy Framework for the Establishment of the African Standby Force and Military Staff Committee* (Addis Ababa: African Union).

African Union (2004), *Report of the Chairman of the Commission on the Establishment of a Continental Peace and Security Architecture and the Status of Peace Processes in Africa* (PSC/AHG/3 (IX)). Solemn Launching of the Peace and Security Council, 9th Session, 25 May (Addis Ababa: African Union).

African Union (2007), *Modalities for the Functioning of the Panel of the Wise.* Adopted by the Peace and Security Council at its 100th Meeting, 12 November, Addis Ababa.

African Union (2008), *Statement on the Situation in Somalia.* Panel of the Wise Fourth Meeting, 28 to 29 November, Nairobi, Kenya.

African Union (2008), *Memorandum of Understanding on Cooperation in the Area of Peace and Security between the AU and the Regional Mechanisms for Conflict Prevention, Management and Resolution* (Addis Ababa: African Union, mimeo).

African Union Assembly (2002), *Rules of Procedure of the Assembly of the Union,* (ASS/AU/2(I)) (Addis Ababa: African Union).

African Union Conflict Management Division (eds.) (2008a), *Meeting the Challenge of Conflict Prevention in Africa: Towards the Operationalization of the Continental Early Warning System* (Leipzig: Leipziger Universitätsverlag).

African Union Conflict Management Division (eds.) (2008b), *The CEWS Handbook* (Addis Ababa: African Union), mimeo.

African Union High-Level Panel (2007), *Audit of the African Union: Towards a People-Centred Political and Socio-economic Integration and Transformation of Africa* (Addis Ababa: African Union).

African Union Peace and Security Council (2005a), *Communiqué of 20 October 2005*, PSC/PR/2(XLII) (Addis Ababa: African Union).

African Union Peace and Security Council (2005b), *Communiqué of 25 February 2005*, PSC/PR/Comm. (XXV) (Addis Ababa: African Union).

African Union Peace and Security Council (2006), *Report on the Status of the Implementation of the Continental Peace and Security Architecture*. 57th meeting, 21 June 2006 (Addis Ababa: African Union).

African Union Peace and Security Council (2007), *Background Paper on the Review of the Working Methods of the Peace and Security Council of the African Union* (Addis Ababa: African Union).

African Union Peace and Security Department (2008), *Panel of the Wise: A Critical Pillar of the African Peace and Security Architecture* (Addis Ababa: African Union), mimeo.

Anderson, M.B. (1999), *Do No Harm: How Aid can Support Peace – or War* (Boulder, CO; London: Lynne Rienner).

Annan, K. (2005), *In Larger Freedom: Towards Development, Security and Human Rights for All* (New York: United Nations).

Ansprenger, F. (1961), *Politik im schwarzen Afrika: die modernen politischen Bewegungen im Afrika französischer Prägung* (Cologne: Westdeutscher Verlag).

Assefa, H. (1987), *Mediation in Civil Wars: Approaches and Strategies – The Sudan Conflict* (Boulder, CO: Westview Press).

Austin, A. (2004), "Early Warning and The Field: A Cargo Cult Science?" in D. Bloomfield, M. Fischer and B. Schmelzle (eds.) *Berghof Handbook for Conflict Transformation* (Berlin: Berghof Research Center for Constructive Conflict Management) <http://www.berghof-handbook.net/>.

Bakwesegha, C.J. (1995), "The Role of the Organisation of African Unity in Conflict Prevention, Management and Resolution," *International Journal of Refugee Law* Special Issue (Summer), 207–19.

Baimu, E. and Sturman, K. (2003), "Amendment to the African Union's Right to intervene. A shift form human to regime security?" *African Security Review* 12:2, 37–45.

Bennett, L. (1991), *International Organizations – Principles and Issues* (New Jersey: Prentice Hall).

Berman, E. and Sams, K. (2000), "Keeping the Peace in Africa," *Disarmament Forum* 3: 21–31.

Bloomfield, D., Fischer, M. and Schmelzle, B. (eds.) (2005–2007), *Berghof Handbook for Conflict Transformation* (Berlin: Berghof Research Center for Constructive Conflict Management) <http://www.berghof-handbook.net/>.

Boutros-Ghali, B. (1992), *An Agenda for Peace* (New York: United Nations).

Brecke, P. (2000), *Risk Assessment Models and Early Warning Systems* (Berlin: Wissenschaftszentrum Berlin für Sozialforschung) <http://www.wz-berlin.de/alt/ip/abstracts/p00-302.de.htm>.

Brown, M. (1996), *The International Dimensions of Internal Conflict* (Cambridge: MA; London, UK: MIT Press).

Brownlie, I. (1979), *Principles of Public International Law* (Oxford: Oxford University Press).

Bush, K. (1998), *A Measure of Peace: Peace and Conflict Impact Assessment (PCIA) of Development Projects in Conflict Zones* (Ottawa: International Development Research Centre) <http://www.idrc.ca/uploads/user-S/10757546941Working_Paper1.doc>.

Buzan, B. (1991), *People, States and Fear: An Agenda for International Security Studies in the Post-Cold War Era* (London: Harvester Wheatsheaf).

Buzan, B. (2003), "Regional Security Complex Theory in the Post-Cold War World," in F. Söderbaum and T. Shaw (eds.), *Theories of New Regionalism: A Palgrave Reader* (Basingstoke: Palgrave Macmillan).

Buzan, B. and Wæver, O. (2003), *Regions and Powers: The Structure of International Security* (Cambridge: Cambridge University Press).

Bøås, M., Marchand, M.H. and Shaw, T. (1999), "The Political Economy of New Regionalisms," *Third World Quarterly* 20:5, 897–910.

Bøås, M., Marchand, M. and Shaw, T. (2003), 'The Weave-World: The Regional Interweaving of Economies, Ideas and Economies,' in F. Söderbaum and T. Shaw (eds.) *Theories of New Regionalism: A Palgrave Reader*, pp. 197–210 (Basingstoke: Palgrave Macmillan).

Bøås, M., Marchand, M. and Shaw, T. (2005), *The Political Economy of Regions and Regionalism* (Basingstoke: Palgrave Macmillan).

Carment, D. and Schnabel, A. (2003), *Conflict Prevention: Path to Peace or Grand Illusion?* (Tokyo, New York, Paris: United Nations University Press).

Carnegie Commission on Preventing Deadly Conflict (1997), *Preventing Deadly Conflict. Final Report with Executive Summary* (New York: Carnegie Commission) <http://www.ccpdc.org>.

Cilliers, J. and Malan, M. (2005), "Progress with the African Standby Force," *ISS Paper No. 107* (Pretoria: Institute for Security Studies).

Cilliers, J. (1999), "Building security in Southern Africa: an update on the evolving architecture," *Institute for Security Studies Monograph Series*, 43 (Pretoria: Institute for Strategic Studies).

Cilliers, J. (2003), *From Durban to Maputo: A Review of the 2003 Summit of the African Union* (Pretoria: Institute for Security Studies).

Cilliers, J. (2008), "The African Standby Force. An update on progress," *Institute for Strategic Studies Paper*, 160 (Pretoria: Institute for Strategic Studies).

Cilliers, J. and Sturman, K. (2004), "Challenges Facing the AU's Peace and Security Council," *African Security Review* 13:1, 97–104.

Clapham, C. (1996), *Africa and the International System* (Cambridge: Cambridge University Press).

Clark, R. (2004), *Intelligence Analysis: A Target Centric Approach* (Washington DC: CQ Press).

Cole, A. (2007), "Lockheed looks beyond Weapons; Contractor Targets Growth with Services in Strife-torn Areas," *Wall Street Journal*, 24 September.

Conference of Independent African States (n.d.), *Declarations and Resolutions* (Accra: Government Printer).

Consilium (2008), *EU Support to the African Union Mission in Darfur – AMIS* <http://www.consilium.europa.eu/uedocs/cmsUpload/080109-Factsheet8-AMISII.pdf> (accessed 4 July 2009).

Cooper, A., Hughes, C. and Lombaerde, P. (eds.) (2008), *Regionalization and the Taming of Globalization* (London: Routledge).

Cowling, M. (2002), "The African Union: An Evaluation," *South African Yearbook of International Law* 27, 193–205.

Davidson, B. (1992), *The Black Man's Burden: Africa and the Curse of the Nation-State* (London: Random House).

De Benoist, J.R. (1982), *l'Afrique Occidentale Française de la conférence de Brazzaville (1944) à l'indépendance* (Dakar: Nouvelles Éditions Africaines).

DeConing, C. and Hussein, S. (1994), "Enhancing the OAU Mechanism for Conflict Prevention, Management and Resolution," *Politeia* 19:1, 13–30.

Department for International Development (DFID) (2002), *Conducting Conflict Assessments: Guidance Notes* (London: Department for International Development) <http://www.dfid.gov.uk/pubs/files/conflictassessmentguidance.pdf>.

Deutsch, K. (1968), *The Analysis of International Relations* (Englewood Cliffs, NJ: Prentice Hall).

Diehl, P.F. (1994), *International Peacekeeping* (Baltimore; London: Johns Hopkins University Press).

Dugué, G. (1960), *Vers les états-unis d'Afrique* (Dakar: Lettres Africaines).

El Abdellaoui, J. (2009), "The Panel of the Wise Working for Peace," *ISS Today* 18 March.

Ero, C. (2000), "ECOMOG: A model for Africa?" in J. Cilliers and A. Hildiung-Norberg (eds.) *Building Stability in Africa: Challenges for the New Millennium* (Pretoria: Institute for Security Studies).

Ero, C. (2005), "ECOWAS and Subregional Peacekeeping in Liberia," *Journal of Humanitarian Assistance* (on-line edition <http://jha.ac/articles/a005.htm>).

European Commission (1996), *The European Union and the Issues of Conflicts in Africa: Peace-Building, Conflict Prevention and Beyond*. Communication from the Commission to the Council, SEC(1996)332 (Brussels: EU Commission).

European Commission (2001), *Communication from the Commission on Conflict Prevention*. COM(2001)211 (Brussels: EU Commission).

European Commission (2004), *Securing Peace and Stability for Africa: The EU Funded African Peace Facility* (Brussels: EC DG Dev), in <http://ec.europa.

eu/development/body/publications/docs/flyer_peace_en.pdf> accessed 10 December 2008.

European Commission (2007), "Africa-EU partnership on peace and security," <http://ec.europa.eu/development/icenter/repository/EAS2007_action_plan_ peace_security_en.pdf> (accessed 4 July 2009).

European Commission (2009), Somalia: Fact Sheet, April 2009.

European Commission, Directorate-General Development (2004), *Securing Peace and Stability for Africa. The EU-Funded African Peace Facility* (Brussels: European Commission).

FEWER (1999), *Conflict and Peace Analysis and Response Manual*, 2nd edn (London: FEWER Secretariat).

FEWER (2000), *Generating the Means to an End: Planning Integrated Responses to Early Warning* (London: FEWER Secretariat).

Field, S. (ed.) (2004), *Peace in Africa: Towards a Collaborative Security Regime* (Johannesburg: Institute for Global Dialogue).

Finnemore, M. and Sikkink, K. (1998), "International Norm Dynamics and Political Change," *International Organization* 52:4, 887–917.

Foltz, W.J. (1965), *From French West Africa to the Mali Federation* (New Haven, CT: Yale University Press).

Francis, D.J. (2006), *Uniting Africa: Building Regional Peace and Security Systems* (Aldershot: Ashgate).

Gallagher, C.F. (1963), "The Death of a Group: Members of the Casablanca Pact Fall Out," *American Universities Field Staff Reports*, North Africa Series, 9:4, 1–11.

Gamble, A. and Payne, A. (ed.) (1996), *Regionalism and World Order* (Basingstoke: Macmillan).

Gurr, T. (1996), "Victims of the State: Genocides, Politicides and Group Repression from 1945 to 1995," in: A. Jongman (ed.) *Contemporary Genocides: Causes, Cases, Consequences* (Leiden: PIOMM, University of Leiden).

Haas, E.B. (1958), *The Uniting of Europe: Political, Social and Economic Forces 1950-57* (Stanford: Stanford University Press).

Haas, E.B. (1983), "Regime Decay: Conflict Management and International Organizations, 1945–1981," *International Organization* 37:2, 189–256.

Haas, P.M. (1993, 2002), "Epistemic Communities and the Dynamics of International Environment Cooperation," in: V. Rittberger et al. (eds.), *Regime Theory and International Relations* (Oxford: Oxford University Press 1993, Reprinted 2002).

Hasenclever, A., Mayer, P. and Rittberger, V. (1997, 2004), *Theories of International Regimes* (Cambridge: Cambridge University Press 1997, 6th reprinting 2004).

Haufler, V. (2002), "Crossing the boundary between public and private: International Regimes and Non-State Actors," in: V. Rittberger et al. (eds.) *Regime Theory and International Relations* (Oxford: Oxford University Press 1993, Reprinted 2002).

Hawkins, V. (2003), "Measuring UN Security Council Action and Inaction in the 1990s: Lessons for Africa," *African Security Review*, 12:2.

Hettne, B. (2002), "The Europeanization of Europe: Endogenous and Exogenous Dimensions," *Journal of European Integration* 24:4, 325–40.

Hettne, B. (2003), "The New Regionalism Revisited," in F. Söderbaum and T. Shaw (eds.) *Theories of New Regionalism: A Palgrave Reader*, pp. 197–210 (Basingstoke: Palgrave Macmillan).

Hettne, B. (2005), "Beyond the 'New' Regionalism," *New Political Economy* 10:4, 543–72.

Hettne, B. and Söderbaum, F. (2000), "Theorizing the Rise of Regionness," *New Political Economy* 5:3, 457–73.

Hettne, B. and Söderbaum, F. (2006), "The UN and Regional Organizations in Global Security: Competing or Complementary Logics?" *Global Governance* 12:3, 227–32.

Hettne, B., Inotai, A. and Sunkel, O. (eds.) (1999), *Globalism and the New Regionalism* (Basingstoke: Macmillan).

Hulme, D. and Goodhand, J. (2000), *NGOs and Peace Building in Complex Political Emergencies: Final Report to the Department for International Development* (Manchester: University of Manchester).

Ibok, S. and Nhara, W. (eds.) (1996), *OAU Early Warning System on Conflict Situations in Africa* (Addis Ababa: OAU Conflict Management Division, mimeo).

Ikome, F. (2007), *Good Coups and Bad Coups: The Limits of the AU's Injunction on Unconstitutional Changes of Government.* Occasional Paper 55 (Johannesburg: Institute for Global Dialogue).

Institute for Security Studies (2008), *Operationalising the AU Panel of the Wise: Progress and Prospects*, Direct Conflict Prevention Programme Seminar Report, 25 March.

International Alert, Saferworld, CECORE, APFO and CHA (2004). *Conflict-sensitive Approaches to Development, Humanitarian Assistance and Peacebuilding.* <http://www.conflictsensitivity.org/resource_pack.html>.

Joint Evaluation of Emergency Assistance to Rwanda (eds.) (1996), *The International Response to Conflict and Genocide: Lessons from the Rwanda Experience*, vols 1–5 (Copenhagen).

Kalk, P. (1971), *Central African Republic: A Failure in De-Colonisation* (London: Pall Mall Press).

Kamto, M. (1996), "Le méchanisme de l'O.A.U. pour la prévention, la gestion et le règlement des conflicts. L'esquisse d'un nouvel instrument régional pour la paix et la sécurité en Afrique," *Ares* 15:2, 61–83.

Kent, V. and Malan, M. (2003), "The African Standby Force (ASF)," *African Security Review* 12:3.

Keohane, R. (2002 [1993]), "The Analysis of International Regimes: Towards a European-American Research Programme," in V. Rittberger et al. (eds.) *Regime Theory and International Relations* (Oxford: Oxford University Press).

Kilner, D. (2008), "AU Official Criticizes Charges for Sudan Leader," <www.voanews.com> (accessed 20 January 2009).

Kinzel, W. (2007), Afrikanische Sicherheitsarchitektur – ein aktueller Überblick, *GIGA Focus Afrika*, No 1.

Kioko, B. (2003), "The Right of Intervention under the African Union's Constitutive Act: Non-interference to Non-intervention," *International Review of the Red Cross* 85, 807–25.

Klingebiel, S. (1999), *Wirkungen der Entwicklungszusammenarbeit in Konfliktsituationen. Querschnittsbericht zu Evaluierungen der deutschen Entwicklungszusammenarbeit in sechs Ländern* (Berlin: Deutsches Institut für Entwicklungspolitik).

Klingebiel, S., Blohm, T.M., Eckle, R., Grunow, K., Heidenreich, F., Mashele, P. and Thermann, A. (eds) (2008), *Donor Contributions to the Strengthening of the African Peace and Security Architecture* (Bonn: German Development Institute).

Krasner, S. (1983), "Structural Causes and Regime Consequences: Regimes as Intervening Variables," in: S. Krasner (ed.) *International Regimes* (Ithaca, London: Cornell University Press).

Krasner, S. (2002 [1993]), "Sovereignty, Regimes and Human Rights," in: V. Rittberger et al. (eds.) *Regime Theory and International Relations* (Oxford: Oxford University Press).

Kratochwil, F. (2002 [1993]), "Contract and Regimes: Do Issue Specificity and Variations of Formality Matter?" in V. Rittberger et al. (eds.) *Regime Theory and International Relations* (Oxford: Oxford University Press).

Kunig, P. (1981), *Das völkerrechtliche Nichteinmischungsprinzip: Zur Praxis der Organisation der afrikanischen Einheit (OAU) und des afrikanischen Staatenverkehrs* (Baden-Baden: Nomos).

Laakso, L. (ed.) (2002), *Regional Integrations for Conflict Prevention and Peace Building in Africa* (University of Helsinki: Department of Political Science).

Lake, D. and Morgan, P. (eds.) (1997), *Regional Orders. Building Security in a New World* (Philadelphia: Pennsylvania State University Press).

Le Billon, P. and Nicholls, E. (2007), "Ending 'Resource Wars': Revenue Sharing, Economic Sanctions or Military Intervention?" *International Peacekeeping* 14:5, 613–32.

Leonhardt, M. (2001a), *Conflict Analysis for Project Planning and Management. A Practical Guideline – Draft* (Eschborn: Deutsche Gesellschaft für technische Zusammenarbeit, GTZ) <http://www.gtz.de/de/dokumente/en-conflictanalysis.pdf>.

Leonhardt, M. (2001b), *Conflict Impact Assessment or Development Projects* (Eschborn: Deutsche Gesellschaft für technische Zusammenarbeit, GTZ).

LeRoy Bennett, A. (1991), *International Organizations: Principles and Issues* (Englewood Cliffs, NJ: Prentice Hall).

Lewin, A. (1990), *Diallo Telli: Le tragique destin d'un grand Africain* (Paris: Editions Jeune Afrique).

Low, D.A. (1982), "The Asian Mirror to Tropical Africa's Independence," in P. Gifford and W.R. Louis (eds.) *The Transfer of Power in Africa: Decolonization 1940-1960* (New Haven, CT: Yale University Press), 1–29.

Lund, M. (1996), *Preventing Violent Conflicts. A Strategy for Preventive Diplomacy* (Washington DC: US Institute of Peace, Carnegie Commission on Preventing Deadly Conflict).

Lund, M. and Betts, W. (1999), "Conflict in the Horn of Africa," in *Searching for Peace in Africa* (Utrecht: European Platform on Conflict Prevention and Transformation).

Makinda, S.M. and Okumu, F.W. (2008), *The African Union: Challenges of Globalization, Security, and Governance* (London, New York: Routledge).

Malan, J. (1997), *Conflict Resolution Wisdom from Africa* (Durban: African Centre for the Constructive Resolution of Disputes).

Marx, K. (1852), *18th Brumaire of Louis Bonaparte* (New York: Die Revolutions).

Mathews, K. (2001), "Birth of the African Union," *Africa Quarterly* 41:1/2, 114–20.

Mathews, K. (2003), "The African Union: From Dream to Reality: Focus on the Maputo Summit, July 2003," *Africa Quarterly* 43:2, 1–16.

Mays, T. (2002), *Africa's First Peacekeeping Operation: The OAU in Chad, 1981-1982* (Westport, CT: Praeger).

Mitrany, D. (1966), *A Working Peace System* (Chicago: Quadrangle Books).

Mortimer, E. (1969), *France and the Africans 1944-1960: A Political History.* (London: Walker).

Muchie, M., Habib, A. and Panayachee, A. (2006), "African Integration and Civil Society: The Case of the African Union," *Transformation: Critical Perspectives on Southern Africa* 61, 3–24.

Munger, E.S. (1961), *African Field Reports 1952–1961* (Cape Town: C. Struik).

Murithi, T. (2005), *The African Union. Pan-Africanism, Peace-Building and Development* (Aldershot: Ashgate).

Murithi, T. (2006), "Practical Peacemaking Wisdom from Africa: Reflections on 'Ubuntu'," *Journal of Pan-African Studies* 1:4, 25–34.

Murithi, T. (2008), "African Indigenous and Endogenous Approaches to Peace and Conflict Resolution," in D. Francis (ed.) *Peace and Conflict in Africa*, pp. 16–30 (London: Zed Books).

Murithi, T. and Murphy-Ives, P. (2007), "Under the Acacia: Mediation and the Dilemma of Inclusion," in K. Papagianni (ed.) *Conflict Mediation in Africa: Challenges and Opportunities*, pp. 77–84 (Geneva: Centre for Humanitarian Dialogue).

Muyangwa, M. and Vogt, M. (2003), *An Assessment of the OAU Mechanism for Conflict Prevention, Management and Resolution, 1993-2000* (New York: International Peace Academy), mimeo.

Mwanasali, M. (2004), "Emerging Security Architecture in Africa," in Centre for Policy Studies, Occasional Paper. *Policy: Issues and Actors* 7:4.

Naldi, G.J. (1999), *The Organization of African Unity: An Analysis of its Role* (London; New York: Mansell).

Nathan, L. (2004), "Mediation and the African Union's Panel of the Wise," in S. Field (ed.) *Peace in Africa: Towards a Collaborative Security Regime*, pp. 63–80 (Johannesburg: Institute for Global Dialogue).

New Partnership for Africa's Development (2001), *Framework Document* (Johannesburg: NEPAD).

Nivet, B. (2006), "Security by proxy? The EU and (sub-)regional organizations: the case of ECOWAS," occasional paper No. 63, March (Paris: Institute for Security Studies).

Nkrumah, K. (1963), *Africa Must Unite* (London: Heinemann).

Organisation of African Unity (1963), Charter. [Online] <http://www.africa-union.org/root/au/Documents/Treaties/text/OAU_Charter_1963.pdf> (accessed 8 April 2009).

Organisation of African Unity (1994), *Report of the Secretary-General on the Operationalization of the Mechanism for Conflict Prevention, Management and Resolution* (CM/1805 (LIX), Council of Ministers, 59th Ordinary Session, 31 January – 5 February 1994) (Addis Ababa: OAU).

Oye, K.A. (ed.) (1986), *Cooperation under Anarchy* (Princeton, NJ: Princeton University Press).

Princen, T. (1992), *Intermediaries in International Conflict* (Princeton, NJ: Princeton University Press).

Révolution Africaine [magazine], February 1963.

Rittberger, V. (2002[1993]), "Research on International Regimes in Germany: The Adaptive Internalization of an American Social Science Concept," in: V. Rittberger et al. (eds.) *Regime Theory and International Relations* (Oxford: Oxford University Press).

Rosamond, B. (2000), *Theories of European Integration* (New York: St. Martin's Press).

SADC (2007), *Memorandum of Understanding amongst the Southern African Development Community Member States on the Establishment of a Southern African Development Community Standby Brigade* (SADC/CM/2007/3.3.3D).

Schachter-Morgenthau, R. (1964), *Political Parties in French-Speaking West Africa* (Oxford: Clarendon Press).

Schoeman, M. (2003), *The African Union After the Durban 2002 Summit*, occasional paper (Copenhagen: Centre of African Studies).

Schümer, T. (2004), "Evidence and Analysis: African Regional and Subregional [G]overnmental Capacity for Conflict Management," *Working Paper Commission for Africa* <http://www.commissionforafrica.org/english/report/background/schumer_background.pdf> (accessed 9 September 2008).

Souaré, I. (2006), *Civil Wars and Coups d'Etat in West Africa* (New York; Oxford: University Press of America).

South Africa Department of Foreign Affairs (2005/6), *Annual Report* (Pretoria: Government Printer).

Söderbaum, F. (2004), *The Political Economy of Regionalism: The Case of Southern Africa* (Basingstoke: Palgrave Macmillan).

Söderbaum, F. and Shaw, T. (eds.) (2003), *Theories of New Regionalism: A Palgrave Reader* (Basingstoke: Palgrave Macmillan).

Söderbaum, F. and Tavares, R. (2008), *The African Union and the Regional Economic Communities. Three Scenarios for 2018-2028*, Report Commissioned by the Swedish Defence Forces (mimeo).

Tavares, R. (2009), *Regional Security: The Capacity of International Organisations* (London; New York: Routledge).

Taylor, I. (2005), *NEPAD. Toward Africa's Development or Another False Start?* (Boulder, CO: Lynne Rienner).

Teló, M. (2007), *European Union and New Regionalism: Regional Actors and Global Governance in a Post-Hegemonic Era*, 2nd edn (Aldershot: Ashgate).

Thakur, R. (2005a), *The United Nations, Peace and Security* (Cambridge: Cambridge University Press).

Thakur, R. (2005b), Speech by Ramesh Takhur at the conference, "Regionalisation and the Taming of Globalisation," 26–28 October, 2005, Warwick University.

Thomas, C. (1985), *New States, Sovereignty and Intervention* (Aldershot: Gower).

Thompson, W.S. (1969), *Ghana's Foreign Policy 1957-1966: Diplomacy, Ideology, and the New State* (Princeton, NJ: Princeton University Press).

Tieku, T. (2004), "Explaining the Clash and Accommodation of Interests of Major Actors in the Creation of the African Union," *African Affairs* 103:11, 249–67.

Touray, O. (2005), "The Common African Defence and Security Policy," *African Affairs*, 104:417, 635–56.

UNDG ECHA (2004), *Inter-agency Framework for Conflict Analysis in Transition Situations* (New York: United Nations).

United Nations (2000), *Report of the Panel on UN Peace Operations, 21 August 2000* (A/55/305, S/2000/809) (New York: UN General Assembly/Security Council).

United Nations (2004), "A More Secure World: Our Shared Responsibility." Report of the Secretary-General's High Level Panel on Threats, Challenges and Change (New York: UN) <http://www.un.org/secureworld>.

United Nations (2007), *Report of the Secretary-General on the Situation in the Central African Republic and the Activities of the United Nations Peacebuilding Support Office in the Central African Republic*, S/2007/376, 22 June.

Uvin, P. (1999), *The Influence of Aid in Situations of Violent Conflict* (Paris: OECD DAC).

Van de Goor, L. and Verstegen, S. (1999), *Bridging the Gap from Early Warning to Early Response* (The Hague: Netherlands Institute of International Relations "Clingendael").

Van Tongeren, P. and Heemskerk, R. (2005), *Reader. UN, Regional Organisations and Civil Society Organisations*. Global Conference "From Reaction to

Prevention: Civil Society Forging Partnerships to Prevent Violent Conflict and Build Peace," 19–21 July (New York: United Nations).

Van Walraven, K. (1999), *Dreams of Power: The Role of the Organization of African Unity in the Politics of Africa 1963–1993* (Aldershot: Ashgate).

Van Walraven, K. (2004), "From Union of Tyrants to Power to the People? The Significance of the Pan-African Parliament for the African Union," *Afrika Spectrum* 39:2, 197–221.

Van Walraven, K. (2005), "Empirical Perspectives on African Conflict Resolution," in: P. Chabal, U. Engel and A.-M. Gentilli (eds.), *Is Violence Inevitable in Africa? Theories of Conflict and Approaches to Conflict Prevention* (Leiden, Boston: Brill Academic Publishers).

Van Walraven, K. (2009), "Decolonisation by Referendum: The Anomaly of Niger and the Fall of Sawaba (1958–1959)," *Journal of African History* 50:2.

Ward, T. Col. (2008), *Interview*. Nairobi, 16 January.

Wallensteen, P. and Möller, F. (2003), *Conflict Prevention: Methodology for Knowing the Unknown* (Uppsala: Department of Peace and Conflict Research, Uppsala University).

Welch, C.E. (1966), *Dream of Unity: Pan-Africanism and Political Unification in West Africa* (Ithaca, NY: Cornell University Press).

Wheeler, N (2000), *Saving Strangers: Humanitarian Intervention in International Society* (Oxford: Oxford University Press).

Wheeler, N. (2001), "Review Article. Humanitarian Intervention after Kosovo: Emergent Norm, Moral Duty or the Coming Anarchy," *International Affairs* 77:1, 112–28.

Williams, P. (2007), "From Non-Intervention to Non-Indifference: The Origins and Development of the African Union's Security Culture," *African Affairs* 106:423, 253–80.

Wolf, K. and Zürn, M. (1986), *International Regimes und Theorien der internationalen Politik* (Tübinger Arbeitspapiere zur internationalen Politik und Friedensforschung 3; Tübingen).

World Bank Conflict Prevention and Reconstruction Team (2005), *Conflict Analysis Framework (CAF)* (Washington DC: The World Bank).

Index